THE OUTSOURCING MANUAL

THE OUTSOURCING MANUAL

Robert White and Barry James
of Lucidus Ltd

Gower

Published by
Gower Publishing Limited
Gower House
Croft Road
Aldershot
Hampshire GU11 3HR
England

Gower
Old Post Road
Brookfield
Vermont 05036
USA

British Library Cataloguing in Publication Data
White, Robert
    The outsourcing manual
    1. Contracting out
    I. Title II. James, Barry
    658.5

    ISBN 0 566 07834 1

Library of Congress Cataloging-in-Publication Data
White, Robert, 1949–
    The outsourcing manaual/Robert White and Barry James.
        p.   cm.
    Includes indec.
    ISBN 0–566–07834–1 (cloth)
        1. Contracting out. 2. Industrial project managemnt. I. James,
    Barry, 1948–   . II. Title.
    HD3860.W48 1997
    658.7'23—dc20   96–32168
                                                                        CIP

Typeset in Great Britain by Bournemouth Colour Press and printed in Great Britain by Biddles Ltd, Guildford.

Contents

Figures

Introduction

Welcome to the world of outsourcing which, rather boringly, we define as 'a contractual relationship between an external vendor and an enterprise in which the vendor assumes responsibility for one or more business functions of the enterprise'.

Expressed like that outsourcing sounds dry and uninteresting but actually it can be very exciting. So much so, in fact, that an 'Indiana Jones' frame of mind might well be helpful as you set off on this particular adventure. We don't, however, expect you fully to understand the analogy until you have roller-coastered your way through your first procurement and fought your way to the end of the resultant agreement's first year – you have been warned!

But what of your reward – the priceless artefact or cache or fabulous treasure? Well, it's there all right as evidenced by the continued rapid growth of outsourcing services across the world. Organizations like Eastman Kodak, Hughes, General Motors, Rank Xerox, British Aerospace, Rolls-Royce and many others have divested themselves of important, but non-core, activities. Even governments are doing it. The British government has outsourced the principal computing functions in the Departments of Inland Revenue and Social Services to name but two. It is hard to imagine that these organizations would have done this without the prospect of some real benefit to them. Interestingly, even small companies are beginning to see advantages in using outsourcing services.

For us, though, outsourcing is just one tool of many in the performance improvement armoury. If you think of it in those terms you will avoid becoming involved with outsourcing for the sake of it. You need to be going somewhere first, and only then can you assess outsourcing on the basis of its suitability as a vehicle for getting you there – not as a means in itself. In that sense outsourcing is a bit like flying. Provided you board the right plane, it is a good way to travel somewhere quickly. Better still, if you take the right precautions, the chances of survival are quite high!

But how do you know whether outsourcing is right for you and, if it is, how do you realize the benefits? Even more difficult, how do you know what benefits are available in the first place and which of them you really want? And how do you manage the risks, presupposing, of course, that you know what they are?

A bewildering array of questions and we've yet to scratch the surface. The difficulties increase, for at least two reasons. First, there are no 'standard' outsourcing agreements that can be used as a template – virtually every agreement needs to be hand-crafted to fit specific customer circumstance and requirements. Second, large and complex agreements require the bringing together of a wide range of information, decisions, judgements and the fruits of a great deal of thinking, badgering, coaxing, arguing and re-thinking. When trying to break in for the first time, you are therefore confronted with a series of disordered fragments from which it is quite impossible to discern a coherent picture.

Outsourcing looks a bit like a double maze – finding the correct way in is extremely difficult and quite bewildering when viewed from the outside. Once you are in, it will remain bewildering until you have been able to make enough of the fragments coalesce. As you step into the subject of outsourcing, then, you should take comfort from the fact that many of our clients have taken considerable time, even with careful guidance, to understand how the many components of an outsourcing agreement actually fit together.

That is why we have written this book. We hope that it will enable you to find the right entrance to the maze and help you successfully navigate once inside. The book is divided into four parts. Part I will help you make sure that you know where you are going and whether outsourcing has a part to play in getting you there. Part II assumes that outsourcing is relevant to your journey and prepares you for the ride. Part III concentrates on making it all work, whilst Part IV offers the outsourcing suppliers' perspective.

Let's examine each of those parts in an attempt to create a mental picture or framework so that, as you 'lose' yourself in the detail, there are sufficient land marks along the way to keep you from getting lost. Figure 0.1 maps out the chapters to show how everything fits together. One word of comfort though – if your requirements are simple and small scale, you will be able to move through the map quite quickly since not all components may be necessary and most will be straightforward to deal with. It is only the larger and more complex agreements that must rigorously follow the route and where very careful thinking will be required for each component.

PART I

Part I of this book is designed to start you thinking! And the first thing to think about is your mission, vision, goals or destination, however you want to express it. Thus chapter 1 is concerned with setting clear objectives. It might seem obvious to say that without a clear mission and goals there can be no sense of direction, no reason to know whether what you are doing is helpful and, worst of all, no way of knowing when the mission is complete or whether successful. Yet

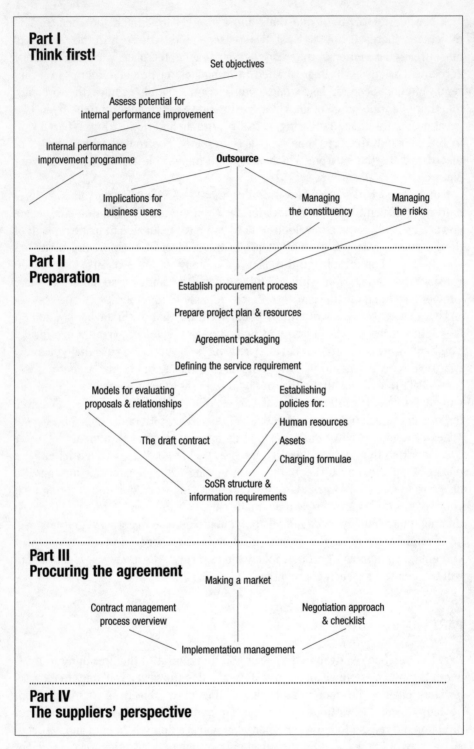

Figure 0.1 The outsourcing road map

the vast majority of organizations find it difficult to set clear, meaningful targets and even more difficult to avoid the distractions that get in the way of achieving them.

Within the context of outsourcing, the objectives you set are critically important because they allow you to test whether you are entering the maze by the correct entrance and which of the many avenues open to you is actually the one you want. There are a great many choices: do I want cost reduction, improved performance or both? If I want both, can they be delivered without external help? If no, what form should the help take? If I want external help to deliver both cost reduction and improved performance, what compromises do I need to make and can I live with them? What functions of my organization must I include in any outsourcing agreement to get the benefits I want? How much control am I prepared to give or lose to the outsourcing supplier? We could continue – the questions and choices are seemingly endless. It becomes obvious then that without a touchstone against which to check, it will be very easy to lose your way.

It will also be easy for you to lay traps to fall in, perhaps even years after your outsourcing agreement has started. Some agreements based upon a single objective to reduce cost, and which were signed three to five years ago, have encountered a rather large snag. It seems that the over energetic pursuit of minimum cost outsourcing agreements has forced suppliers to be inflexible in terms of the way in which they deliver the contracted services. Unfortunately for some organizations, the world in which they operate continues to change at an increasingly rapid rate, a rate that cannot be matched by the outsourcing supplier because of the contractual constraints under which it is forced to operate. The outsourcing agreement, once heralded as 'the solution', has now become a real constraint to business development. Chapter 1 examines these issues to make sure that you set off on the right foot and avoid difficult and expensive problems at some future point in your journey.

Setting off on the right foot may not, of course, mean selecting an outsourcing route. In fact, outsourcing makes no sense at all if you can achieve the performance targets required through the use of your internal resources, since there is no need to incur the cost of the outsourcing supplier's profit nor the cost of the procurement.

Chapter 2 'Assessing the potential for improving performance' will help you come to an informed judgement about the real capabilities of your internal team. Your team will, of course, believe that they can achieve what you want. They must, however, operate under a number of constraints to do with the relevance of their current skill set, the time available to deliver the target, the cost and time, if necessary, of refreshing the skill set and the availability of funds both capital and revenue.

Quite often, the combination of significant constraints and insufficient management skills and resources to overcome them will lead to a decision to outsource. In these circumstances, it is important to understand the extent to which performance can be improved since it provides a baseline against which to assess the proper cost of an outsourcing agreement. Without a baseline, or bid threshold as we call it and will discuss later, you run the risk of passing 'super profit' to your outsourcing supplier. Chapter 2 attempts to offer some insights into these issues together with a means by which you might start to measure the potential for internal performance improvement.

As you start to improve performance, by whatever means, the customers of the function in question *will* feel the effects. The effects tend to come in two forms. First, assets are worked harder. This means that any 'cushion' of spare capacity will have gone. In other words, if the service customers (users) continue to perform at the same level, any service contingency thought to exist will probably have been eroded. Second, in circumstances where the service function is dependent upon inputs from its customers in order to provide back the service, it becomes obvious that the customer will need to match the improved performance of the service function otherwise the cycle breaks down and no service improvement will result.

Thus, if there is to be an improved performance from the service function, it is more likely than not that a matched improvement will be needed from its customers. Therefore it is better to consult with the customers prior to inflicting the change and Chapter 3 'implications for business users' endeavours to offer some advice.

There are yet more obstacles to overcome. Outsourcing is a sensitive subject for any organization. In your organization there are people who will be pleased to help and there are those who will not. There will also be people from whom you will need help and those from whom you will not. The trouble is that rarely is there that happy coincidence of willing and desired help. All too often those from whom you need help find ways not to provide it and vice versa. The impact upon the procurement of an outsourcing agreement of absent, unhelpful or inefficient interventions is substantial and must be managed. We have invented a simple process, constituency management, to help with this task and Chapter 4 'Managing the constituency' gives you the details.

To bring your initial 'thinking' phase to a close, there is the little matter of risks and their mitigation. The risks that surround outsourcing are considerable but, with care, manageable. Remember that risks change as the procurement project develops. It will not be enough simply to list all the risks to emerge from an intensive brain storming session. You will need a process to manage the risks, and their mitigation strategies, as they change both in terms of old risks disappearing and new ones arriving and the way in which individual threats heighten and diminish.

Chapter 5 'Managing the risks' offers a simple risk management process and a view of the likely risks to be encountered.

PART II

Part II assumes that the initial thinking has been completed and that you have decided to proceed with an outsourcing procurement. There are now a wide range of issues for you to begin to think about – bringing together all those fragments that we discussed earlier. It's time to prepare, remembering that a good finish depends almost entirely upon the quality of the preparation.

Chapters 6 and 7 discuss the issues surrounding the procurement process and project planning. The procurement process itself is straightforward; provided that you follow the basic disciplines as suggested by the process set out in Chapter 7, you will be safe. Project planning, and the resources associated with it, is altogether another story. Just about every organization we have worked with has, initially, underestimated the project resources needed to procure an outsourcing agreement in terms of both the skills and amount of effort required.

One leading organization with which we worked quite correctly appointed a very senior executive to lead a large and complex outsourcing procurement. He asked us how much time he would need to give to the project – would it be as much as 25 per cent? We responded that, initially, he would need to spend 25 per cent of his time on the project but that within three months it would require 50 per cent and two months after that 100 per cent of his time. Translating loosely from the vernacular, he informed us that 'anything more than 25 per cent would be quite impossible'.

Over the following weeks we watched the load on him steadily increase. He finally had to concede that our estimates were correct and began reorganizing his responsibilities. The story had a happy ending since he ultimately spent 100 per cent of his time on the project, delivered it successfully and was promoted. Do not underestimate the huge amount of work that has to be done if the resultant agreement is going to fulfil your business objectives. Chapter 7 has some important messages for those who intend to succeed.

Having brought your project team together and confirmed your procurement process, you must now deal with the details. Before you can safely proceed, you will need to establish the outer boundaries of the potential outsourcing agreement. In other words, you need to define the agreement 'package' and this is the point where you could either make or lose a great deal of benefit depending upon the quality of your judgement. The simple rule for valuing (note that we did not say 'pricing') outsourcing agreements is 'volume over time', that is a large volume of service required for a long period of time has the potential to give the biggest return, of which only part is the lowest unit cost. So, the agreement 'package' is central to delivering your performance objectives whatever they might be. Note that the 'value' you are seeking need not be restricted to simple cost reduction. Indeed, we would argue strongly that unless there are very specific reasons to aim for cost reduction alone, you should always endeavour to gain other value added benefits.

In addition to reduced costs, value added benefits might include the attainment of new or improved skills, the delivery of a changed culture, the movement of capital costs off balance sheet, the transfer from fixed to variable costs and a wide range of other benefits, limited only by your imagination and the total capability of your chosen outsourcing supplier. Chapter 8 'Packaging the agreement' will help you break into this important area.

Having defined the outer boundaries of your agreement, you have now reached the point where a number of detailed activities can begin, leading to the development of a Statement of Service Requirement (SoSR), which suppliers will use to develop their responses. Your first task is to define more precisely the services you require within the boundaries of your agreement package. Chapter 9 'Defining the service requirement' offers an approach that should keep you safe. Safe is a key word here because if there are omissions or ambiguities in the SoSR that remain undiscovered until after the agreement has been signed, the supplier may well need to increase its charges in circumstances where your negotiating levers have gone. A lack of attention to detail when preparing your service requirement could cost you a lot of money.

Chapters 10, 11 and 12 discuss the various policy decisions you will need to make regarding, respectively, human resources, assets and the basis of charging for the deal, i.e. the charging formulae to be used.

The issues surrounding staff and outsourcing are difficult for both employees and employer. Employers must pick their way through a range of difficult ethical and legal issues, balancing the needs of the organization with those of its staff and all within the relevant legal framework for their particular part of the world. For staff it is far worse. It matters little what you say to them – they will be traumatized. And it is not surprising. They will be acutely anxious and angry because their future is uncertain; they have lost control of their lives; and they have, in their terms, been abandoned by the organization to which they have given their loyalty. Do not forget their families either. The uncertainty flows through the family, which can exert a very considerable influence. Therefore determine your staff policies very carefully and your staff communications strategy even more so.

Assets are difficult also, but in a less obvious way. Tangible assets are reasonably straightforward when disposing of them to the outsourcing supplier, but what happens at termination of the agreement? It is quite likely that what were your assets will have been thoroughly integrated into the supplier's portfolio and are now indistinguishable from its own. You need an exit strategy that gives you certain rights and confers obligations upon the supplier to co-operate in either the transfer of service to a third party or back in-house. If, however, you fail to negotiate these rights and obligations at the outset of the contract, one day it could ruin your whole day. Intellectual property is just as interesting. You will obviously protect your position regarding current intellectual property, but what of that created in the future by the outsourcing supplier on your behalf? Rules will need to be formulated before the contract is signed.

Charging formulae can keep you up at night on at least two counts. They are potentially difficult to put together since they are, effectively, the heart of the agreement and if you get them wrong the following few years will provide you with a challenging opportunity. Our first advice is to avoid the price escalation trap by achieving pricing certainty. Pricing certainty simply concerns making sure that, no matter what your future requirements might be, the price can be mechanically calculated without the need for negotiation. Remember that if the charging approach selected allows any kind of negotiation to take place after the contract is signed, you are likely to be on weak ground since most of your negotiating levers will have gone with the initial contract signature. With pricing certainty firmly in mind, you will need to select a charging approach that is based on inputs, outputs, risk/reward or a mixture of each. Input charging is generally well understood and is based upon the costs associated with delivering the service, to which is added a contribution to supplier profit. Output charging is less well understood, particularly for complex service based contracts, and relies upon a detailed understanding of service outputs for each of which there is an agreed unit price. Risk/reward based charging is where the outsourcing supplier's charge is related directly to your business performance. In this way a direct link can be created between the outsourcing supplier's services and the value they add to your business. This approach is relatively new and, although at first glance fairly simple, may have some hidden consequences.

Whatever approach is chosen, the resulting charging formulae must be straightforward to administer and monitor, leave you in strategic control and leave the outsourcing supplier in day-to-day control of resources and incentivized both to reduce operating costs and to improve your business performance.

Chapter 13 explores the components of the contract that will emerge from all this work. It will be helpful to publish in the SoSR the draft legal framework that you intend to use, hence the need to think about it at this point in the procurement process. Notwithstanding the anticipation of a warm, friendly and mutually beneficial relationship between you and your supplier, there has to be a legal document that, if nothing else, sets out the 'rules' for the relationship. The importance of a correctly constructed and drafted legal document cannot be overemphasized. It is advisable, therefore, to ensure that legal advisors are properly engaged in the procurement project at the earliest appropriate moment and that sufficient time is spent getting the contract right.

Chapters 14 and 15 offer some insights into the ways in which prospective suppliers and their offerings may be evaluated. Again, it will be important to publish in the SoSR the basis upon which supplier proposals will be evaluated, so the thinking must be done prior to release of the SoSR. The whole area of evaluation is potentially very difficult because in amongst the 'hard' issues are an array of 'soft' ones. This would not normally pose a problem but if you overlay the emotion that normally surrounds the procurement of an outsourcing agreement, then all of a sudden objectivity can be in very short supply.

Experience has led us to an approach that places great reliance upon supplier references. By requesting structured information from a large number of referees (up to 30 for large procurements) any bias can be reduced and selection is based more upon actual experience then supplier sales propaganda. In addition, we have found it helpful to use a large number of selection criteria since this tends to make the evaluation models less sensitive to small movements in any one criterion.

There is a neglected aspect of evaluation that in the context of an outsourcing agreement is particularly important. It is the whole question of establishing and maintaining relationships. Outsourcing agreements typically run for a number of years and if they are to deliver their best, both parties to the agreement must work closely together. Invariably, the cultures of the two organizations are different and it is important to test the ability of suppliers to form and maintain working relationships appropriate to the type of agreement required. Chapter 15 gives some clues as to how this difficult area might be tackled.

Well, once you have completed everything from Chapter 1 through to Chapter 15, you will have a large cache of fragments from which to make a picture. Chapter 16 gives you the template for assembly of the fragments from which will emerge a Statement of Service Requirement – the SoSR. Once the SoSR has been prepared you will have the clearest idea of how everything fits together and will be ready to proceed to Part III.

PART III

Part III explains how to make it all work! Chapter 17 'Making a market' offers some thoughts on how to engage suppliers in the procurement process in a manner that gains their confidence, assures their enthusiasm and, ultimately, has a positive commercial and performance impact on your deal. You may find it surprising that you need to take positive action to create a market for your requirements. It is because there are relatively few competent outsourcing suppliers. Those that are competent are, to some degree, able to be selective about the procurements with which they become involved. If you fail to set your stall out correctly, they may not bid or, if they do, may not offer you the best terms. Better to approach the market correctly and get the best deal possible.

Chapter 18 'Negotiating the agreement' suggests an approach for delivering an effective agreement, notwithstanding all the complexities that stand in the way. During negotiations all of those fragments that we have so carefully put together to create a coherent agreement will be taken apart to be negotiated and, if we are not careful, put back together again in a different shape or with pieces missing. Chapter 18 gives some helpful hints on how to be organized in the negotiation phase so that you emerge with at least as much as you went in with.

Then, having successfully secured an outsourcing contract, Chapter 19 'Managing the contract' and Chapter 20 'Implementing the contract' discuss the really difficult tasks of implementing and managing the contract to get the best from the relationship over the next few years.

PART IV

Our experience has shown us that most suppliers are reputable and generally honest. We also know, of course, that they have stakeholders to satisfy and therefore need to make a profit. And because you know that, you are forced to a position of, shall we say, healthy scepticism when discussing the ways in which they might help you and your organization. This 'scepticism' or lack of trust constitutes a real barrier to effective communication between you and your potential suppliers. The trouble is that most of the time you are right to behave in this way as, sadly, there are suppliers who cannot be trusted. In a conventional customer/supplier relationship, the world, over thousands of years, has developed strategies for managing the risks associated with a lack of trust.

In the case of outsourcing, however, a lack of trust is more problematic. This is because an outsourcing agreement will usually run for a number of years and will therefore require a good working relationship between the parties if maximum mutual benefits are to be delivered. In the early stages of 'getting to know' you, a mature and competent outsourcing supplier will, by definition, have a much greater understanding and practical experience of the issues surrounding outsourcing. The supplier will therefore seek to pass on some of this knowledge in an attempt to help you avoid the more obvious pitfalls which, in the longer term, will give both of you a problem. If, however, you are 'on guard', you are in danger of discounting much of what the supplier has to say to the ultimate long-term detriment of the relationship.

In an attempt to circumvent this barrier to effective communication, we invited three of the world's leading providers of outsourcing services to offer some advice to potential customers in the hope that, through the medium of this book, we may all take what they say at face value.

Having fought your way through to the end of Part IV you will, we hope, be a little wiser about outsourcing and more able to judge whether it is right for you. On balance, and after active involvement in more than fifty different agreements, we believe that outsourcing services do have an important role to play and should be regarded as an important weapon in your performance improving armoury. It is, however, only one weapon and, in many respects, you will end up swapping one set of management challenges for another if you choose to use it. The swap will have been worthwhile if in so doing you have gained access to resources and capabilities that were hitherto unavailable or potentially unattainable. Your new management challenge will be to work with your 'partner' to focus and drive the combined resources to achieve the objectives that you so carefully set out at the beginning.

We wish you every success.

Bob White and Barry James

Part I
Think First!

Introduction to Part I

The trouble with outsourcing is that it has become fashionable – and when something becomes fashionable there's always a rush to buy. Whilst there *are* real business benefits to be had from outsourcing, experience shows that winning them requires much careful thinking *before* you sign a deal and a lot of robust management afterwards.

Therefore the first important message is *don't rush* – do nothing, do not pick up the phone and call your local friendly outsourcing dealer. All you have to do is think – at this stage, it's the only safe thing to do and, believe us, it will save you much money in the long run!

Part I of this book, then, is aimed at setting you off on the right foot. That means being clear about what you are trying to achieve before you do anything, and Chapter 1 will offer some thoughts on how to set some relevant objectives. Once clear targets have been identified, you then need to know whether outsourcing is relevant to their achievement. Chapter 2 provides some clues as to how you might assess its relevance and, at the same time, if outsourcing proves not to be relevant, assess the potential to improve your internal performance.

If you do decide to pursue an outsourcing agreement, you will need to know some of the more immediate implications. Chapter 3 will give some insights into the implications for users of the function under consideration, Chapter 4 will remind you about all those people who are going to have an interest in what you are doing, each one of whom will need careful management, and Chapter 5 will expose some of the risks.

If, after all that, you still want to proceed, Part II will begin to show you how – but before you reach that far – think on!

1 Setting clear objectives

WHY OBJECTIVES ARE IMPORTANT

The importance of setting objectives correctly cannot be overstated. Outsourcing agreements typically run for a number of years and involve two, usually disparate, organizations attempting to work closely together. More particularly, outsourcing agreements can take many different forms and have many different components. You may be confronted with a bewildering range of options which could lead to what will seem like a life sentence if you make the wrong choices.

The nature of the objectives set profoundly influences both the direction and the outturn of the outsourcing agreement. Correctly set objectives will fulfil the following functions:

- Guide the assessment of internal options and suitability for external partnering.
- Guide the design of the external partnering contract or internal improvement programme.
- Provide the basis for measuring progress towards the delivery of benefits.
- Facilitate the ultimate delivery of planned benefits.
- Provide a datum against which proposed courses of action may be tested.

The absence of objectives will frustrate the ability to test the appropriateness of proposed courses of action and deficient objectives may lead to the adoption of inappropriate courses of action.

Setting meaningful and measurable objectives is, therefore, a critical success factor. It is also more difficult than most people believe.

HOW OBJECTIVES INFLUENCE THE OUTCOME

The skill with which objectives are set will affect the outcome of both an investigation into the appropriateness of outsourcing and, if judged to be relevant, the resultant outsourcing agreement itself. The illustration that follows shows how.

Assume that a single objective to reduce costs is set. The resulting service or contract principles will be as follows:

- There must be an *exact* definition of service requirement – poor definition that excludes a service component will result in increased charges or lower service
- Tight cost constraints will mean *total* adherence to the supply of those closely defined services – the supplier will have no scope to vary the service since it is tightly constrained by the need to provide a service and make a profit for the price agreed.
- There will be minimal service flexibility and no value added services.
- Constraints to the rate of business development may be imposed because the supplier is forced to a position where it is unable to agree to changes in the service requirement without the ability to see how existing poor margins will be improved or, as a minimum, not be diminished still further.
- Changes to service requirements will be subject to potentially difficult negotiation because the supplier will either perceive an opportunity to improve weak margins or, more negatively, work to avoid a further weakening of margin.
- Increased charges for changed requirements will be used to lever up the supplier's margin. The most basic of business dynamics must make this so.
- Budget constraints may constrain the desire or ability of the service provider to respond to changes in the customer's market sector, leaving the customer trailing its competitors.

If forced to operate within the principles defined above, the service provider is likely to behave in the following way:

- The service supplier may be forced to a position of inflexibility by the twin constraints of low costs or margins and a tight work specification. Low costs and low margins may mean reduced investment, research and loss of continuity, remembering that resources are tuned to the precise requirement and unnecessary resources are removed or re-assigned.
- The service supplier's priority will be the maintenance of either low margins or tight cost budgets since this is the primary demand of the customer's objective.
- The implications of the above inevitably result in a lack of emphasis on helping to deliver the customer's wider business objectives. The requirement has placed no obligation on the supplier to take a broader view and the commercial constraints make it quite impossible for the supplier to react differently.
- The supplier may seek to use every change in requirement to improve margins, which, over time, will have a debilitating effect upon both the relationship and value for money.
- There will be maximum job losses and possibly unforeseen consequences

because the pressure to reduce costs will result in the apparent need for fewer people and for assets to be worked harder. The ability to respond to upward variations in service demand or recover from unplanned problems will therefore be reduced.

- There will be a low level of supplier management input. If the service requirement is very clear and the supplier is providing a low value service, the supplier management will have neither the need nor incentive to invest any management effort in the arrangement.

Notwithstanding the points above, a low cost basic service *should* be satisfactorily delivered against the single objective. However, were a number of objectives to be set, the effect would be quite different.

Assume now that the following multiple objectives are set:

- Reduce *unit* costs and minimize capital expenditure.
- Gain access to modern technologies.
- Achieve earliest delivery of new technology benefits.
- Maximize staff career opportunities.

The resultant contract will have the following characteristics:

- Service supply will emphasize value for money since the supplier, through access to a greater scope and mix potential, is now being asked to deliver a wider range of business benefits for the lowest unit and capital costs consistent with the delivery of the other objectives.
- From the supplier's viewpoint, the requirement is now of greater commercial interest since it offers the possibility for expanded involvement and reward against the delivery of new technologies and business benefits.
- The service supplier and customer will have the potential to achieve a symbiotic relationship where pursuit of individual goals benefits the other party.
- There will be a continuous downward pressure on *unit* costs and continuous upward pressure for innovation because, despite the pressure to reduce *unit* costs, there is a clear intention to seek and exploit up-to-date technological advances to mutual benefit.
- There will be scope for charging formulae that give service flexibility but maintain pricing certainty. Since the objectives do not concern reduced costs alone, charging formulae can be devised that provide flexibility.

If asked to operate within the principles defined above, the service provider is likely to behave as follows:

- The service provider will be flexible and keen to maintain the relationship because, where the agreement appears to offer real scope for the profitable use of new technologies and developed skills, the supplier will be keen to exploit these opportunities.

- The supplier will give priority to the delivery of the customer's business objectives rather than maintaining low margins. Where the supplier does not have to concentrate on the maintenance of narrow profits, it can afford to invest time, effort and resources on both existing delivery obligations and future opportunities.

- Service variations will be a normal part of the relationship. Since both parties will appreciate the need for change and, if appropriate, the need for controlled amendments to the price, processes dealing with change can be easily devised and readily subscribed to by both parties.

- There will be minimum job losses and a higher level of supplier management input. Tight margins mean that supplier management must respond appropriately to circumstances. With less financial pressure, supplier management is likely to take a more measured view of skills, apply training (as an investment) and seek alternative methods of dealing with surplus resource.

THE OBJECTIVES SETTING PROCESS

Setting objectives is apparently straightforward but actually very difficult. It requires considerable thought and understanding and a significant commitment of time. Sufficient time is rarely allocated to the development of objectives, which places the procurement at risk before it has really begun. This is because objectives set a direction and, as a result, provide a test against which progress may be measured and any deviations identified. Figure 1.1 provides a schematic view of an objectives setting process.

Setting objectives is an imprecise task by nature and the results are often difficult to corroborate or confirm. When managing a project, even the most experienced director, manager or project leader will be unsuccessful if there are no objectives by which to measure progress and success. After all, without formal and robust objectives, how can expectations be properly set? This section provides some thoughts on how one might go about setting appropriate objectives for an outsourcing agreement.

INFORMATION REQUIRED

Within the context of outsourcing, the following information will be required:

- **High level corporate objectives and measures**
  There will be little point to an outsourcing agreement if it does not, either directly or indirectly, further the corporate goals of the enterprise. The initial thinking surrounding the outsourcing approach and its relevance must therefore take account of both the corporate goals and their associated measures.

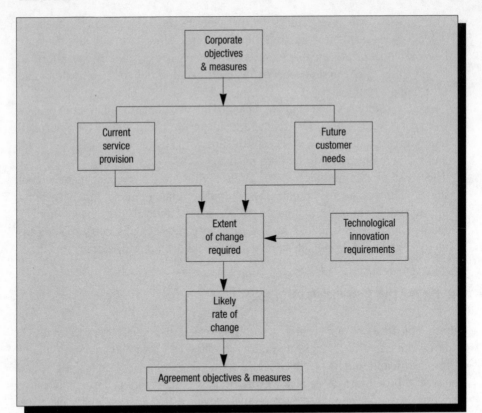

Figure 1.1 Objectives setting process

- **An understanding of future customer needs**
  If user requirements, both current but particularly future, are not understood, it will not be possible to set objectives that assure the alignment of the outsourcing agreement to those requirements.
- **A view of the gap between current service provision and customer needs**
  Without such a view it will not be possible either to determine the nature and size of any gap or to formulate a likely solution to its closure should it exist.
- **An assessment of the extent to which technological innovation is important**
  Such a view will inform judgements surrounding the general nature of any potential outsourcing agreement in terms of requirements for skills and products relating to technology, its cost effective acquisition and its exploitation.
- **The likely rate of change**
  All business sectors are feeling the pressure of accelerating rates of change but some sectors change faster than others. Any requirement for rapid change

will bear heavily upon the structure of an outsourcing agreement, the type of supplier selected, the requirement to lever technology and, most of all, cost – because 'change' has a significant cost. If you are clear about the likely rate of change, the potential costs can be negotiated into the outsourcing agreement at a better unit rate than would be achieved later through change control.

Careful consideration of the factors listed above should result in clearly articulated and written objectives and measures for each objective. The combination of the two will provide both a target for management action and a means by which progress can be measured.

SOME EXAMPLES OF GENERIC OBJECTIVES

There follow some examples of generic objectives that may provide some insights into the development of objectives more specific to individual circumstances.

SKILLS, TOOLS AND TECHNOLOGIES

Objective

To gain, and maintain, access to those skills, tools and technologies appropriate to the maintenance of operational systems and the attainment of corporate objectives.

Measures

- Minimize direct investment in developing or acquiring tools and technologies. Specific financial limits may be specified if appropriate.
- Minimize direct re-skilling investment in the use of new tools and technologies. Specific financial limits may be specified if appropriate.
- Business strategic and tactical requirements not constrained by a lack of appropriate tools and technologies. Measures can include the number, nature and cost of constraints where cost can be defined as financial, performance, time to market and so on.

COST-EFFECTIVENESS

Objective

To maintain a continuous downward pressure on *unit* costs without detriment to delivery of business objectives.

Measure

- [x per cent] reduction in the *unit* cost of outputs over a five-year period.

RESPONSIVENESS AND FLEXIBILITY

Objective

To improve, by [x per cent], the identification of, and response to, customer needs.

Measures

- Maintenance of a qualitative and quantitative view of customer needs.
- Cycle time for significant innovations not to exceed [x] months.
- Cycle time for minor innovations not to exceed [y] months.

STAFF

Objective

To maximize career opportunities for existing staff.

Measures

- Retention of mission-critical skills.
- Assure the existence of, and active participation in, personal development plans.
- Avoidance of compulsory redundancy.

2 Assessing the potential for improving performance

THE NEED TO ASSESS

A FUNDAMENTAL QUESTION

The fundamental question when thinking about whether to outsource is:

- do I need a source of service supply other than that currently in place?
    - If the answer is yes, what will be the basis upon which I judge the relevance and acceptability of alternatives?
    - If the answer is no, what improvements, if any, could I make to the current environment?

The answer to these questions may be found only in a detailed understanding of the disposition and effectiveness of the *current* environment. Without such an understanding, there can be no measures with which to assess both the need for change and the options for change.

THREE FUNDAMENTAL MEASURES

An understanding of the potential for performance improvement will provide the following important measures which, *in conjunction with the business objectives*, give a basis for assessing the need for change and for testing the options for change:

1. The internal improvement baseline
    A view of the extent to which performance could be improved without recourse to significant external support.
2. The external improvement baseline
    A view of the extent to which performance could be improved through the use of external services.
3. The bid threshold
    If external service supply is judged to be appropriate, the internal improvement baseline may be used as the threshold below which external suppliers must bid.

THE INTERNAL IMPROVEMENT BASELINE

The internal performance improvement baseline will define, in quantitative terms, the extent to which efficiency may be increased or costs reduced or both. In reality, there are two baselines. The first defines a *theoretical* maximum for efficiency/cost improvement that assumes the absence of constraints, whilst the second takes account of constraints to give a *practical* maximum.

The difference between the theoretical and practical baselines is governed by those internal constraints imposed upon the business. For example, significant performance improvements might be achieved following capital investments but insufficient capital funds are available, or expensive resources that are under-utilized cannot be released or re-assigned because of a need to maintain operational resilience or meet unexpected peaks in demand.

Logical development of these thoughts reveals a number of interesting insights. Establishment of the theoretical baseline will lead us to determine the extent to which we are constrained internally from achieving our full potential, which, in turn, leads us to establish the number and nature of internal constraints. A quantitative understanding of these constraints will lead us either to challenge the constraints and remove them or, reduce our theoretical potential for improvement to determine the practical baseline for internal improvement.

Having calculated the theoretical and practical maxima and gained a clear view of internal constraints, we can develop our logic a little further. Given the extent to which we can, in a practical sense, improve our internal performance, we must ask ourselves whether that new level of performance is sufficient to deliver our business objectives. This question creates a simple, but quantified, test to determine the extent of need for alternative sources of service supply.

If the new performance level *is* sufficient to meet our business objectives, no new sources of service supply will be needed and the practical baseline provides a clear target for internal performance improvement. Note, however, that business objectives will invariably contain a reference to cost improvement and future service demand. The difference between the theoretical and practical baselines will, therefore, always bear upon the decision to outsource. Under these circumstances, it will always be prudent to determine whether the internal performance improvement programme can be enhanced by external contributions.

If the new performance level *is not* sufficient to meet our business objectives, judgements may then be made regarding the applicability of the 'buy' route, the decision making process for which may be supported by the following:

● The theoretical baseline provides a price ceiling against which alternative sources of supply may be assessed (the bid threshold). For alternative suppliers to be able to add value, they must be free of the constraints imposed upon your business and must, therefore, be judged against the theoretical, and not the practical, baseline.

- The fact that alternative suppliers will be judged against the theoretical baseline (the bid threshold) avoids the possibility of excessive profits falling to the supplier.
- Since the constraints to theoretical performance improvements are known, a service requirement that is free of those constraints can be designed, and the ability of suppliers to meet the new, and unconstrained, service requirement can be tested.

Figure 2.1 shows the relationship between the two baselines and constraints.

THE EXTERNAL IMPROVEMENT BASELINE

The external improvement baseline provides a datum for comparison against the bid threshold to determine the likely contribution of external suppliers. It is, of course, relevant only where alternative sources of service supply have been identified and, although it cannot be accurately determined, it is possible to determine an indicative range of probability. This relies upon knowledge of the likely supplier profit margin, the ability of suppliers to remove any constraints identified as part of the internal improvement baseline and their ability to add value beyond that currently available.

REMOVING CONSTRAINTS AND ADDING VALUE

The work associated with calculating the internal improvement baseline will have

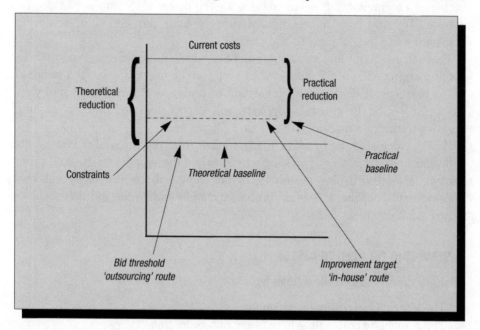

Figure 2.1 Relationship between baselines and constraints

identified a range of internally imposed constraints. If these could be removed through external intervention, there would be, all other things being equal, a net gain. If, in addition, suppliers could bring other benefits, the net gain would be enhanced.

We can therefore take the performance capability and resource disposition of each supplier and map them against the characteristics of each constraint. For example, let us assume there is an operational requirement to remove rubbish across a national network of depots. Sixty per cent of rubbish is already being removed from the 'hub' depots cost-effectively. The remaining 40 per cent is fragmented across the network and it is impossible to implement any further economies of scale or other internal efficiencies. The fragmented nature of the depots has therefore created a constraint to further internal performance improvement.

However, supplier x has both a broad geographic spread and an established collection network. It is therefore able to include the fragmented requirements within the margins of its current operation for a modest incremental cost. Given an understanding of the supplier's geographic spread and general mode of operation, a profile of possible synergy savings can be created. The supplier may, however, be able to add even more value. In addition to a good geographic spread, supplier x has invented new technology for the disposal of central rubbish – a technology that will not be made available to non-clients. Applying this technology to the central disposal requirement will reduce the number of journeys to the disposal site and hence the cost. An understanding of the effects of this new technology allows us to calculate the potential for improved value for money. We now have a preliminary view of both the effects of removing constraints and the potential to add value.

There is one more important ingredient to add – the supplier's profit margin. Profit margins will vary from sector to sector and could easily be in a range of 5–100 per cent. It is, therefore, important to understand the dynamics of your particular sector. In general, suppliers will expect service contracts of long duration to return a margin in the range 7–25 per cent.

Having calculated the benefits, if any, to flow from the removal of constraints and value added capability, you simply need to add the supplier's estimated profit margin. The result, plus or minus 15 per cent, will be the likely external improvement baseline and, in all probability, will straddle the bid threshold as Figure 2.2 illustrates.

SUMMARIZING THE NEED TO ASSESS

We have now identified the following:

- The internal improvement capability.
- The remaining constraints to delivery of business objectives.

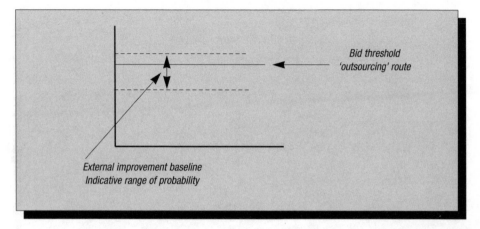

Figure 2.2 The external improvement baseline

- The extent of any external contribution to the delivery of business objectives.

Sufficient information should now be available to allow the development of a range of performance improvement options to support the outsourcing decision. Figure 2.3 shows schematically the importance of assessing the potential for performance improvement.

CALCULATING THE IMPROVEMENT BASELINES

The performance characteristics and associated metrics must inevitably vary considerably for each business. We can therefore offer only generic advice and guiding principles. Also, empirical performance related data is likely to be in short supply. For the outsourcing assessment, a high degree of accuracy in the measurement of performance is unnecessary; an indicative range of performance will suffice. Greater accuracy demands a disproportionate amount of effort and situations may change over the, potentially long, life-cycle of the outsourcing assessment and implementation. In addition, the resource and commercial disposition of potential alternative suppliers governs their pricing response. The life-cycle of the outsourcing decision means that supplier responses have the potential to move through a relatively wide range.

There are three primary components to be considered when seeking to calculate the improvement baselines:

- Internal staff utilization.
- Internal staff efficiency.
- Utilization of assets.

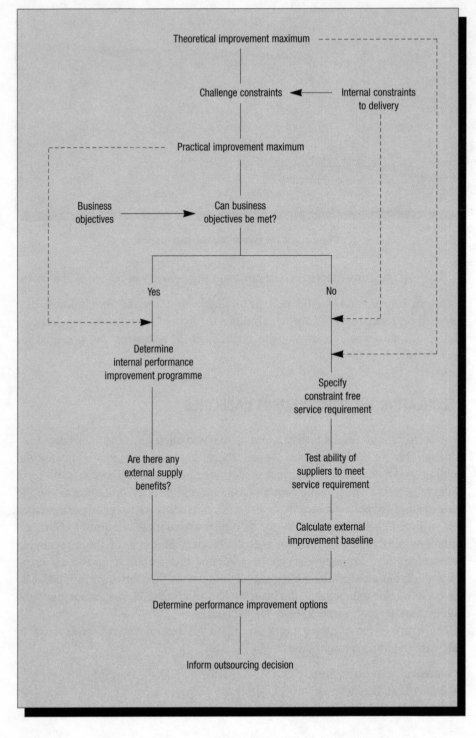

Figure 2.3 Assessing the potential for performance improvement

INTERNAL STAFF UTILIZATION

What is staff utilization?

Staff utilization is a measure of the proportion of staff time spent on productive activities. It is not concerned with how efficiently the time is spent, merely the proportion of time spent productively.

Environments that have not been subjected to a rigorous improvement programme will typically utilize staff productively for between 45 per cent and 60 per cent of their time. 'Best of breed' companies who operate within a competitive environment will generally achieve a utilization figure of at least 75 per cent and we can use this number as a datum from which to measure.

Assessing staff utilization

An assessment of staff utilization will depend upon some form of activity or process analysis. These can range from traditional O & M exercises through simple timesheet analyses to sophisticated computer-assisted modelling. Whatever approach is selected, the generic sampling steps may be summarized as follows:

- Identify the number of different roles or processes within the domain to be sampled.
- Select one person to represent each role or process.
- Calculate the average manpower cost for each role or process.
- Determine the activities *actually* performed by the role or process.
- Note the difference between a person's perception of what they believe to be required of them relative to what they actually do and be sure to collect 'actuals' rather than 'beliefs'.
- Assess the time consumed by each activity.

One approach is to assess effort over a twelve-month period. This information is best captured with computer assistance via interview and takes the following form:

- For each activity:
  - determine the time it takes to execute one cycle;
  - determine the number of times the activity is performed per annum taking note of any 'seasonal' variation;
  - calculate the total amount of effort expended on the activity;
  - compare this with the total theoretical effort available (research shows that people overestimate by a factor of two, the amount of effort they believe they expend); and
  - refine the cycle times and number of executions to give an agreed annual profile.
- Once the activities within a role or process have been agreed with the

representative, seek confirmation and agreement from peers involved in the same role or process.

- Categorize each activity in terms of its contribution to the value chain.
- Calculate the percentage of unproductive effort.
- Identify those non-staff costs associated with each unproductive activity.
- Calculate the cost of unproductive effort relative to the best practice datum of 75 per cent productive.
- Calculate the total unproductive cost by summing the two previous bullets.
- Calculate the potential headcount reduction.

Summing up

To assess staff utilization relative to best practice:

- Determine the manpower cost by process or role.
- Select a role or process representative.
- Determine the percentage of productive and non-productive work for each role or process.
- Test the findings with peer groups and gain agreement.
- Determine the industry norm for utilization – if in doubt use 75 per cent.
- Calculate the potential for performance improvement as follows:

  75 – per cent productive/75 x 100 = % possible improvement

- Calculate the potential headcount and cost reductions.

INTERNAL STAFF EFFICIENCY

What is staff efficiency?

Staff efficiency is a measure of the number of useful outputs delivered within the period of productive activity determined by the staff utilization calculation. The metrics associated with efficiency depend heavily upon the field of activity. Each field of activity will have its own industry norms.

Insights into measuring staff efficiency

The wide variation in the metrics for each field of activity makes it impossible to give precise guidance here. Some insights into specific sector performance may be gained from informal discussions with commercial organizations within relevant sectors. The underlying principles may be summarized as follows:

- Identify, in broad terms, the primary outputs associated with either a process or role. This can turn into a protracted exercise if driven to too great a level of detail. It will suffice to keep the view of outputs to a high level since we are looking for only an *indication* of relative performance. The activity analysis undertaken to determine staff utilization will help – take each activity or

Primary output	Total outputs produced per month	Total staff time consumed (hrs)	Total staff cost £	Non-staff costs £	Total cost of output £	Unit cost of output £	Unit effort of output (hrs)
Output 1	125	62	434	94	528	4.22	0.5
Output 2	12	526	4045	2561	6606	550.5	43.8
Output 3	3250	17023	127672	2147	129819	39.9	5.2
Output 4	1	54	830	0	830	830	54
Output 5	15700	2616	19620	1570	21190	1.35	0.17
—		20281	152601	6372	158973	—	—

Figure 2.4 Staff efficiency matrix

related groups of activity and ask the question 'what actually results from the performance of this activity?'

● Determine the total number of outputs produced within the period.
● Determine the amount of staff time consumed in the production of outputs identified above. The analysis of staff utilization will assist.
● Identify non-staff costs associated with each output.
● Calculate the total cost for each output.
● Calculate the unit cost for each output.
● Calculate the unit staff effort associated with the production of each output.

You are now able to construct a matrix as illustrated in Figure 2.4. You can test this information against known industry norms to provide an indication of the extent to which current service performance is in advance of or behind industry norms and input to the calculation of the external improvement baseline.

UTILIZATION OF ASSETS

The extent to which synergy exists between current assets and those of potential suppliers will play an important part in determining the external improvement baseline.

Assessing the impact

A simple way to assess the impact may be summarized as follows:

● Identify your asset base by setting out all of the asset components. Remember that there may be a wide range of relevant assets, not just those directly associated with the mainstream task. For example, if the mainstream task is engineering, there will obviously be machinery and other directly relevant

19

equipment. However, there will also be buildings, perhaps motor transport and stock holdings of different varieties.

- Determine the extent to which these resources are utilized, i.e. the extent to which there is spare capacity or the need for greater capacity.
- Determine broad replacement costs and timescales.
- Match these assets to those of potential suppliers and look for those areas where they overlap.

You can now assess the extent to which service suppliers may be able either to reduce the overall requirement for assets or avoid a direct replacement cost, and the likely effect of this on the external improvement baseline (see Figure 2.2).

Example

Current engineering equipment is under-utilized by 15 per cent and will need a capital outlay of £3m for replacement/refurbishment within the next two years. Supplier x has appropriate assets but a larger critical mass. If supplier x were to assume responsibility for the current workload the impact might be as follows:

- The supplier's critical mass means that just enough capacity to meet the exact needs of the actual workload can be purchased – no more, no less. This means that what was an over capacity of 15 per cent can now be released; the financial benefits of which can contribute towards the external improvement baseline (see Figure 2.2).
- In addition, it will not be necessary to incur the replacement/refurbishment cost of £3m, since this will be factored into the unit pricing of the supplier's price. It is possible that the current workload can fit into the supplier's critical mass of resources allowing a more competitive unit price, the supplier's critical mass of resources will allow the potential benefits associated with the under-utilised capacity to be unlocked, and the outlay of £3m in capital is avoided.
- The combination of these factors may result in a unit price that is below current costs, the avoidance of capital investment, and a more flexible and scaleable service. All of these factors may then be taken into account when calculating the external improvement baseline.

3 Implications for business users

The effects upon customers of service supply moving to a third party will vary considerably depending upon the complexity of the service requirement. Where the nature of the service is 'simple', i.e. cleaning services, little impact will be felt. Where the service requirement is more complex and, as a consequence, requires routine customer input or refinement over time, the impact will be much greater. Here, the principal effects of a move to third party supply will be seen in the interplay between better performance and lower unit costs. This is because the objectives for the new service will almost certainly include the need to reduce unit costs and improve service performance.

Customers play a key role in both service performance and the level of unit cost since they define the requirement and may provide critically important inputs to enable the service provider to deliver the service. Service performance will increase and unit cost will reduce *only* if there is a matched improvement in performance from both the service provider *and* the customer. Suppliers may therefore be unable to deliver projected benefits from the new arrangements unless there is a *matched* performance improvement from customers.

IMPLICATIONS FOR CUSTOMERS

WORKING THE ASSETS

Seeking tough value for money targets will cause transferred assets to be worked much harder. One effect of this will be to squeeze out the bulk of contingent resource. Resource requirements will move to a position where their provision will be on a 'just in time' basis against predetermined minima. A failure on the part of the customer to meet agreed target dates for its inputs, whatever they might be, (e.g. plans, specifications, data, decisions, investments, etc.) may disrupt finely balanced resource planning mechanisms and cause additional costs to be incurred or timescales to slip. The new supplier will accommodate the delays that normally come upon these issues but the resource, cost and timetable effects will be much more obvious to customers. It is apparent, therefore, that unless customers are clear about their contribution to the whole performance equation, the delivery of predicted benefits may be put at risk.

PERFORMANCE LEVELS

Service performance may fall below that which has historically been achieved but still remain within the agreed performance window, for example historical performance may have been delivered at a level of, say, 99 per cent but the agreed level is 98 per cent. The supplier is likely to optimize service around the 98 per cent figure as a contribution to delivering higher value for money and is able to do so because it remains within the contractually agreed service level. Alternatively, the cost of delivering 99 per cent is likely to be higher and the value for money correspondingly less.

PLANNING

Base resource requirements will be established within the specification for each service and will be set at levels sufficient to achieve known demands. The price for this minimum agreed resource will probably be lower than the price for unplanned resources purchased at short notice above the agreed threshold. This is because price is a function of volume over time (see Chapter 12).

It should always be possible to regulate the minimum agreed resource level up or down over time but adjustments will most likely be made over an agreed planning horizon of, say, 12 months. Under circumstances such as these, maximum value for money will be achieved only if customers are able to participate in regular and focused analyses of their future base resource requirements. It is probable therefore that the ability of customers to plan effectively over appropriate planning horizons will more directly affect the delivery of value for money.

THE SERVICE CYCLE

One objective of the new service may be to reduce the amount of time it takes to complete one service cycle. Depending upon the nature of the cycle and the demands it places upon customer inputs, acceleration of the cycle through the application of improved external services may imply the need for a matched acceleration of customer inputs. An accelerated service environment is forced to be much less tolerant of any lapses in customer performance. The clear implication is, therefore, that customers must be in a position to develop and refine their interfaces with the service provider to enable the whole service to be provided with precision and at a pace appropriate to the accelerated cycle.

IMPLICATIONS FOR THE OUTSOURCING PROCUREMENT TEAM

The general impact of a third party service provider upon customers will be significant and sometimes subtle. It will range, ultimately, across all aspects of service supply. For this reason, it becomes important for customers, at all relevant operational levels, to be positioned properly to understand and question the implications for them of the proposed new arrangements. To this end, the procurement team should offer a number of workshops aimed at informing customer staff, at appropriate management levels, about the nature and implications of the proposed agreement and beginning a dialogue with customers that will focus more precisely upon the business issues about which they are most interested and concerned.

4 Managing the constituency

One of the more worrying aspects of managing an outsourcing assessment and procurement programme is the possibility of an unexpected intervention by a person or body not directly concerned with the project but who has authority, influence and the ability to cause delay. Conversely, programme delays may occur if those from whom a contribution *is* required are unprepared or inefficient. It is therefore worth giving some early thought to those who will influence the programme and then to compile a full list of potentially interested constituents. You will then require a simple device within the programme management routine to control constituent interventions.

WHAT IS A CONSTITUENT?

A constituent is defined as 'Any person or body who has, *or believes they have*, a direct or indirect interest in the programme or its outcome and who has sufficient authority, influence or ability either to make a significant contribution or inflict significant delay if not properly managed or consulted.'

WHY WORRY ABOUT CONSTITUENTS?

By definition, a constituent has the potential either significantly to improve or significantly to damage the programme. Thus, in large organizations running large and complex programmes, the potential for disruption from constituents is enormous.

For example, often lawyers are not consulted until the end of the process, when a contract is needed within which to enshrine the agreement principles. However, if legal advice is not sought earlier, an opportunity to gain valuable input may have been lost and, more importantly, disruption is now likely to ensue as the lawyer, perhaps, begins to identify a range of issues that should previously have been considered.

Alternatively, there may be those within the organization who actively oppose the purpose of the programme or wish to ensure a different outcome. In such circumstances it is helpful to engage them in the process in an attempt both to influence them and to understand their point of view and activities.

Some individuals or organizations may have an interest in the programme after the event, for example audit authorities. An understanding of their interest will have some effect on the conduct of the programme and, if required, ensure that adequate records are kept.

IDENTIFYING THE CONSTITUENTS

The purpose of active constituency management is to ensure that the programme manager has a satisfactory understanding of expectation, from all quarters. The first task will be to devise the full list of interested parties – the constituency.

AUTHORIZING BODIES/DECISION MAKERS

The authorizing body and decision makers are clearly important. The programme manager must know the identity of the decision makers and if decision making is conducted by a committee or group, its composition and *modus operandi*.

COLLEAGUES

There may be colleagues who are not directly involved in the programme but have a vested interest in its outcome. Examples include those with implementation or financial control responsibilities.

USERS

The ultimate users of the function under consideration for outsourcing must be identified and involved. User involvement could take the form of representation on the programme management team, attendance at workshops or involvement with regular communication events. Alternatively the programme manager may consider setting up a small working group(s) to provide informal opinion on some elements of the programme.

STAFF AND STAFF REPRESENTATIVES

Clearly if the programme is to affect staff in any way, the programme manager must be aware of existing staff representation arrangements (see Chapter 10, p. 63).

INTERNAL SPECIALISTS AND EXPERTS

The input of all relevant specialists and experts must be available to the programme manager. Some internal specialists and experts will be members of the programme team, others may have only a brief or intermittent involvement. It will be necessary for the programme manager carefully to consider such involvement since inappropriate exclusion from meetings may generate resentment and unnecessary internal obstacles while over-attendance may lead to ineffective meetings.

SUPPLIERS

Existing suppliers may become unsettled at the prospect of moving to an outsourcing arrangement and the programme manager will need to maintain contact with relevant suppliers so that their indirect influence can be monitored. Aggrieved suppliers can cause delay. Remember that the outsourcing supplier may already have working relationships (good or bad) with existing suppliers – a situation which may help or hinder. Equally, other opportunities may emerge from relationships between existing suppliers and the new outsourcing supplier.

EXTERNAL BODIES

There may be external government or trade bodies that should be considered or consulted, for example Data Protection Registrar, National Audit Office, Customs & Excise, Industry Training Boards.

THE CONSTITUENCY LIST

Identify the constituents as indicated above and generate a list. The purpose of the list is to facilitate a regular debate and rolling assessment of their interests relative to the current status of the programme. Since the list must be reviewed on a regular basis, it may be helpful to make it a standing agenda item for each programme board/steering group meeting. If programme boards are infrequent, the list should be reviewed as part of the routine programme reporting procedures.

MANAGING THE CONSTITUENCY

Managing the constituency appears to be deceptively simple. In fact, it requires a great deal of careful thinking and even more discipline – without either in the right amount, influence upon the constituents will be reduced and significant project advantages lost.

The following issues are central to successful constituency management:

- Ensure that all main constituents have been identified.
- For each constituent, determine their likely disposition, needs, potential impact upon the project and timing of intervention.
- Against the view established above, prepare an approach for each constituent that is specifically designed either to respond to their needs or to control an unhelpful intervention.
- The approach must be carefully prepared and *logically unassailable*.
- Launch each intervention *just ahead* of the natural point at which the constituent would look to become involved.
- Monitor the effects of the intervention and update the approach.
- Launch the next intervention if necessary and repeat the cycle.

In the early stages of the programme the constituency management list will probably require weekly monitoring. Once the constituents are fully engaged, the review period may be extended, depending upon demand.

5 Managing the risks

The management of risk must always begin with the identification of risks – but it must not end there! Risks change as projects develop – threats heighten and diminish, risks appear and disappear. Risk management is not, therefore, a 'one shot' exercise to be forgotten when the risk register has been compiled. It requires not only a structured register of risk, but also a process for its maintenance and a process for managing the risks.

THE RISK REGISTER

The information required to describe, classify and effectively manage risk is substantial and potentially complex, but if risks are to be managed effectively, there are no known short cuts. Effective risk management depends upon a combination of effective controls, an appropriate allocation of resources, and sufficient allocation of planned time and effort in the project plan. Effective controls begin with the risk register, which will be at the heart of any risk management system.

The risk register supports four primary functions:

- It facilitates the identification of project risks and their potential impact.
- It provides key input to, and therefore enables, an effective management review of project risks.
- It facilitates the assessment of risk by providing consolidated risk management information.
- It provides a basis for recording and monitoring risk management actions.

THE RISK REGISTER FRAMEWORK

There are a number of components to the risk register and Figure 5.1 broadly illustrates their relationship.

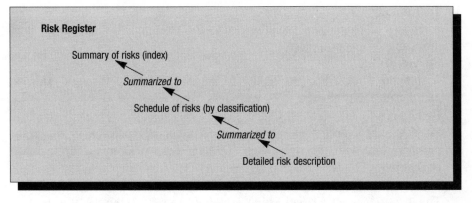

Figure 5.1 The risk register structure

DETAILED RISK DESCRIPTION

RISK DETAIL SHEET – CONTENT

Each risk will be entered onto a risk detail sheet which will have the following fields:

Reference number

A unique number allocated by the risk manager.

Version number

Perception of risks will change through the project life-cycle and risk parameters will change accordingly. As risks change the version number will increment by one to enable the trend in risk movement to be tracked.

Risk classification

It will be helpful to organize the various project risks into common groupings or classifications. There are a number of general categories into which risks will fall as follows:

● **Complexity**
  The project may demand the bringing together of a number of different organizations, components or systems, the complexity of which becomes difficult to understand and manage.
● **Constituency**
  It may be that those people or other organisations who have an interest in the project create unforeseen difficulties (see Chapter 4).
● **Effectiveness**
  Assumptions surrounding the direction or solution selected may change to a point where they either no longer support the project aims or their effectiveness is diminished.

29

- **Technology**
  A chosen technological solution may, for example, be unproven, late, unreliable or inappropriate.
- **Serviceability**
  Assumptions regarding the ability to assure availability through effective maintenance may change.
- **Resources**
  Project, supply and customer resources must all coalesce in the right numbers and with the right skills. Deficiencies will dramatically increase project risks.
- **Experience**
  The experience of project, supply and customer resources will have a profound effect upon the effectiveness of the project and the delivered solution. Any deficiencies will dramatically increase both the risks to project and outcome.
- **Safety**
  Assumptions surrounding the safety of staff and customers may change.
- **Security**
  Security requirements or assumptions may change, or suppliers may fail to comply with security standards.
- **Management**
  Management difficulties may arise or be predicted for the project, or with the ultimate service supplier.
- **Legal instruments**
  Poorly drafted contracts, schedules and service agreements may give rise to dispute and litigation.
- **Project plan**
  Deficiencies within the project plan or events outside the control of the project team may change the delivery parameters.
- **Finance**
  Pressure on funds may force a reduction of quality or remove entire project plan strands or service components.

Risk description and title

A concise description of the risk together with a brief title for ease of reference.

Risk domain and source

A statement naming the organization from which the risk originates and the functional area in which it occurs.

Risk owner

The person who has direct responsibility for the risk.

Reason to occur

A record of any information which sheds light on why the risk is likely to occur.

Likelihood of occurrence

An estimate of the percentage likelihood of the risk occurring.

Risk effect and timing

An assessment of the likely effect to both project and outturn in terms of cost, timescale and effectiveness, with an indication of when the effect is likely to occur. The effect is rated separately for cost, effectiveness and time on a 50 point numeric scale where 1 = nil effect and 50 = catastrophic effect.

Risk score

The *likelihood* percentage and *effect* scores are multiplied to give a risk score which when combined with the version number gives a scale and, if monitored over time, a trend of risk. Figure 5.2 illustrates the point. The version 1 risk assessment indicates the existence of a time threat to the procurement calculated as 2.5 (likelihood of 10 per cent x effect of 25) but indicates no threat to either effectiveness (likelihood of 0 per cent x effect of, say, 10) or cost (likelihood of 0 per cent x effect of, say, 15). When the risk was next assessed at version 2, the time threat had reduced to 10 but in the process of responding to the time pressure, effectiveness had been affected giving rise to an effectiveness rating of 7.5 (likelihood of 75 per cent x effect of 10). A third assessment at version 3 shows a worsening picture in that the time risk is slipping back out, the effectiveness risk is remaining stable but problems of cost have now emerged with a rating of 5.

Version No	Cost	Risk scores	
		Effectiveness	Time
1	—	—	2.5
2	—	7.5	10
3	5	7.5	12

Figure 5.2 Risk score and trend

Mitigation strategy

The mitigation strategy defines the actions to be taken to reduce or eliminate the risk. It will include the following:

- A statement of the actions to be taken.
- The individual(s) responsible.
- The target deliverable(s).

- The completion date and time.
- Status of the actions.

RISK DETAIL SHEET – EXAMPLE

Figure 5.3 illustrates the risk detail sheet format.

SCHEDULE AND SUMMARY OF RISKS

There will be a great many risks associated with each outsourcing programme and the accumulation of risk detail sheets will make the management of risk cumbersome. Therefore, a more manageable format is needed for day-to-day review and it is provided by the schedule of risks and the summary of risks.

SCHEDULE OF RISKS

The schedule of risks simply takes selected data items from each risk detail sheet and brings them together for ease of review, ordered by classification and highest risk score. Figure 5.4 illustrates its content and format.

SUMMARY OF RISKS

The summary of risks is the highest summation level and provides an overview of risks and an index to the risk register. Its format is illustrated in Figure 5.5.

RISK REGISTER OVERVIEW

Figure 5.6 brings together all of the risk register components to give an overview of the final document.

THE RISK MANAGEMENT PROCESS

Figure 5.7 illustrates schematically the risk management process (see p. 38).

SAMPLE RISKS

The following main risk headings are used:

- Project plan and project team.
- Constituency management.

Risk Detail Sheet

Review domain .... *Risk title* .... **Part A**

Description	Domain	Classification
	Source	Owner

Reason to occur	Time to occur

Effect rating **Risk score**

	Cost		Effectiveness		Time				
Version	Rating	% Likely	Rating	% Likely	Rating	% Likely	Cost	Effectiveness	Time

Risk Detail Sheet

Review domain .... *Risk title* .... **Part B**

Risk mitigation strategy

Action to be taken

Target deliverables	Status	Completion	Responsible

Figure 5.3 Risk detail sheet format

33

Schedule of Risks

Review domain . . . .   *Issue date* . . . .   *Version* . . . .
Classification . . . .

Ref.	Risk score		Owner	Description	Mitigation deliverables	Status
	Cost					
	Effect.					
	Time					
	Cost					
	Effect.					
	Time					

Figure 5.4 Schedule of risks format

Summary of Risks

Review domain . . . .   *Issue date* . . . .   *Version* . . . .

Ref.	Risk title	Status	Cost	Effect	Time	Version
Complexity						
1.01	Risk Title One Point One	Resolved	2	2	2	2
1.02	Risk Title One Point Two	Current	10	8	25	2
1.03	Risk Title One Point Three	Current	10	15	30	2
Constituency						
2.01	Risk Title Two Point One	Current	25	12	32	2
2.02	Risk Title Two Point Two	Current	30	8	12	2
2.03	Risk Title Two Point Three	Current	5	2	2	2
2.04	Risk Title Two Point Four	Current	45	32	41	2
Effectiveness						
3.01	Risk Title Three Point One	Current	10	0	0	2
3.02	Risk Title Three Point Two	Current	15	10	0	2
3.03	Risk Title Three Point Three	Current	12	5	10	2
3.04	Risk Title Three Point Four	Current	3	8	20	2
3.05	Risk Title Three Point Five	Resolved	0	0	0	2
Technology						
	etc.					

Figure 5.5 Summary of risks format

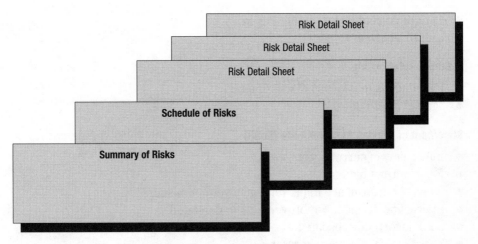

Figure 5.6 Risk register overview

- Making a relationship.
- Statement of service requirements.
- Short-listing.
- Launch.

Each risk under the above headings should be assessed separately to identify underlying causes and effects. The probability (risk) of each cause or event should be classified as low, medium, likely or high where low has up to a 10 per cent probability of occurring, medium has an 11–50 per cent probability of occurring, likely has a 51–75 per cent probability and high a probability of 76 per cent or over. The assessment of these probabilities will change as the programme develops. Some example risks follow.

Project plan and project team

- Fail properly to plan project.
- Fail adequately to scope relationship.
- Ineffective project management mechanisms.
- Inexperienced skills on project.
- Delay to project from project definition stage.
- Lack of project resources.
- Insufficient time left for detailed work.
- Fail to identify objectives of partnership.

Constituency management

- Fail to manage constituency.
- Staff demotivation, impact on cost/quality/schedule.
- Staff demotivation, loss of key people.
- Service sabotage.

- Lack of customer community buy-in.
- Industrial action by staff.

Making a relationship

- Fail to manage informal discussions.
- Market does not exist.

Statement of Service Requirements (SoSR)

- Initial view of current costs wrong.
- Fail to attract bidders.
- Internal performance improvements over-optimistic.
- Internal performance improvements understated.
- SoSR incorrectly specified.
- Specification of resources wrong.
- Suitability of draft contracts.
- Security/confidentiality.
- Internal changes affect SoSR.
- Inventories incorrect.
- SoSR too detailed (preferential selection).
- SoSR not detailed enough.
- SoSR misleading.
- Delay to project from preparation of SoSR.

Short-listing

- Choose 'wrong' short list (exclude 'good' supplier).
- Internal changes affect requirements.
- Inadequate information provided by suppliers.
- Evaluation inconclusive – delay to project from short-listing.
- Insufficient time for reference visits and evaluation.
- Suppliers slow to provide additional information.
- Litigation/complaints from short-listing evaluation.
- Insufficient time for bidders to respond.
- Suppliers withdraw without submitting a bid.
- Unable to achieve expected value for money.
- Suppliers withdraw bid during evaluation.
- Delay to project from evaluation procedure.
- Negotiating position undermined by constituency.
- Difficulty in choosing partner.
- Lack of negotiating skills.
- Fail to see significance of contract terms.
- Breakdown of partnership during negotiation.
- Commercial pressures.
- External factors.

- Supplier delays (perhaps leading to later withdrawal).
- Poor assessment of company stability.
- Poorly written contract.
- Pricing too aggressive.
- Complexity of contract leads to disputes.
- Wrong choice of company.
- Change in company capabilities.
- Insufficient control given to partner.
- Partner does not provide necessary skills.
- Internal performance improves.

Launch

- Disruption to business.
- Partner slow to build re-engineering team.
- Inability to manage contract.
- Insufficient business skills.
- Change in senior management.
- Failure to extract benefits from the business.
- Change in objectives.
- Change in policy as a result of a change in government.
- Poor measurement of partner performance.
- Failure of partnership approach.

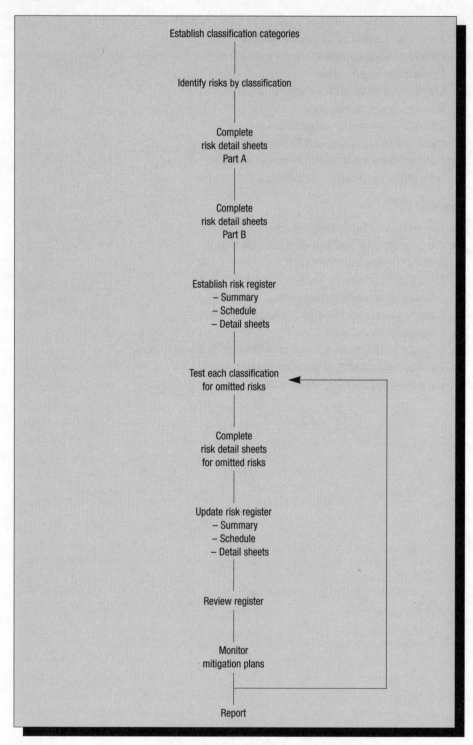

Figure 5.7 The risk management process

Part II
Preparation – The Key to a Good Job

Introduction to Part II

Having thought clearly about your objectives and determined the need to engage an outsourcing supplier, you are ready to begin to assemble the components, of which there are many, for a successful agreement.

Part II will examine the range of issues about which you will need to think deeply and formulate a position. The issues in question are as follows:

- Establishing the procurement process.
- Planning and managing the project.
- Packaging the agreement.
- Defining the service requirement.
- Human resources.
- Assets.
- Charging formulae.
- The contract.
- Evaluating the proposals.
- Evaluating relationships.
- Statement of Service Requirement.

As you work through Part II, the context of some chapters may seem a little obscure. The reason for this is that creating an outsourcing agreement is a bit like doing a jigsaw puzzle – you must have all the pieces before the picture can be completed. We hope you will find that when you reach Chapter 16 the issues discussed in prior chapters will start to find a home and the picture will begin to emerge. You may also find it helpful to study the procurement process illustrated in Chapter 6 (Figure 6.1, p. 43).

6 Establishing the procurement process

The process for procuring an outsourcing agreement, which is summarized schematically in Figure 6.1, contains the following steps.

PREPARING THE PROJECT PLAN

Once you have determined the agreement objectives, scope and procurement process, a project plan should be developed from which will emerge a firm timetable, an indication of the scale and nature of resources required and a view of individual responsibilities (see Chapter 7).

DEFINITION OF SERVICE REQUIREMENT

A definition of the services required may now be prepared, which will define the boundaries of outsourced activity, the services that are to fall within those boundaries and the service levels required for each of the services elements (see Chapter 9).

FORMULATE PRINCIPAL POLICIES

In parallel with the definition of service requirements, a number of policies will need to be formulated and agreed. Each policy will, to a greater or lesser degree, govern supplier responses by establishing the boundaries within which they may bid. By way of example, two significant policies will be those regarding the handling of any internal bid and staffing issues in general. An example of an important contract mechanism is the means by which costs are to be controlled and flexibility retained without the possibility of price escalation over time.

You should identify all of the policies and mechanisms likely to be required and formulate an agreed position for each. The primary policy issues and mechanisms are as follows:

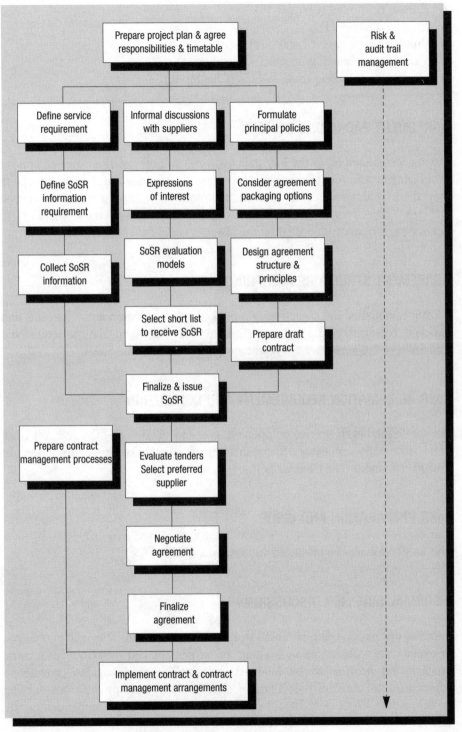

Figure 6.1 The procurement process

- Human resources (Chapter 10).
- Assets (Chapter 11).
- Charging formulae (Chapter 12).
- Models for evaluating proposals (Chapter 14).
- Model for evaluating relationships (Chapter 15).

AGREEMENT PACKAGING OPTIONS

Having formulated all of the key policies, you can now detail a range of options for packaging the required service components. The most appropriate package may then be determined in light of the requirements to service the agreed 'business' objectives, implications for any internal bid and the constraints to service performance identified by the internal study (see Chapter 8).

AGREEMENT STRUCTURE AND PRINCIPLES

Having established the objectives, scope, key policies, contract mechanisms and package required, you may now finalize and document the structure and principles of the agreement in readiness for inclusion in the SoSR.

SoSR INFORMATION REQUIREMENT AND COLLECTION

Having defined each service component, you now need to identify and collect all of the information necessary to construct the Statement of Service Requirement (SoSR) document (see Chapter 16).

SoSR PREPARATION AND ISSUE

The SoSR may now be prepared and issued.

INFORMAL SUPPLIER DISCUSSIONS

Informal discussions with potential suppliers can be useful. They will enable you to explain your objectives in seeking an agreement and describe the general procurement process to be followed. Informal discussions also provide an opportunity to test the objectives of suppliers for entering into outsourcing arrangements. Both sets of objectives should be broadly complementary to become joint objectives for the relationship (see Chapter 17).

EXPRESSIONS OF INTEREST

Some organizations are bound by legislation to follow certain procurement processes. For example, there may be a statutory requirement to post an 'expression of interest' advertisement. Responses to this advertisement provide the basis for a short-list selection.

For those organizations subject to such procurement rules the advertisement is a vital part of the procurement process because, if not constructed properly, it has the potential both to frustrate the process and allow a judicial challenge from unhappy losers. Careful consideration must therefore be given to both its content and timing of placement. It is not unknown for an organization to find its procurement project under substantial time or political pressure at an early stage because the obligation to advertise was not understood or the advertisement was posted too late.

Those organizations who are not formally required to advertise may wish to consider such an approach as a means of establishing a short list, particularly in circumstances where the market is immature and few suppliers are known to operate. An advertisement of this type may encourage new, but credible, suppliers into the market.

SUPPLIER SHORT LIST

Use the evaluation models provided in Chapter 14, suitably modified to accommodate your requirements, to compile a short list of suppliers to receive the SoSR.

THE SoSR EVALUATION MODEL AND PROCESS

The evaluation of outsourcing tenders is complex and carries significant risks. Notwithstanding the prescriptive quality of the SoSR, supplier proposals *will not* conform to the required format and the nature of proposed service charges *will not be obvious*. The evaluation models set out in Chapters 14 and 15 offer some guidance in this difficult area but they will, of course, require refinement to meet your precise needs.

NEGOTIATE CONTRACT

The extent to which an enduring and effective contract may be created is largely determined by the ability to achieve a balance of obligations between the parties and a *fair* price/profit ratio. Issues surrounding contract negotiation are discussed in Chapter 18.

PREPARE CONTRACT MANAGEMENT PROCESSES

In many senses, the procurement of a partnering contract is merely the beginning of a very long road. The contract simply provides the *potential* for benefit delivery. Benefits will be delivered in proportion to the quality and vigour with which the contract is managed. It is therefore essential that sufficient resources be allocated to the challenge of contract management and for appropriate and robust processes to be developed to ensure effective performance but to avoid micro-managing the partner. The issues surrounding contract management are discussed in Chapter 19.

IMPLEMENTATION MANAGEMENT

Although implementation of the agreement will be the responsibility of the outsourcing supplier, you will be required to participate. Chapter 20 discusses the issues.

7 Planning and managing the project

The acquisition of a robust outsourcing agreement is a particularly complex undertaking with many disparate, and potentially difficult, strands of activity. The quality with which the project is managed therefore represents a critical success factor, particularly given the long-term nature of most outsourcing agreements.

WHAT IS PROJECT MANAGEMENT?

Project management is the planning, organizing and managing of tasks and resources to achieve a defined objective, usually within defined cost and time constraints. Virtually any group of tasks can, and should, be treated as a project and be subject to project management techniques and practices.

Given a clear objective, the project should be broken down into easily managed tasks or activities. The timescales associated with the completion of the activities should be identified, scheduled and recorded. Ownership of the tasks must be identified, agreed and recorded. Use of equipment or service facilities must be planned.

Activities must be tracked and progress recorded. Such monitoring of progress will allow the project manager to assess the following:

- The likely completion date for activities within the project plan and the project as a whole.
- The effect of delays on the project.
- Which activities are critical to the project.
- The appropriateness of resources allocated to the project both in terms of numbers and skills.
- Alternative sequencing of activities.

PROJECT MANAGEMENT ELEMENTS

Project management divides neatly into the three primary elements of planning, managing and reporting.

47

PROJECT PLANNING

Planning is the most important part of the project management cycle. Careful planning will allow the project length and resource requirements to be determined.

Planning the project will also enable the project manager to identify the difficult areas, the risks and the resources needed. Note that projects frequently overrun not because planned tasks take longer than expected, but because time critical tasks were omitted from the original plan. Another reason for project overrun is the optimistic assessments of progress. Project participants will often claim that a task is complete when in fact it is not or is only partially complete. This trap can be avoided by assigning an 'output' or 'deliverable' to each activity, asking to see the 'output' and then testing its quality. This approach has the added benefit of improving the definition of tasks since, if it is difficult to identify the output, there may be little point in attempting the task.

MANAGING THE PROJECT

Managing the project is concerned with tracking and corroborating the completion of activities and adjusting the plan to meet the early or late completion of tasks and deliverables. It is not uncommon within outsourcing procurement projects for the business of managing the project to be confused with the formulation of policies and contractual mechanisms. This occurs because project meetings are called to discuss progress but, instead, discuss the merits or de-merits of a particular policy or mechanism. This creates a distraction to the primary business of the meeting with the result that neither project progress nor the policy mechanism is sufficiently well examined.

We suggest an approach that selects and maintains a clear focus of action so that the matters under discussion receive the fullest attention of everyone and the duration of the meeting is reduced.

REPORTING THE PROJECT

Project reporting is a vital ingredient of project management. Comprehensive and accurate reporting:

● provides a record of progress;
● provides early warning of potential failure;
● enables achievements easily to be communicated;
● enables difficulties easily to be communicated; and
● contributes to the audit trail.

THE PROJECT MANAGER'S ROLE

Project managers are ultimately responsible for delivery of agreed outputs and should hold the following responsibilities:

- Project initiation.
- Project plan creation.
- Identification and recording of dependencies.
- Acquisition of resources appropriate to the task.
- Securing approvals, as required.
- Setting and following quality standards.
- Monitoring progress.
- Providing appropriate documentation.
- Project administration.
- Managing communications within the project team.
- Managing communications with interested parties outside the project team.
- Assuring effective team working within the project.
- Utilizing effectively all project resources.
- Identifying the need for and using effectively any external support.
- Assuring that appropriate control systems are in place and function correctly.
- Establishing and operating change management processes.
- Managing the project budget.
- Establishing an audit trail and co-operating with audit activity.
- Identifying and responding to all project threats.
- Corroborating the delivery and quality of activity 'outputs'.
- Assuming full responsibility for delivery, or non-delivery, of project objectives.

INITIATING A PROJECT

TERMS OF REFERENCE AND OBJECTIVES

The terms of reference for the project must be agreed with the responsible executive or manager. Terms of reference define responsibilities for all members of the project team and set the scope of the project. They will typically include the following:

- Scope and purpose of project.
- Objectives – corporate/project.
- Project assumptions.
- Quality requirements.
- Project budget.
- Timescales.
- Outputs.

- Procurement price expectations.
- Expected benefits.
- How success/benefits will be measured.
- Risks.

Note that the establishment of correctly defined objectives and associated measures are critically important to the ultimate success of the project (see Chapter 1).

PROJECT PLAN

A comprehensive and well-structured project plan provides the basis for allocating work, monitoring progress, controlling deliverables and the completion of tasks and activities. Setting the plan is best achieved by systematic definition of the work elements and tasks, beginning at a high level and working downwards into increasing levels of detail. Break the plan into discrete groups of tasks usually associated with a higher level element, with each group taking no more than five to ten days of effort. In this way it is less likely that important tasks will be missed and monitoring of progress will be easier. Time spent carefully and logically constructing the plan to minimize the risk of missing out key tasks will be well rewarded towards the end of the project.

Wherever possible, always seek an independent quality check of the initial plan.

PROJECT BOARD/TEAM

The project team should be established as early as possible after project initiation. The project team will consist of full-time and part-time members. The full-time members should be few in number and will form the core of the team. Experience suggests that greatest control will be exercised by a core team no larger than six people. It will consist of the project manager, who in the case of large-scale high value procurements should be a senior executive; an able administrator capable of administering the project plan; members of the function to be outsourced who are technically expert; and, if the team is inexperienced in the business of outsourcing, an external outsourcing advisor.

Part-time members of the project team will cover the following professional domains depending upon the nature of the procurement:

- Legal.
- Human resources.
- Asset valuation/leasing/disposal.
- Property valuation/leasing/disposal.
- Building and site maintenance.
- Finance.
- Audit

An early meeting of all participants will enable working contact to be established and everyone will have an opportunity to discuss prominent issues and the project plan as a whole at an early stage. Part-time members of the team must receive regular updates to the project plan and minutes from all project planning meetings.

Projects fail for two main reasons. The first is a failure to identify all tasks at the outset, the second is to underestimate both the numbers and skills of people required. There will always be more work to do than can be imagined at the beginning of the project. If the project is to be conducted within the scope of 'best practice' it is not uncommon for original resource estimates to be *at least 100 per cent wrong.* Be prepared, therefore, to refine the composition and constituents of the team as the project develops. While expert advice may be needed at the beginning or end of the project, mid-project activities like, say, the large-scale collection of information, will need different people with different skills.

DECISION MAKING AUTHORITY

Regardless of the quality of the terms of reference, many decisions of a policy nature will need to be made during the project. Ensure that the project manager sets up direct lines of communication with the decision maker and the appropriate decision making authority. Ideally, the project manager should be sufficiently senior to take most project decisions. The project manager must take account, in the project plan, of the appropriate lead time for gaining formal decisions. This means identifying all appropriate decision points as milestones within the plan.

A TYPICAL PROJECT MANAGEMENT CYCLE

Figure 7.1 provides a schematic view of a typical project management cycle.

AN ILLUSTRATIVE PROJECT PLAN

An extract from a large Information Technology outsourcing procurement will be found at Appendix A, p. 233.

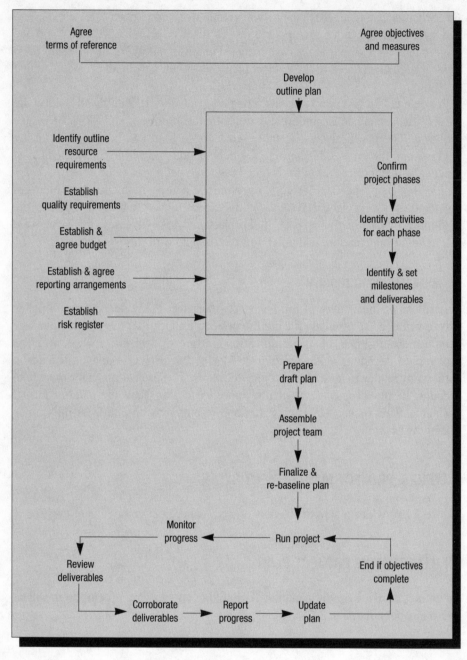

Figure 7.1 A project management cycle

8 Packaging the agreement

Commercial charges will usually be a function of volume over time, that is a large volume of service required for a long period of time will give the lowest unit cost and vice versa (see Chapter 12). The purpose of this chapter is to discuss the implications of different agreement packaging approaches, that is volume and time packages, insofar as they affect ultimate service charges and the attainment of added value.

WHAT IS AN AGREEMENT PACKAGE?

Often, when considering the potential service requirement of a large department or function, the service boundaries can be drawn in a number of different ways simply by including or omitting different permutations of functional activity. An agreement 'package', in this context and at its simplest, can therefore be described as those functional activities included within the boundary. It becomes more interesting, however, when one begins to consider the commercial leverage afforded by a 'package'.

Since price is a function of service volume and service duration, there comes a point where, if volume and time are large enough, a commercial lever emerges. The nature of the lever may not be obvious and care will need to be exercised in its use. For example, it is relatively straightforward to use the lever to reduce the price, but this can be counter-productive, resulting in adverse service performance and poor supplier relationships. If the point is reached where further cost reductions are either unsafe or unavailable, the lever can be redirected to other value added services. In this context, then, an agreement 'package' may be defined as those functional activities within the service boundary *plus* any value added services.

DEFINING THE PACKAGE

SETTING THE BOUNDARIES

There is usually a temptation to restrict the service boundary or engage more than one supplier so as to minimize whatever might be the perception of risk. Unless there are very pressing operational or strategic reasons, it is always more commercially advantageous to make the scope and duration of services relevant to one supplier as wide and large as possible. This is because the 'volume/time' equation is at its most effective but it also allows the supplier to invest in the service in the certain knowledge that there will be time and scope to recover its investment.

This argument works against splitting the service requirement across two or more suppliers. In circumstances where no one supplier is large enough, or operational requirements demand, consideration should be given either to dividing the service on a basis that is likely to deliver the best added value opportunities or to inducing suppliers to form consortia (see the following section).

GAINING ADDED VALUE

Added value is defined, in this context, as services that are either in addition, or complimentary to, those contained within the service boundary and are provided at either a reduced price or are included within the base cost.

Added value can be created from a great many sources and derives from a combination of supplier capability and agreement size. Thus, greater added value will typically come from larger suppliers with the broadest range of services and resources. Examples of added value are discussed below.

Management input

Every service will require managing and, therefore, some management expertise will be made available by the outsourcing supplier and included within the base cost. If an agreement is large enough and of long duration, it will be of strategic importance to the supplier and attract an additional weight of management. Careful construction of the agreement package can therefore bring with it an enhanced management capability beyond that strictly required by the agreement, which, in turn, can be used to help improve customer business performance.

Additional services at reduced prices

Service requirements change in ways that cannot easily be foreseen when an agreement is struck. One way to add flexibility and increased value is to identify those services and facilities that, currently, are not required but for which there *might* be a future use, and lever down the price of these services as part of the

54

base service negotiation. This implies that likely additional service requirements must have been thought through prior to contract negotiation and, ideally, should have been specified as part of the total requirement.

For example, the supplier may be capable of supplying a wide range of skills only a subset of which are required for the base service. You might define a wider skill set and negotiate its unit price as part of the base negotiation such that, when the wider skill set is finally required, the price is already agreed and is lower than would otherwise have been the case. In this way, greater service flexibility and greater added value can be negotiated.

Benefits by association

If the supplier is selected on the basis of its total capability and size, it may well have world class resources and skills. Under these circumstances, it may be possible to have access to its research and development activities or to be kept informed of technological and business developments that may be of great benefit and that might otherwise have been missed.

Specialist industry knowledge

Increasingly, suppliers are seeking to add value to their customers through specialist and highly focused industry knowledge. Quite often, specialist knowledge is packaged into tools that are proprietary to the supplier and are not sold directly to customers but used by the supplier on behalf of the customer. Negotiating increased access to these tools could lead to considerable business advantage.

9 Defining the service requirement

We have defined the 'package' of services required and the boundaries within which they sit. Now we need to define the services themselves.

Both you and potential suppliers will require a clear understanding of the services that are to pass to the outsourcing supplier in the event that a contract is agreed. A clear articulation of the service requirements and responsibilities should therefore be included in the Statement of Service Requirement (SoSR) against which prospective suppliers will respond. Note that if there are omissions or ambiguities in the SoSR that remain undiscovered until after the agreement has been signed, the supplier may need to increase its charges in circumstances where your substantive negotiating levers have gone. Preparation of the service definition is therefore one area where a lack of attention to detail will certainly cost you money in the long term.

Construction of the service definition should be conducted in three simple steps.

1. Write down the general activities of the service to be outsourced, e.g. are buildings cleaned, is equipment maintained, are computers operated?
2. Write down the basic resources and service characteristics associated with each primary activity. The principal issues will be as follows:
   - *Staffing* General staffing information to do with organisation structures, staff numbers, job titles, job descriptions and skills requirements provide a good insight into the service responsibilities and give a sound base upon which suppliers can construct their bids.
   - *Service recipient(s)* A description of the customers or users of the service should be provided including any that may be external third parties.
   - *Relevant locations* The service may be provided centrally, remotely, at a specialized base, in customer locations, etc. A description of relevant locations should therefore be provided.
   - *Timeliness* There are normally some time-critical aspects of service that could have a commercial effect on the agreement. All service schedules and components of a time-critical nature should therefore be identified.

- *Assets used* This section should list assets utilized in providing the service, e.g. equipment, building, licences, patents, leases, intellectual property, etc.
- *Materials and consumables* The service may involve extensive use of materials or consumables, which may need to be purchased, stored, distributed or disposed of. Equally, there may be large materials stocks which are to transfer. A general description and approximate volumes (or value) should be given.
- *Costs* It may be helpful to set out some headline cost values to aid the general understanding of the requirement, i.e. gross revenue of organization, departmental costs total by budget heading and amounts spent with main suppliers. In addition, costs will need to be described in detail in the SoSR and special sections or appendices should provide full details. This aspect of the SoSR is discussed in Chapter 16.
- *Volumes* Sometimes it is difficult to convey the scale of a service merely in resource terms. The provision of volume statistics, e.g. tonnes per day or calls per hour, will help convey the scale of the service and the pressures under which it works. Potential suppliers will then be able to relate the current resources applied to the volume of output and decide the scope, if any, for performance improvement.
- *Service performance and quality issues* Some indication of quality standards and service levels will enhance supplier understanding of the service definition and requirement.
- *Technical specifications* Where the service to be outsourced is of a technical nature, it will be essential to provide technical data to ensure that the technical implications of the service requirement are understood.
- *Internal suppliers* Service functions will often enjoy support from other internal functions. An indication of such support, and the nature of any interfaces, should be described.
- *External suppliers* Virtually all service functions take services from third parties. Where a third party plays a central role, such involvement must be clearly articulated to avoid later problems or difficulties. Care must be taken, however, to avoid breaching existing contracts.
- *Other issues* Ensure that suppliers are aware of all issues associated with the undertaking of service responsibilities, e.g. historically poor performance or the intention to close a large customer department at some time in the future.

3. The service definition, once drafted, should be circulated for comment and review amongst interested parties, examples of which include the project board, managers in the service function to be outsourced and customers of that service. This step provides an opportunity for the service definition to be refined so that it adequately reflects all aspects of the service requirement.

When drafting the service definition text for the SoSR, avoid falling into the trap of including too much information. The detail should be contained in annexes and may well be extensive depending upon the scale and nature of the function to be outsourced (see Chapter 16). Use existing documentation wherever possible in the annexes, since this will save time and give suppliers an authentic feel for the service function.

10 Human resources

The decision to outsource may be significantly influenced by matters relating to human resources. The maintenance of staff rights and benefits through transfer to a new employer has the potential to reduce the commercial attractiveness of an outsourcing opportunity and diminish the financial value of any subsequent proposals. However, an alternative view would be that the formality of human resources legislation actually reduces the risks associated with staff transfer to a third party because the legislation provides a practical framework within which the transfer may safely occur. Whichever view is favoured, unless great care is taken in the management of staff through the procurement process, significant damage will be done to individuals, their families, their morale, their performance and the general standing of management.

IMPACT ON STAFF

For most employees, the prospect of a forced move to a new employer, possibly the first move in their career, is traumatic. The trauma manifests itself in the form of acute anxiety, which derives from uncertainty about the future, a loss of control regarding one's future, anger at the lack of choice, feelings of abandonment and a feeling that one's loyalty has no value. Quite obviously, unless these feelings are carefully managed, there will at best be a measurable decline in performance and at worst, industrial action. So what might a relevant staff strategy look like?

The most important lesson to learn is that, *no matter what you say or do*, it is virtually impossible to remove the anxiety felt by most staff. The keys to managing staff anxiety are, first, communicate effectively and, second, keep the period between the announcement of the intention to outsource and actual staff transfer as short as possible. Before announcing your intentions to outsource, you must therefore have a staff communications strategy.

STAFF COMMUNICATIONS STRATEGY

The primary elements of a staff communications strategy are as follows.

Pre-announcement

Depending upon the scale and complexity of the function to be outsourced, the procurement timescale can be anywhere between 6 to 18 months. Staff, at the point of announcement, will wish to know, in great detail, precisely how they will be affected. It will not be possible to give them the detail they seek since much of the work will not have been done nor the potential supplier's intentions gained. It follows that a flow of information will be needed, which argues for a carefully constructed communications plan. The plan must be available, and sufficient work done to satisfy the initial communication, prior to the announcement event.

The plan should relate to project plan milestones and Figure 10.1 provides a typical example. Note that when implementing the plan, it is best to keep communications short, factual and as open and honest as the circumstances will allow. Avoid open forum question and answer sessions and deal with staff questions through written answers, which can be circulated to all staff to ensure that absentees receive the right message. Ensure that you always do what you have said you will do. If, for example, a plan of communication events has been published, *stick to it*. Open and honest communication will help to establish feelings of trust, which in part will help to mitigate the feelings of acute anxiety

Communication 1	Communication 4
Announcement	**Progress report**
Objectives	Preferred supplier name & details
Scope	Timetable update
Procurement process	Question & answers
Timetable	
Communications plan	
Communication 2	Communication 5
Staff policies and support	**Supplier presentation**
Redundancy & early retirement	Overview of supplier
Choice	Supplier's intentions
Helpline	General employment package
Written questions & answers	Approach to personal development
	Outline implementation plan
Communication 3	Communication 6
Progress report	**Detailed implementation plans**
Names of suppliers invited to tender	
Timetable update	
Written questions & answers	

Figure 10.1 Sample staff communications plan

Announcement

The announcement event should, as a minimum, communicate the following issues:

60

- The business objectives associated with the decision to outsource.
- The scope of the outsourcing exercise, clearly defining those functional areas to be outsourced and those that are excluded.
- The process and associated milestones to be used for procuring the outsourcing service.
- The anticipated timetable for the procurement, bearing in mind the need to manage staff expectations by taking account of the potential for the timetable to slip.
- The communications plan and associated communications events that will be used to keep staff informed of intentions, progress and, when possible, more detailed information regarding terms and conditions of future employment.

Staff policies and support

The staff policies and support communications event should provide information on how staff are to be treated in terms of job security, the potential for redundancy or early retirement and the choices, if any, they may have. These issues are dealt with later in this chapter.

Given that these are such difficult and emotive subjects, it will be worth establishing a telephone helpline that can be used to collect questions to which written replies to all staff can be given and, in addition, can provide immediate counselling support.

The production of regular written question and answer documents are important since they provide informative documents that staff members may take home to their families. Families, too, may be traumatized by the apparent threat of outsourcing, and any information that comes to them first hand from the employer, if properly and sensitively prepared, will help to address their anxieties.

The early staff policies and support communications event(s) should therefore concentrate upon the following:

- Set out the policies, where appropriate, on redundancy, early retirement and choice.
- Indicate the existence of the telephone helpline and how to use it.
- Hand out the first written question and answer document.

Progress reports

A number of progress reports will be necessary depending upon the length and scale of the procurement exercise. We suggest you avoid a routine 'monthly' update and stick to reporting against agreed milestones. This means you will actually have something of substance to report and in situations where there is little to communicate, avoids the event or document generating a hostile reaction.

Staff will be keenly interested in any information relating to potential suppliers and their human resources track record. The initial progress report should therefore indicate the names of those suppliers that have been invited to submit proposals together with a thumbnail sketch of each. A subsequent progress report will name the preferred supplier, subject to contract, and can give more details. Even in the best managed procurement programme, timescales are likely to slip because there is so much that is outside direct project control. Communicate to staff any slippage to the plan and, most importantly, any changes to the milestone dates and associated communications events.

In addition, maintain a rolling written question and answer document and issue the next update. This is desirable as everybody's understanding grows through the life of the procurement.

Supplier presentation

Once a preferred supplier has been selected with whom to enter into contract negotiations, mount a supplier presentation event. This event should take the form of a presentation from the preferred supplier and, as a minimum, focus upon the following:

- Overview of supplier, its business, achievements and outsourcing track record.
- Supplier's intentions in terms of its general approach to the requirement and whether redundancies and relocations are anticipated.
- Supplier's general employment package as it relates to this procurement.
- Supplier's approach to personal development and who will be eligible to participate.
- Supplier's outline implementation plan with particular emphasis on how the supplier will induct each transferring staff member.

Detailed implementation plan

Probably the last formal communications event will feature the detailed agreement implementation plan (see Chapter 20). The implementation plan will be the responsibility of the supplier but will require a significant amount of input from the customer. From the staff perspective, the most significant issues will be those dealing with the following:

- When, how or to where they are to be transferred.
- The process for discussing and agreeing individual terms and conditions.
- How their working routine is to change, if at all.
- To whom they will report.
- The process for agreeing individual development programmes.

ISSUES FOR CONSIDERATION

Once the staff communication plan has been established, the following issues will require careful consideration:

CURRENT HUMAN RESOURCES POLICIES

Existing human resources policies will need to be reviewed within the context of the outsourcing procurement; some may impose specific constraints upon the procurement whilst others may need to be changed. Those relevant to the procurement will need to be set out in the Statement of Service Requirement (SoSR).

Existing policies are unlikely to cover all aspects of the outsourcing procurement and it will be necessary to allow sufficient time for them to be reviewed, new policies to be drafted, and for all to be debated and authorized by the outsourcing procurement team and human resources experts.

TRADE UNION CONSULTATION

Where there is trade union representation, there may well be either legislation or internal agreements that demand a minimum level of consultation. These agreements are likely to specify both the nature of any consultations required and any minimum time periods before work may begin on the procurement proper. Contravention of these agreements may lead to disputes, which, in turn, may give rise to disruption of both the procurement project and working environment.

HUMAN RESOURCES LEGISLATION

Many countries have employment protection legislation of varying degrees of complexity. Whatever legislation exists must be properly understood by the procurement team and an expert in the field will be needed to support the development of appropriate policies.

In the United Kingdom, employment protection is provided by the Transfer of Undertakings (Protection of Employment) Regulations (TUPE) (as amended by the Trades Union and Employee Rights Act 1993), which confers specific 'consultation' obligations on the Transferor (i.e. the outsourcing customer) and the Transferee (i.e. the outsourcing supplier). TUPE indicates that consultation must commence as early as possible and requires the holding of meaningful consultation 'with a view to seeking', amongst other things, 'agreement'.

This is the usual legal framework for the transfer of employees from one employer to another as part of an 'undertaking'. The Regulations set out to preserve employees' rights and benefits associated with the transfer of the undertaking, although TUPE may not cover everything. If staff are due to transfer to a new employer as a result of an outsourcing procurement, you will need to provide substantial information about staff in the SoSR so that proposals can be accurately costed. The time needed to collate such information could be significant and must be considered as part of the programme plan.

CHOICE

Among the very early questions asked by staff when faced with the possibility of an outsourcing agreement are the following:

'Must I transfer to the new supplier?'

'If I must transfer, I presume that I will receive a redundancy payment?'

'May I choose between remaining with my current employer or transferring to the new supplier?'

When thinking about the issue of choice, the following points are relevant:

- Under the auspices of TUPE, employees have no right of choice. The intent of the legislation is to assure the *continuity* of employment on the same terms and conditions. To all intents and purposes therefore, TUPE assumes that the transferring individual, and the job they perform, continues and all that has changed is the name of the employer. Thus there is no 'alternative' from which to make a 'choice' and no need for redundancy payments since the job continues.
- Remaining with the current employer should not be an option open to staff, for the following reasons:
  - TUPE and its provisions only work when transferring either the entire 'undertaking' or a coherent part of the 'undertaking'. If some staff are given the option *not* to transfer, it could be argued by opponents of the outsourcing procurement, of which there may be many, that a coherent 'undertaking' has not been transferred, thus removing the transfer from the auspices of TUPE. This in turn puts all transferring staff in a position where they may argue for redundancy payments.
  - Notwithstanding the fact that staff will transfer from one employer to another, there is still the need to maintain provision of their operational function. The outsourcing supplier, at least initially, is wholly dependent upon transferring staff for the maintenance of operational services. Were staff to be given the option to transfer or remain with their current employer, there is a strong possibility that key resources, in terms of numbers and skills, would not be available to the outsourcing supplier for the maintenance of operational services and some disruption to services would almost certainly occur.
- Practically all staff, when first hearing about the possibility of outsourcing, jump to the conclusion that they will receive redundancy payments and then transfer to the new employer with all rights and benefits preserved. A redundancy approach can be adopted but it is important to understand the implications for both you and transferring staff.
  - Allowing *some* staff to be made redundant, even without jobs with the new

employer, may compromise the TUPE transfer because a coherent 'undertaking' will not have been transferred; potentially unnecessary redundancy costs will be incurred and an opportunity for legal challenge in the courts may be created.

– If it is decided to make staff redundant, then *all* transferring staff must be included, the implications of which are as follows: The transferor will incur potentially substantial redundancy costs that would not be incurred under a TUPE transfer. Although staff would receive a redundancy payment, they would not maintain the rights associated with 'continuity of employment' as envisaged by TUPE. This means that the transferee would not legally be obliged to offer employment. Those who were to be offered employment would therefore have the status of 'new starters' with all that that means, including no substantive employment protection for the initial years of their employment, and their employment package would be at the discretion of the transferee.

In effect, the application of TUPE largely eliminates the existence of any choice for the individual although any challenge or dispute will revolve around the definition of the 'undertaking', which occasionally can be open to interpretation.

You should by now be aware that this area is fraught with difficulty. Not only is the subject matter complex but decisions and conclusions on the myriad issues will vary according to geography, circumstances, disposition and even the commercial effect of the proposed contract. Moreover, employment legislation frequently changes. The acquisition of human resources and legal advice must be considered mandatory and should be sought as early as possible and certainly before any staff communications are made.

POLICY FOR EARLY RETIREMENT

Those staff nearing retirement would perhaps prefer to take early retirement than transfer to a new employer. Where this is judged to be of benefit to both the company and relevant staff, existing early retirement policies will need to be reviewed to ensure that they are still appropriate or a new policy developed.

PENSIONS

The TUPE regulations, as amended by the Trades Union and Employee Rights Act 1993 (for the UK), do *not* provide a legal framework for the transfer of pensions. Caring employers will require the new employer to provide benefits in respect of the employee's pension transfer values which are, in the opinion of the transferor's actuary, broadly equivalent to the value of the accrued benefits in the transferor's fund. The prospective outsourcing supplier (new employer) should be asked to give an early indication as to how they are to comply with the transferor's pension requirement.

REDUNDANCY RULES

Different organizations have different terms for redundancy situations. The prospective supplier will need to be informed of the current policies. The outsourcing procurement team should understand the distinction between contractual obligations and discretionary benefits as staff may expect discretionary benefits to be included in the transfer package. TUPE does not transfer policies – just rights. Discretionary benefits will be carried forward only if specific provision is made in the contract with the supplier and the customer accepts the consequential commercial effect, should there be any, on the agreement.

Early discussions with human resources advisers, legal advisers and other interested persons will be necessary to ensure the following:

- The latest legislation is contemplated.
- The commercial effect is calculated and considered.
- Any special polices are prepared and agreed.
- Alternative strategies can be discussed.
- Staff can be correctly briefed.

REDUNDANCY INDEMNIFICATION

TUPE has the effect of transferring continuity of employment, including redundancy rights, to the new employer. Thus the customer actually passes the accrued redundancy liability for each employee to the new employer. In many circumstances this liability will lapse, in the fullness of time, as each employee resigns or retires. However, should the supplier wish to sever some of the transferred staff, notably at the end of the outsourcing contract term, then the liability is realized as a result of redundancy payments. Therefore, a transfer of redundancy rights will have a commercial effect on any agreement since the outsourcing supplier must seek to protect its commercial position by either requesting an indemnity regarding the accrued redundancy liability or by building its perception of the accrued redundancy liability into the agreement price.

You will need to decide which approach is appropriate for you. If you agree to indemnify the outsourcing supplier for the term of the outsourcing agreement, no cost is incurred unless transferred staff are made redundant. This may be an attractive option should there be a real likelihood that the transferred staff will be fully absorbed into the supplier's workforce and remain with the supplier beyond contract termination. On the other hand, there are potential disadvantages:

- The outsourcing supplier will control the timing of any redundancies which could demand payments, the timing of which might be unhelpful and give rise to funding difficulties.

- Integration of transferred staff into the new organization may be delayed, to the detriment of individuals, because, if the outsourcing supplier needs to make *any* staff redundant, it is possible that those staff for whom redundancy costs are covered, will be made redundant first.
- Because redundancy costs are covered, it may be that the number of transferred staff who are made redundant is higher than otherwise might be the case.

Alternatively, you may wish to buy out the liability. Should this be the case, then within the boundaries of a procurement competition, it would be reasonable to ask potential bidders to include the liability in their price but on a fully disclosed basis. The competition can then be used as a means of driving down the total cost.

CODES OF PRACTICE

If the prospective outsourcing supplier is satisfactorily to cost its bid and meet transfer requirements, it will need to review its own human resources policies to see if there are any potential difficulties in matching your policies, practices and other non-contractual terms. Full details of your provisions will be required. By way of example only, the provisions may include the following:

- Early retirement.
- Trade union representation.
- Long service awards.
- Training.
- Leave for military training purposes.
- Youth group leave.

Other provisions and associated details should be obtained in consultation with the human resources representative on the procurement team.

USE OF CONSULTANTS AND CONTRACTORS

If the function to be transferred currently employs consultants or contractors, this may provide an opportunity for substantial cost efficiencies if they can be replaced by the outsourcing supplier's staff. If appropriate, a detailed statement about the use of consultant/contractors will assist with the construction of supplier bids.

STAFF TRAINING AND DEVELOPMENT

Training and career development may be an important area for staff, particularly in technical departments/functions. Your ability to deliver training in these areas may be an important consideration for internal improvement programmes. The prospective outsourcing supplier's track record and willingness to train may be an essential element of both the transfer programme and future supplier performance. Thought should be given regarding the importance of staff training and development to the longer term performance of the function and, where special requirements are needed, these must be determined and specified in the SoSR.

STAFF DETAILS

For suppliers to make adequate proposals, full details of staff who will transfer are required so that potential suppliers can price their proposals. Details will include the following:

- Salary, pension and fees.
- Overtime, travel and subsistence.
- Other benefits and entitlements.
- Any unfilled vacancies that the supplier will be expected to fill or that it will need to fill in order to achieve the appropriate service requirements or service standards.
- Human resources policies – general codes of practice.

11 Assets

Assets are possessions owned by a person or business which can be used to pay debts, produce goods or, in some way, help the business make a profit. There are a number of different types of assets, not all of which may apply to a particular function or outsourcing procurement.

CAPITAL ASSETS

Capital (or fixed) assets are used for making or selling the services or products of the business and are not themselves intended for sale or liquidation as long as they are useful to the business. There are four logical groups of capital assets:

- **Replaceable assets**
  Replaceable assets would include equipment or plant used directly for the business, e.g. rolling stock, heavy plant, mainframe computers.

- **Infrastructure**
  Infrastructure assets divide into those that are renewable, like fixtures and fittings, and that are used indirectly to support the business, e.g. furniture, special environmental equipment, local area networks and other telecommunications equipment, and non-renewable assets like property and accommodation. Real property assets comprise land and buildings or other immovable property. Property and accommodation may be leased or rented, rather than owned, but nevertheless may provide opportunities for cost savings, improvements or changes that can bring benefit.

- **Current assets**
  Examples of current assets include consumables, materials or stock in hand used in the provision of the service.

- **Intangible assets**
  Intangible assets are assets that have value to the business but are not a physical entity. They include intellectual property, copyright, patents, trademarks, goodwill, ownership in documented techniques and routines. Intangible assets have positive benefit and should not be underestimated – an outsourcing supplier may be able to exploit these assets to mutual benefit in

ways not open to the customer. As a consequence, care should be taken to retain ownership of intangible assets and if subsumed within an outsourcing agreement, specific clauses will be needed for their exploitation.

ISSUES RELATING TO ASSETS

A number of issues relating to assets with which the outsourcing procurement team should be familiar are discussed below.

FUNDING AND SALE OF CAPITAL ASSETS

The funding of capital assets can frequently be difficult particularly within tight funding limits. Outsourcing suppliers are increasingly disposed to funding capital items since it represents an opportunity for them to add value to their services. They will, of course, only do so if they are guaranteed a return on their money within the life of the agreement.

Two primary benefits flow from passing the acquisition of capital assets to the outsourcing supplier:

1. There is no longer the need to find large amounts of capital, although the outsourcing supplier's service charge will be higher to take account of capital funds recovery.
2. The assets will be off balance sheet, which for some organizations can be helpful.

Note, however, that for existing assets that are sold to the outsourcing supplier, tax advantages may have been previously taken through permissible capital allowances. If assets are sold, the relevant tax authorities may seek to recover some or all of the allowances previously granted.

The outsourcing procurement team should establish the medium- to long-term requirements for capital funding and identify any commercial opportunities potentially available within an outsourcing agreement.

SALE AND RETURN OF CAPITAL ASSETS

If existing assets are sold to an outsourcing supplier as part of the outsourcing arrangement, you may wish to secure the right to recover the assets at contract termination. This matter may have more significance should a contract fail rather than terminate normally. The issue of service continuity in the event of both early and natural agreement termination should therefore be considered.

USE OF SPARE CAPITAL ASSET RESOURCES

Where capital assets may not be fully utilized, the outsourcing procurement team should establish the extent of under-utilization and identify what opportunities exist for exploitation either internally or externally with third parties. The external exploitation of capital assets, that is selling spare capacity to third parties, may be problematic for a number of reasons including the following:

- A lack of marketing expertise.
- The need for additional investment.
- Political constraints.

The outsourcing supplier may be in a far better position to exploit available resources because of the following advantages:

- An existing marketing infrastructure.
- An existing client base.
- Synergy with existing resources.

The outsourcing procurement team should therefore establish the extent, if any, of any under-utilization of resources and determine the potential for exploiting these resources within an outsourcing agreement.

INTELLECTUAL PROPERTY

Opportunities exist for the exploitation of intellectual property and other intangible assets. External exploitation may be problematic for the same reasons given for tangible assets above. Carefully consider the transfer – intentional or otherwise – of intangible assets as part of an outsourcing arrangement. Contract provisions will almost certainly be required to protect existing and new intangible assets and any proposals for their potential exploitation.

As a general rule, there is so much to do in order to create and negotiate the outsourcing agreement that it is simpler and safer merely to retain ownership within the initial contract and once the contract is signed and implemented, the issues associated with exploiting intangible assets may be discussed and agreed in a calmer and less pressured environment.

PROPERTY AND ACCOMMODATION

Rationalization of property may yield considerable benefits, assuming that existing properties can be either adequately disposed of or re-assigned for alternative purposes. The outsourcing procurement team will need to investigate the potential for the alternative use of existing properties and the potential for partial or complete vacation.

12 Charging formulae

Charging arrangements within simple contractual relationships take many forms and are well understood. Charging mechanisms suitable for regulation of long-term relationships within which requirements will change in unpredictable ways are more difficult and, therefore, less well understood.

This chapter discusses the general principles that guide the formulation of charging mechanisms. Note that although the outsourcing procurement team requires some idea of how it wishes the charging mechanisms to work, the precise mechanisms for charging will evolve only from detailed discussions with suppliers post-tender response. For this reason, no attempt is made here to prescribe actual formulations.

SUPPLIER PERSPECTIVES

There are, at its simplest, two types of suppliers: those who are experienced in striking long-term flexible outsourcing agreements and those who are not. It is essential to understand the difference between the two for the following reasons.

For long-term commercial relationships to succeed, they must be founded upon a mutually acceptable and practical financial base. As will be discussed later, if price escalation over time is to be avoided and maximum value for money delivered, a degree of 'imagination' may have to be applied when developing pricing mechanisms and they may take on a complexity not usually encountered in conventional contracts. Experienced suppliers will have little difficulty in assimilating unusual approaches or with the concept of 'open book' accounting, allowing discussions to proceed without having to consider a negative reaction to any unusual proposals. Inexperienced suppliers may struggle to understand unusual proposals and, in extreme cases, have been known to take offence and leave the table (see Chapter 17). This occurs principally where open book accounting or controls based upon the purchaser's understanding of the supplier's cost structure are suggested.

Thus it is important to gauge the extent of the potential supplier's experience. If the likely supplier *is* inexperienced, you should embark, either overtly or covertly, upon a structured education process to ensure that the relationship remains intact through the negotiation process.

THE PRICE ESCALATION TRAP

The charging mechanisms of many long-term agreements are structured upon the simple precept of an agreed price for an agreed package of work. Indeed, experienced suppliers will often urge the purchaser to 'keep it simple'. There is much to commend 'simplicity' within the realms of charging and every effort should be made to achieve it.

The reality is, however, that simple charging mechanisms may be applied only to simple service requirements. Within this context, simplicity means a stable requirement that is unlikely to vary over the long term either in terms of its volume or characteristics. Under these conditions you can closely define and price the requirements and the price may easily take account of any minor variations. If, however, a price is agreed for the requirements and in, say, year four, unforeseen and significant changes to the requirement are needed, the charging mechanism will be unable automatically to calculate the new price and a negotiation must therefore ensue.

Once the supplier has achieved a negotiating position post-contract signature, most of the purchaser's negotiating levers associated with the initial contract procurement are gone. Under these circumstances, some suppliers regard themselves as well positioned to increase margins through carefully structured pricing changes as each change of requirement emerges. Over time, some suppliers may attempt progressively to escalate their price without, perhaps, a matched increase in value for money. Therefore, if requirements are likely to change significantly over time, charging mechanisms must be designed to avoid re-negotiations.

Since most businesses are unable to see beyond a three-year horizon and the only certainty is that things will 'change', charging mechanisms must, as a minimum, deliver pricing certainty within service flexibility. If charging mechanisms fail in this respect, the contract has the potential to become either a significant constraint upon business flexibility or administratively burdensome.

CHARGING MECHANISMS

The key to attaining pricing certainty and service flexibility is to be found in the construct of the charging formulae. Charges can be calculated on the basis of inputs, outputs, risk/reward or a mixture of each.

Input charging is generally well understood and is based upon the costs associated with delivering the service to which is added a contribution to supplier profit. Output charging is less well understood, particularly for complex service based contracts, and relies upon a detailed understanding of service outputs for each of which there is an agreed unit price. Risk/reward based charging is where the outsourcing supplier's charge is related directly to the business performance of the customer. In this way a direct link can be created between the outsourcing supplier's services and the value they add to the customer's business. This approach is relatively new and, although at first glance fairly simple, may have some hidden consequences.

Whatever approach is chosen, the resulting charging formulae must be straightforward to administer and monitor, leave the outsourcing supplier in day-to-day control of resources, leave the customer in strategic control and incentivize the outsourcing supplier both to reduce operating costs and to help improve the customer's business performance.

INPUT CHARGING

Input based charging mechanisms can take a great many forms. If, however, they are to achieve pricing certainty and service flexibility, they must have the following basic building blocks:

- A *standard* component that deals with the known and routine base requirement.
- A *variable* component that deals with known requirements, the frequency and volume of which do not fit a standard pattern.
- An *additional services* component that provides for unpredictable or unknowable service requirements that are within the scope of the service provider's capabilities and range of service offerings.
- A *transitional* component that deals with charges associated with service initiation, examples of which would include the transfer of assets and staff or severance liabilities.

The standard charge

Commercial charges will usually be a function of volume over time, that is a large volume of service required for a long period of time will give the lowest unit cost and vice versa. Suppliers will seek to levy a standard charge that covers all routine activities likely to be required for the foreseeable future. The effect of the standard charge is therefore to create a commitment for a large volume of service which, broadly, will be required for the duration of the agreement. This allows the supplier to offer a low unit price against the certainty of a significant, long-term, volume of work.

The standard charge is an agreed price to cover the routine and predictable services associated with the service requirement. It will relate to the cost of transferred resources *as rationalized by the supplier* to which will be added supplier costs and contribution to profit. Note, therefore, that the standard charge is not a 'cost plus' charge. The standard charge will *not* relate directly to the cost of transferred resources but will reflect the supplier's total costs, comprising transferred costs from which superfluous costs have been removed and any possible synergy advantage taken, new supplier costs and profits. Moreover, the standard charge, for it to be credible, will need to be less than the predicted performance improvement cost, i.e. the bid threshold (see Chapter 2). Examples of primary cost components follow but it will be for each supplier to submit its own standard charge construction:

- Equipment lease/rental/amortization.
- Known and routinely quantifiable materials.
- Accommodation (rent, Council Charge, maintenance, infrastructure).
- Environment (air conditioning, electricity).
- Transferred staff.
- Supplier management team and staff.
- Supplier specialist equipment.
- Contribution to supplier profit.

A standard charge for the service will be submitted by suppliers, which will be compared, not with the projection of current costs, but with the projection of costs to flow from the internal performance improvement programme, i.e. the bid threshold, and this comparison will form the basis of determining the value of the supplier's offering.

The basis for calculating the standard charge will remain fixed for the life of the agreement. The precise charge may, however, vary in line with movements in resource requirement and indexation (see the section on regulatory mechanisms in this chapter) but the unit cost will remain fixed for the life of the agreement.

The variable charge

The variable charge relates to those items of routine service that are not easily predictable, examples of which might include stationery, consumables and overtime. These items are usually charged at cost, in arrears, sometimes with the addition of a small handling charge.

The additional services charge

The additional services charge prescribes the basis of charging for any service *not* included within the standard charge. It is the additional services charge that allows requirements outside of the standard charge to vary but within a framework of pricing certainty. If a new service is required, the additional services charge will give the agreed basis of charging and the price may be calculated either as an increase to the standard charge or as a short- to medium-term increment. As indicated earlier, commercial charges will usually be a function of volume over time. If, therefore, additional services are required for a short period, one should expect the unit price to be greater than that contained within the standard charge.

Some guiding principles should be set to distinguish between manpower and non-manpower charges and give varying unit cost rates depending upon volume and time requirements. For example:

- As it relates to manpower, the additional services charge provides the means by which medium-term resource peaks may be serviced, at a cost that is below normal list price but above the long-term rates contained within the standard charge.
- Favourable additional services charge rates might, by way of example, be provided by the supplier only within the following constraints:
  - A contractual commitment to purchase, say, 20 man years above those contained within the standard charge.
  - If the elapsed period for delivery of the requirement is less than, say, 6 months, there will be a minimum volume purchase of, say, 5 man years.
  - Any mix of resource or profile of usage may be specified.
  - Should the committed view of the total number of man years required exceed an elapsed planning period of 12 months or a minimum volume requirement of 20 man years, the requirement will qualify for standard charge rates.
- Requirements other than manpower will most likely involve a need for capital associated with infrastructure costs, in addition to that which may have been required for the initial purchase of transferred assets. These requirements could be dealt with on the following basis:
  - Capital items may be acquired either on a pass through basis at an agreed cost or amortized over a number of years.
  - The formula for amortization will be agreed prior to contract. Note that where capital items are amortized, residual costs beyond the end of the agreement should be avoided.

The transitional charge

There may be one-off charges relating to the transitional period, examples of which could include the purchase of assets in situ at the start of the agreement, transitional management and overhead costs and severance payments.

These charges may be dealt with either through a single direct payment or, as is more likely, factored into the standard charge against an agreed payment profile.

Input charging summary

The total charge based upon inputs will be calculated by bringing together, usually on a monthly basis, all of the charging components to give a charge for the period as follows:

$$SC + VC + ASC_m + ASC_n + TC = \text{input charge}$$

where:

SC   = standard charge
VC   = variable charge
ASC_m = additional service charge for manpower
ASC_n = additional service charge for non-manpower
TC   = transitional charge

OUTPUT CHARGING

Output charging, as its name implies, is based upon an agreed price per identified unit of output. Experienced suppliers favour output pricing because it is believed to be simple to administer. There are, however, at least three questions to be considered before agreeing to a contract based upon output charging:

1. Can the output units be identified?
2. Can the units of output be accurately counted?
3. Can the price per unit of output be tested to assure its reasonableness?

Identifying the outputs

In many cases outputs may be obvious, e.g. number of rooms cleaned, overalls washed, length of cable laid, etc. In other cases it is more difficult. For example, what might be the outputs of the finance or personnel departments? Thus, although outputs can be determined, the task may require a substantial amount of effort.

Counting the outputs

Once you have determined the construct of the output units, a reliable means of counting them must be found. If the supplier is to be paid on the basis of, say 'the number of new starter queries' to the personnel department, there must be a robust mechanism that accurately and easily delivers the output count – remembering that it will be the supplier who is managing the service environment and therefore probably doing the counting.

Testing the unit price per output

Many experienced suppliers will simply offer a unit price per output unit. Where the price offered can be tested against equivalent market offerings to determine its competitiveness, calibration is straightforward. Where equivalent market offerings are not available, calibration is more difficult and it will be harder to satisfy yourself that the unit price being offered represents good value for money, even though it may. Under these circumstances, there is no alternative but to resort to an input based calculation, which will match input costs with unit volume. The negotiation may then centre upon supplier overheads and the contribution to profit, both figures often calculated as a direct percentage of cost. Once the output unit price has been identified, sensitivity analyses should be conducted to test potential supplier charges against a likely range of output volumes including the minimum and maximum. The actual unit price may then be agreed and there should be no further need to monitor input costs.

RISK/REWARD CHARGING

Charging based upon risk/reward is potentially simple to operate and has the benefit of forging a direct link between the services provided by the outsourcing supplier and the actual performance enhancing value of those services to the customer. It may be particularly appropriate where the outsourcing service is for a critically important service, for example distribution, information technology, finance. However, agreeing some overarching principles is one thing, constructing a mutually acceptable and robust charging mechanism is more problematic.

There are a great many ways in which performance based charging mechanisms may be constructed. What follows merely represents one approach from which some general principles may be extracted.

There are a number of components to a risk/reward based charging mechanism:

- Behavioural drivers.
- Behavioural implications.
- The cost baseline and charge cap.
- The margin cap.
- Sensitivity analyses.
- New capital investments.
- Market discontinuity.

Behavioural drivers

The risk/reward based charging approach should be designed to stimulate the outsourcing supplier to facilitate the following:

- A reduction of the outsourcing supplier service costs.
- A reduction of the customer's business costs.
- An improvement in customer revenue.
- Increases in customer margin.
- Resistance to poor investment decisions.
- The injection of a high degree of rigour into the development of investment business cases.

Behavioural implications

Both parties will need to modify their normal business behaviour or be prepared to compromise, if the risk/reward based charging approach is to work. The primary behavioural implications are as follows:

- The customer must be prepared to accept, within the core customer business, both pressure and support from the outsourcing supplier if true business benefits are to flow.
- The linkage to customer margin may give the outsourcing supplier some difficulty since, unlike revenue, there is scope to 'manipulate' customer margin.
- Where 'open book' audit access is needed, this should be a reciprocal process to avoid the opportunity unreasonably to manipulate margins.

The cost baseline and charge cap

The outsourcing supplier service charge, in this model, will be linked to the customer's actual turnover or revenue. A multiplier is therefore required by which the customer's annual revenue can be multiplied and which will govern the maximum permitted charge. This multiplier is the charge cap and can be derived as follows:

- Future service costs, over the duration of the agreement should be projected and an average annual cost calculated. Note that these costs should *exclude* any contribution to the outsourcing supplier's profit.
- An average of customer revenues for the previous three years should be calculated.
- The multiplier may then be calculated by dividing the average service customer revenue by the average future cost.

This baseline percentage, when multiplied by the customer's annual revenue, creates the maximum limit of the supplier's price to the customer and, as a result, operates as a cap to supplier charges. The ultimate supplier charge will, of course, be generated from a combination of the revenue cap and the margin cap (see below).

Figure 12.1 illustrates the calculation of the charge cap.

The supplier margin cap

The charge cap alone is an insufficiently sensitive measure with which to regulate the supplier charge because the charge cap conceptually drives up revenue without a matched improvement in margin. The necessary link to margin is provided by the margin cap, which may be derived as follows:

- The supplier margin is linked to its own performance and to movements in the customer margin.
- The supplier margin is capped at a base percentage plus x times the customer margin. The base percentage may or may not be needed and is used to regulate differences in both the markets and organizational infrastructures of the parties.

	£m
Total costs to be outsourced	136.6
Customer revenue – last three years	
1994	898.1
1995	1025.3
1996	1254.7
Average revenue	1059.4
Charge cap = 13.66/1059.4 x 100 =	1.23%

Figure 12.1 Calculating the cost baseline and charge cap

Note however:

- The supplier should be permitted to regain losses derived from funding agreed investments before the margin cap operates.
- When the cap is operating, the supplier's margin will follow the customer's margin up or down from the agreed base percentage.
- Depending upon the agreed base percentage chosen, the supplier is automatically afforded some degree of protection against losses, subject always to the ability of customer revenues to support the payment.

This mechanism provides the supplier with an incentive to keep both its own and the customer's costs low to increase the supplier margin. As the supplier helps to increase the customer's margin it will drive both its own revenue and margin upwards.

Sensitivity analyses

A range of sensitivity analyses will be needed from which can be derived an appropriate margin cap.

New capital investments

For this illustration, the general principles associated with capital investments are as follows:

- Either party may identify opportunities for new capital investments.
- The supplier will always provide the capital.
- Each investment proposal will be accompanied by a business case.
- The business case will determine the percentage return anticipated for the proposed investment.
- In the event that the parties fail to agree the anticipated percentage return, the external auditors of the customer will arbitrate.

- If the percentage anticipated return is agreed to be [x per cent] or above, and the customer wishes the investment to be made, the investment will proceed.
- If the percentage anticipated return is agreed to be [x per cent] or above, and the customer wishes *not* to proceed, the supplier may invest anyway if the project is purely related to the supplier's infrastructure base. In this case the parties must recognize that benefits will flow to the customer before the supplier sees a return on its investment.

  If, however, there are organizational implications for the customer arising from the investment, then an investment by the supplier without guaranteed co-operation from the customer would be foolish.
- If the percentage anticipated return is agreed to be [x per cent] or above, and the supplier does not wish to proceed, then the supplier is compelled to proceed because the agreed percentage return on investment is above the threshold.
- If the percentage anticipated return is agreed to be below [x per cent], and the customer wishes to proceed, the rules for market discontinuity will apply (see below).
- Assuming the write down period for investments is usually five years, the supplier may be disinclined to invest in the later years of the agreement since it will be unable to obtain a return from its investment before the natural termination of the agreement. The supplier must, at the natural termination of the agreement, be able to recover its residual investment costs together with a contribution to profit, which could be at the rate of the supplier margin base excluding the multiplier, whatever that is determined to be from the sensitivity analyses.

Market discontinuity

Normal market movements will usually be accepted by suppliers as a routine business risk within a risk/reward arrangement. However, over the life of the agreement, some form of discontinuity is likely to occur, driven either by profound changes in the market or by decisions from the customer. The nature of any discontinuity may undermine the baseline assumptions built into the charging model, that is customer margins or revenue may change profoundly, either up or down, for reasons unconnected with supplier activity. In these circumstances a mechanism will be needed which allows a controlled re-alignment of supplier charges without substantial re-negotiation and in a way that does not prejudice either party's 'contractual' investments. This mechanism should be used only in extreme and predicted circumstances and by agreement between the parties. No retrospective adjustments should be envisaged. A suggested mechanism follows:

- There is an event that will have a marked effect upon customer margins. The years affected should be agreed and the extent of margin movement predicted and agreed. The customer margin line should be adjusted for those years during which the effect applies, prior to being fed to the charging mechanism and prior to the margin cap being applied.

- There is an event that will have a marked effect upon customer revenues. The years affected should be agreed and the extent of margin movement predicted and agreed. The customer revenue line fed to the charging mechanism should be adjusted for those years during which the effect applies, prior to the calculation of potential supplier charges and before the margin cap is applied.
- There is an event that will have a marked effect upon both customer revenues and margins. Both the adjustments above should be undertaken. In the event that agreement upon the precise percentage effects cannot be reached, the customer's external auditor should arbitrate.
- Where the supplier believes that the customer has without prior consultation undertaken actions that have substantially affected the supplier's earning capability during the previous year, the supplier should calculate what it believes the effect to have been. Following this, agreement regarding adjustments for the future years should be undertaken using the mechanisms above. There should be no retrospective payment. The retrospective calculation merely informs the argument for future adjustment.

REGULATORY MECHANISMS

There are at least five regulatory mechanisms that may be required:

- Regulating the standard charge.
- Third party use of assets.
- Sharing performance gains.
- Maintaining price competitiveness.
- Indexation.

REGULATING THE STANDARD CHARGE

The standard charge relates to the volume of service resources required within each service strand and, as a consequence, a means of measuring each service component will be required. The subject of service measurement is complex and will be resolved only after detailed pre-contract discussions with the preferred supplier. The primary service components will be identified and the standard charge for each service strand will be projected by the supplier. From this information can be derived the unit cost of the primary service components, which, in turn, can be used as the basis for varying the actual standard charge as volume requirements change. However, there will be a critical mass of resources below which it will not be possible to meet the service requirement. The costs associated with these resources will be the *minimum charge*.

It should therefore be possible to vary the total service strand charge above the minimum charge by regulating the number of units of service components required. The service strand charge will be a function of the total service volume related to the required time period. The implication is, therefore, that the supplier will be looking for a minimum commitment of volume over time and will be less concerned about the actual make up of the work itself.

The optimum time period, which balances maximum value for money with the uncertainties of longer range planning, will vary depending upon the volatility of the business function. Once determined, this period will act as a rolling planning horizon against which resources can be planned and charges levied. The volume of services required can thus be regulated up or down whilst maintaining the discounted standard charge pricing rates, provided that a forward commitment to service volume equivalent to the planning period is given. The following points should be noted:

- At least the same degree of flexibility regarding the deployment of resources as is currently available should be maintained since the supplier is principally concerned with committed volume of revenue.
- The charges associated with an increase or decrease in resource requirement will not necessarily be proportional since the supplier may be close to a resource step function. In other words, a small reduction in resource requirements may be insufficient to release the associated cost, or a small increase in requirement could trigger the need for significant additional costs. For example, a requirement for an extra 1000 sq ft of office space may simply increase the service charge by 1000 times the square foot charge or, alternatively, may trigger the need for new premises.
- It will be possible to adjust the make-up of service strands on a rolling planning period basis provided that a forward commitment equal to the planning period is made.
- Any reduction in service strand charges will be subject to the agreed minimum charge.
- Service strand resources may be increased and qualify for the standard charge rate if the total number of man years required exceeds either the agreed planning period or an agreed minimum volume requirement.

THIRD PARTY USE OF ASSETS

Suppliers may wish to exploit the use of 'spare' resources by selling them on to third parties and, as a consequence, there may be an opportunity to enhance value for money targets by seeking a share of the profit. The creation of a profit sharing arrangement would, at first sight, appear to be straightforward and, indeed, from a mechanical point of view, it is. Whether benefits will actually accrue from a profit sharing arrangement is debatable. The following points are relevant:

- All assets and staff associated with a service strand, including any 'spare' resources, will transfer to the supplier who will purchase the assets, take on running costs and assume the cost liability for staff. The 'spare' resources are then available for sale to a third party because, by definition, they are no longer required by the customer and, indeed, the 'spare' resources will have been identified as not being required for the service requirement and marked as a cost reduction. In this circumstance, the supplier would argue that it has fulfilled any performance improving obligations imposed upon it and that you had therefore received a contribution to the value for money objective.
- The only circumstance in which the point above would not apply is if buildings or other assets were rented to the supplier at a peppercorn rate and were then used to service third party clients. Under such circumstances it would be appropriate to levy an additional charge.
- Were you to seek a profit sharing arrangement, where opportunity existed for third party sales the supplier could divert the work to some other part of its resource base to avoid sharing the profits. When preparing your business case, you should therefore avoid relying upon the inflow of profit sharing funds that are not contractually guaranteed and should regard them as a welcome bonus if they materialize.

SHARING PERFORMANCE GAINS

It is possible, as part of the bid process, to commit the supplier to delivery of the potential performance improvement gains resulting from activities identified in the performance improvement assessment (see Chapter 2). The supplier is excluded from sharing those benefits as they are delivered and will not be positioned to make excessive profits.

There should be, however, continued pressure for performance improvements above those identified by the internal performance improvement assessment and both parties will require incentives to deliver them. Where performance improvements are sought from resources transferred to the supplier, discrete performance targets, together with mandatory programmes of work for their delivery, could be developed and the benefits quantified. The resulting performance improvement programmes will form one of the primary inputs to the rolling forward plan and will contribute to movements in the total resource requirement.

The actual benefits to flow from the performance improvement programmes will be identified and apportioned between the parties on an agreed basis – possibly 50:50, although this will depend upon the nature of any investments needed. The following points should be noted:

84

- Suppliers must ensure that their contracts make a contribution to non-attributable corporate costs and corporate overheads. These costs will need to be controlled as they can have an adverse effect upon the benefit flowing from the agreement as a whole. The simplest way to deal with this is to insist that suppliers bid a price inclusive of corporate costs and overheads and declare their contribution to profit as a gross figure including net contribution to profit. The gross contribution to profit will be forced down in the initial competitive bid and will provide a base against which all future profitability calculations may be tested.
- In order to deliver the benefits, the supplier may require resources within the current planning period and, as a result, they will be purchased at the higher rate (and hence margin) contained within the additional services charges. The supplier will therefore derive a benefit over and above that declared by the investment itself. This benefit should be included in the total calculation of benefits to be apportioned.
- Your benefits will probably be taken in the form of an annual rebate calculated against performance improvements achieved in the previous year. Supplier benefits will be taken in the form of reduced operating costs, the effect of which will be to increase the contribution to profit above the standard charge gross contribution to profit baseline.
- The calculation of additional performance benefits for the supplier will, at all times, be related to the initial standing charge percentage gross contribution to profit and can be monitored through the open book accounting arrangements.

MAINTAINING PRICE COMPETITIVENESS

The general and continued pressure to drive out performance gains, facilitated by incentives, will tend to keep prices in line. There will, however, be a requirement to monitor prices in the market-place and this will be a key function of contract management arrangements (see Chapter 19).

Lower prices for any single service component of the services provided can always be found. Moreover, some suppliers may propose to sell services at a loss deliberately to dislodge the incumbent supplier. As part of the contract management arrangements you should construct a formula that recognizes the added value component provided by the supplier, investments the supplier has already made in the relationship and the cost and disruption of change from one supplier to another. Should monitoring reveal a misalignment of prices beyond that determined by the formula, the contract management team will need to conduct an investigation to determine whether the misalignment derives from inflated supplier costs, margin or both. If the supplier is found to be at fault, notwithstanding application of the 'value added' formula indicated above, an agreed programme of remedial action should be undertaken to be concluded within an agreed timescale and culminating in a favourable realignment of supplier charges.

A misalignment of charges may, however, result from a lack of *customer* investment, in which case appropriate judgements will need to be made as part of the normal planning cycle.

Whatever the circumstance, the right to test service requirements in the market should always be retained. Care must be taken, however, since testing on too frequent a basis will damage relationships with the incumbent supplier and will cause other suppliers to avoid bidding (or bid frivolously) if they believe that there is little prospect of winning business.

INDEXATION

An indexation mechanism for the contract should be considered for the following reasons:

● Suppliers are unlikely to accept a long-term contract without one.
● Those suppliers that will proceed without an indexation provision have no option but to increase their initial price to take account of the likely rise in their cost base without a matched price improvement.
● Under these circumstances, bids without an indexation provision may appear less competitive when compared with others.
● It will be virtually impossible accurately to evaluate against bids in which indexation is included or priced separately.
● Without an indexation clause and with open book accounting, supplier costs may be allowed to move upwards as a result of pay awards and other cost changes that are well above inflation and therefore outside of your control.

Indexation therefore offers both parties some protection.

There should be no automatic right to full price indexation – the indexation mechanism should simply provide a ceiling for any potential price increase. The need for, and extent of, any indexed price movement should be discussed and agreed according to current conditions. Not all service costs will move in line with inflation and the mechanism must define those that do and, specifically, those that do not. For organizations in the UK, a possible formula for calculating the revised cost ceiling for each indexed service component is as follows:

$$P^1 = P^0 \times (Y/100(M^1/M^0) + (Z/100(L^1/L^0))$$

where :

P^1	= new price of indexed charges
P^0	= old price of indexed charges
Y	= percentage of contract price attributable to materials/equipment
M^1	= index reading at present base
M^0	= index reading at old base

Z   = percentage of contract price attributable to labour costs
L^1 = index reading at present base
L^0 = index reading at old base

Relevant indices may be obtained from the Central Statistical Office *Monthly Digest of Statistics*, published by HMSO.

13 The contract

Underpinning every outsourcing arrangement is a legal contract. Notwithstanding the anticipation of a warm, friendly and mutually beneficial relationship between supplier and customer, there has to be a legal document which, if nothing else, sets out the 'rules' for the relationship. The importance of a correctly constructed and drafted legal document cannot be overemphasized and the procurement manager will do well to ensure that legal advisers are properly engaged in the procurement project at the earliest appropriate moment, and that sufficient time is spent getting the contract right.

Commercially adept suppliers will, almost certainly, attempt to introduce their own draft contracts because this places you in a position where you are forced to argue for changes to their document, giving them a negotiating advantage. This should be resisted. Control of the process should be established by the introduction of a comprehensive draft contract as part of the SoSR. The following observations cover the principal issues that will need to be dealt with in the draft contract. It is not necessarily an exhaustive list and a review of the specific requirement may unearth topics or circumstances unique to the specific procurement in hand for which your legal adviser must provide specific terms.

Early detailed consultation with legal advisers is strongly advised.

THE BASIC COMPONENTS

A good outsourcing agreement will be highly structured and, depending upon its scope and complexity, may contain the following basic components:

- Terms and conditions.
- Staff transfer conditions.
- Asset transfer conditions.
- Accommodation conditions.
- Other matters, e.g. service definition, contained in attached schedules.

If the scale of the agreement is large enough, lawyers will probably wish to create separate contracts for, say, staff transfer, asset transfer and accommodation arrangements, each of which will need its own terms and conditions and schedules. The various contracts and associated schedules then come together to form the complete outsourcing agreement.

Arranging an outsourcing agreement into logically segmented contractual documents provides the following advantages:

- It becomes easier to conduct parallel negotiations, which can be helpful where time is of the essence.
- The use of specialist skills may be directed more effectively.
- Given the potential complexity of some outsourcing agreements, greater clarity of the issues surrounding specific negotiation points is likely to be gained as a result of a narrower focus.
- Documents that deal with transient matters, e.g. staff transfer, can be filed away once transfer has been successfully achieved.

Creating multiple contracts in this way, however, increases the need for careful co-ordination across the different agreements to ensure that the objectives, policies and principles required for the outsourcing agreement as a whole are consistently applied to all contracts. Care must be taken to ensure that hard-won gains in one document are not diminished in another – this is no mean task so do not underrate it! The alternative approach is to integrate all issues into a single document comprising a single set of terms and conditions and a full set of detailed schedules, which would probably include a schedule each for staff transfer, asset transfer and accommodation.

THE BASIC COMPONENTS EXPLORED

TERMS AND CONDITIONS

The terms and conditions of the contract set out the rights, obligations and duties of each party to the agreement and will, as a general rule, contain the following provisions.

Preamble

The preamble identifies the parties to the agreement and makes an opening statement that provides a context for the contract. Although not necessarily contractually binding, a statement here of the procurement objectives (see Chapter 1) will provide a permanent reminder of the 'spirit' of the agreement as originally intended and may also provide a useful means by which both parties can check their progress towards achieving the original objectives.

The services

This section will set out the general obligations to fall upon the supplier regarding supply of the required services. The detailed description of the services will, almost certainly, be described in the supporting schedules. Should there be any specific exclusions or qualifications to the service obligation, these will also be dealt with here.

It may, for instance, be helpful if certain aspects of the agreement were settled at a time later than the contract commencement date. For example, there may be value in allowing the supplier to spend some time managing the service, and therefore confirm or refine its rationalization plans, before making it commit to certain cost elements, for example use of equipment or accommodation. In such circumstances, the facility would be highlighted in the terms and conditions and would be supported by a schedule to the agreement that would unambiguously specify the timing and terms upon which the supplier could elect, say, either to take up an accommodation lease or, because refined rationalization plans might improve benefits to both parties, decline to take up the lease.

Implementation

Implementation of the agreement will be a critically important activity. Where the supplier is to manage all implementation activity, it will be useful, from a contract management point of view, to impose a commitment on the supplier to supply named individuals and to make available the proposed implementation plan. The obligation would be described in the terms and conditions and the detailed implementation plan itself would form the basis of a schedule to the contract (see Chapter 20).

Term

The contract should specify the term or duration of the agreement. This statement would include reference to any break points, whether the agreement is to continue until notice to terminate is served and, if so, what notice period would apply.

Outsourcing agreements can be defined with a fixed natural termination date or they can run continuously until a notice period, usually of at least 12 months, is served. If the agreement is to run continuously, it is usual to specify a minimum period before any such notice of natural termination may be served.

It is also usual for customers to want an 'escape' route in the form of a break clause. Great care is needed with break clauses as they will, almost certainly, have commercial implications. They are discussed below under Termination.

Change control

A change control mechanism will be needed to facilitate changes to both the contract terms and service requirement. The obligation to be bound by the change control mechanism will be set out in a contract clause and the precise mechanism itself will probably be contained in a schedule.

Current and future intellectual property

Rights to existing intellectual property must be protected and the same protection must also be extended to enhancements, modifications or changes to existing intellectual property provided or developed by the supplier, particularly where the resulting intellectual property will contain a mixture of original and new property. This section should secure all rights to existing intellectual property together with subsequent refinements.

Rights to new intellectual property, generated as part of the service, should also be preserved. Care will need to be taken here because copyright law may vest ownership in the originator, depending upon legal jurisdiction, and not, as you might automatically think, in the organization that pays the bill. A customer must make specific provision if ownership is not to pass unnoticed to the originator. Incidentally, it is possible to leave ownership of intellectual property with the supplier, ideally in return for a better price, and still secure satisfactory rights 'to use'. Do ensure, however, that such rights allow for use by a third party, probably one of your supplier's competitors, should you wish to place future outsourcing business elsewhere. For this reason, advice on this matter from your legal adviser is crucial. In all cases formally claim ownership unless specific advantages have been secured within the agreement with which your advisers are content.

Third party intellectual property

Where the intellectual property of a third party is being used by the customer, special provision may be needed for the transfer of licences or other documents to an outsourcing supplier. Third party licensors will probably wish formally to novate licences and some may wish, probably unreasonably, to re-negotiate terms. If there are many licences to novate, it will take longer to complete the novations than you imagine – so start early.

Title and risk

Where ownership of specific resources and assets, used by the outsourcing supplier in the provision of service, is retained by the customer, it is important to set down in this section a declaration to the effect that title to the resources and assets resides with the customer. However, you will also need to agree, and set down in the contract, which party carries the risks associated with asset renewal and fitness for purpose.

Apart from the need to be neat and tidy, clarity regarding title and risk will become important in untangling the assets when the agreement is finally terminated.

Charges and charging structure

The precise terms of agreed charging formulae should be set out in a schedule to the contract. This section of the terms and conditions should deal with general attributes of the charging arrangements and will cover items such as the following:

- Restricting the submission of charges only to those services contemplated by the agreement or those services additionally agreed, in writing.
- Payment terms and invoicing.
- Value added tax.

This section should also include details of any bonds or guarantees that may be required from the supplier and arrangements for checking the accuracy of the financial statements given to the supplier in the SoSR. This process will take the form of either a pre-contract due diligence or post-contract verification exercise. An exercise of this nature is necessary because outsourcing agreements frequently rely on 'transferred' costs. Suppliers will bid on the basis of the financial information included in the SoSR and will wish to verify the accuracy of the information against the actual costs transferred to them. Whichever form of cost verification is selected, it is likely to result in adjustments to the contract price. The process to be followed must be clearly described in the charging approach schedule.

Financial remedies

This section will reflect the general terms associated with any agreed financial remedy schemes, with detailed descriptions held in a schedule. In this context, financial remedies is another way of saying 'penalties for poor performance'. While it may be prudent to consider financial remedies for poor performance, such devices may impede the development of a working relationship and require significant additional resources and effort if they are to work effectively. The supplier will certainly include in its price the cost of meeting complicated financial remedy schemes and some financial cover to its risk – in other words, you will probably pay more.

Warranties

This section reflects the warranties and any specific obligations made or undertaken by each party. By way of illustration, the customer may wish the supplier to warrant the following:

- The supplier has sufficient resource capacity to provide a satisfactory service.
- Supplier representatives will be suitably skilled and qualified.
- The services will be carried out using reasonable skill and care.
- Service will be provided in compliance with laws, statutes and regulations.

On the other side, where a transfer of staff and equipment is involved, the supplier may wish to ask for warranties regarding the condition of equipment, that is its fitness for purpose, and that there are no outstanding staff difficulties, for example any ongoing disciplinary cases.

Limitation of liability

Some suppliers will seek to limit their financial liabilities in the event of service failures, for example by setting liquidated damages for non-performance and disallowing consequential loss. In some industries this is accepted practice. However, formal advice should be sought before any limitations of liability are agreed.

Indemnities

Indemnities are a return for something lost or suffered, usually through the fault of another, and are frequently sought by purchasers when contemplating strategically important services. Great care is needed when considering indemnities and none should be finalized without a clear understanding of the financial consequences or without detailed advice from your legal and financial experts.

The following questions should be considered:

1. Will the customer and its employees and agents require indemnification resulting from:
   - The provision of the contracted service?
   - A failure to provide the contracted service?
   - The supplier's negligence?
   - Any breach of supplier obligation?
   - Any breach of representation or warranty by the supplier?
   - Loss or damage to property?
   - Loss or damage to data, information or software?
2. What will be the scale of indemnification:
   - Unlimited in all respects?
   - Unlimited for specific categories of risk? for example
     - death or personal injury?
     - loss of, and subsequent recreation of, data?
     - infringement of customer intellectual property rights?
     - infringement of third party intellectual property rights?
     - infringement of confidentiality?
     - damage to tangible property?
   - Include consequential loss?
   - Limited to a specific sum for all events – if yes, what sum?
   - Limited to a specific sum for each event – if yes, what sum?
   - Limited to a specific sum in any one year – if yes, what sum?
3. What insurance cover, if any, will be required of the supplier:
   - Arrangements to cover supplier liabilities?
   - The interest of the customer to be noted on the policies?
   - If a consortium, are policies to be in the names of both suppliers?
   - Policies to be taken out jointly by the customer and supplier?

- Supplier to provide proof that premiums are being paid?
- In the event of default by the supplier, should the customer be able to make appropriate insurance arrangements and pass the costs plus handling fee to supplier?

4. Will the customer require a performance bond?
5. Will the customer require a corporate guarantee?
6. Will the customer be prepared, under *force majeure*, to waive some or all of its indemnity rights – if so, what might be those circumstances:
   - Labour disputes by supplier staff, agents or contractors?
   - Payments due?

The subject of indemnification is wide and complex and no rules can be indicated here except that considerable thought must be applied and knowledgeable advice obtained.

Confidentiality

Ensure that you protect any commercially sensitive information that relates to the customer's private affairs. Some outsourcing services will inevitably involve the supplier having legitimate access to confidential information. It will be important to place the supplier and its staff under certain obligations which protect such information.

Security/safety

The customer will wish to impose, where appropriate, its security and safety rules and regulations. An overview of these should be given in this section with detailed requirements set out in a schedule.

Termination

This section should set down the rules for termination of the contract in the light of a range of different circumstances. You will need to decide what rules are to pertain under the following termination conditions:

- By virtue of material supplier breach.
- By virtue of material customer breach.
- By virtue of supplier insolvency, liquidation or inability to pay debts.
- By virtue of change of supplier ownership.
- By virtue of government legislation.
- By virtue of the customer's desire to withdraw for no cause.

In addition, consider partial termination. This may be needed in circumstances where some aspects of the agreement can be terminated but without prejudice to others.

If there are grounds for termination by virtue of partner breach:

- Will a period for remedy be permitted and, if so, how long?

- Will compensation be required and, if so, how much?

In the event of termination for both breach by the partner and natural termination, the consequences need to be considered and the following questions answered:

- To whom will the assets belong?
- If the supplier has to provide equipment or is forced to vacate a building, who pays the cost and will compensation be paid?
- What provisions will be needed:
  - for reassignment of intellectual property?
  - for access to or return of assets and documentation?
  - regarding access to or re-recruitment of key members of staff?
  - for customer access to supplier premises to assure maintenance of service levels and facilitate transfer to third party or customer?
  - to assure supplier co-operation in transfer to third party?
  - for third party access to supplier premises?
  - to maintain service levels and facilitated transfer?
  - for use of proprietary products used by the supplier in the provision of service?
  - to determine who pays the cost of service transfer?

Dispute

In the event of a dispute, will the courts, an 'expert' or an arbitrator be called upon to provide a solution? If the contract specifies the appointment of an 'expert' as the means by which disputes will be resolved, which independent body will make the appointment? For example:

- President of the Law Society.
- Director General of the relevant services association.
- Relevant institute of specific service or manufacturing sector.

Take care with the above list. While the President of the Law Society may be an obvious choice for a legal document, an industry specialist may be more appropriate.

Break

Often customers will wish to have an 'escape route', or break clause from outsourcing contracts that last for more than five years. Although it makes sense to have a break clause, some very substantial commercial implications flow from their improper use. This is because the supplier's charges will be based upon a combination of volume of service required over the length of the contract (see Chapter 12) and the amount of investment and rate of return over time. 'Time' is therefore a critical feature in the pricing of any outsourcing agreement. If, therefore, you ask the supplier to give a price for a five-year agreement and then place a break point at, say, the end of year three, the supplier is forced to base most of its pricing calculations on a three, and not five, year agreement. Needless to say this has the effect of pushing the price up, which is unhelpful, particularly since, in actuality, you may not need to invoke the break.

There is a way to have the best (well nearly) of both worlds. By attaching the notion of compensation to the 'no cause' break option, the supplier may base its charges on the full term of the agreement knowing that, should it be terminated, it has some protection, and the customer can terminate at a cost that declines as the remaining contract term reduces. The principles of the approach may be summarised as follows:

- The agreement may be broken at any time by the customer.
- The customer must give at least [12] months notice of its intention to break.
- The supplier will have no right to break.
- The supplier will be indemnified by the customer in respect of:
  - all fair and reasonable residual costs incurred on behalf of the customer;
  - all fair and reasonable transition costs;
  - loss of profit;
  - fair and reasonable residual costs.
- Transition costs will include:
  - training new supplier;
  - shadow or parallel running with the new supplier;
  - handover costs;
  - costs incurred arising from the transferring of staff to new supplier;
  - preparation of any additionally required procedural or practices documentation that does not already exist and has not previously been a normal (best practice) requirement of service provision;
  - legal costs arising as a result of break.
- Loss of profit will be calculated as follows:

([say, 75%] x profit element of the anticipated fixed standing charges) + ([say, 50%] x profit element of the committed additional services charge)

The following interpretations would apply:

- 'Anticipated fixed standing charges' means a sum equal to any fixed standing charges with respect to committed forward requirements beyond the date of termination and the then current estimate of future requirements identified by the customer with respect to all services commenced prior to the date of exercise of the 'break option', which, were it not for the exercise of the break option, would be payable by the customer to the supplier if the agreement were to expire five years following the commencement date.
- 'Committed additional services charges' means a sum equal to the additional services charges with respect to committed forward requirements beyond the date of termination identified by the customer, which, were it not for the

exercise of the break option, would be payable by the customer to the supplier'.

- 'Profit element' means the agreed target gross margin reduced by [x per cent] in respect of overheads.
- 'Residual costs' means those supplier related costs for which a fixed liability exists. It may be sensible to suggest that the customer's liability for such residual costs shall not extend beyond year five following the outsourcing agreement commencement date, on the grounds that five years is a sufficiently long time to absorb any such costs.

Audit access

Customers may have audit obligations that must be maintained even if the service is being provided by a third party. Equally, the customer may wish to assure audit access to supplier records under circumstances where charging arrangements rely upon 'open book'. All audit access obligations on the supplier will therefore need to be set down in this section.

Contract management

Contract management is an important function in any outsourcing agreement (see Chapter 19). The contract must place the supplier under an obligation to meet contract management requirements in so far as the supplier is involved, for example the delivery of performance reports. The details of such obligations should be described in an accompanying schedule. A central element of the contract management schedule will deal with the issue of service performance and particularly the master service level agreement or service level agreements.

If there is a satisfactory history of service requirements and performance related information, the precise service requirement can be collated and recorded in service level agreements after contract commencement. The point of this is to place an obligation on the supplier to conduct the actual work, an activity that is best achieved after contract commencement when the supplier is fully engaged in the agreement.

Standard clauses

There will be a range of standard clauses that legal advisers will wish their clients to consider for inclusion in a draft contract. Some examples follow.

Publicity   Customers may wish to control press announcements and other publicity.

Corrupt gifts   Customers may want to make the payment of illegal inducements from the supplier to customer staff a breach of contractual obligations.

Force majeure   This provision may or may not exclude both or either parties from contractual liability from the effects of circumstances outside the control of the obligated party (see Indemnities above).

Transfer and subcontracting   It is normal practice not to allow assignment of the outsourcing contract by the supplier to a third party. Suppliers are, however, often permitted to subcontract parts of the agreement to specialist organizations, e.g. cleaners, portering, deliveries, equipment maintenance, provided that they remain the primary contractor and are not released from any of the contractual obligations, e.g. cleaning.

STAFF TRANSFER AGREEMENT

The staff transfer agreement describes the contractual terms associated with the transfer of staff at commencement of the contract. The staff transfer agreement will cease to be relevant once all the staff have transferred. It will be derived from the work undertaken to define the human resources policies as discussed in Chapters 10 and 16. The staff transfer agreement itself will define the 'rules' for staff transfer whilst the staff and their details will be set out in the relevant schedule to the agreement.

ASSET TRANSFER AGREEMENT

The asset transfer agreement describes the contractual terms associated with the transfer of assets at commencement of the contract. The asset transfer agreement will probably cease to be relevant once all the assets have been transferred. It will be derived from the work undertaken to define the policies surrounding assets as discussed in Chapters 11 and 16. The asset transfer agreement itself will define the 'rules' for asset transfer whilst the assets themselves will be set out in the relevant schedule to the agreement.

ACCOMMODATION AGREEMENT

The accommodation agreement describes the contractual terms associated with the use of relevant accommodation. It will define the 'rules' surrounding the accommodation, its use and any other related matters. Whether this agreement has lasting relevance really depends on the circumstances surrounding the agreement. Accommodation contracts are potentially complex and a contractual error can be very expensive. It is strongly recommended that the structure and content of the accommodation agreement be discussed with an appropriately qualified legal adviser.

SCHEDULES

Schedules have been mentioned a number of times earlier in this chapter. A contract schedule is a record of additional details describing or extending the scope of the terms and conditions or providing a factual record of matters affected by the terms and conditions. Schedules can also contain detailed descriptions of processes or mechanisms or copies of relevant documents to which the contract directly refers.

The following list describes some of the subject matter to be typically found in service contract schedules.

- **The services**
  A description of the services to be provided.
- **Implementation plan**
  A copy of the agreed implementation plan.
- **Change control process**
  A description, in detail, of the change control process for agreeing and implementing agreed service changes.
- **Invoicing procedure**
  A description of the formal payment arrangements.
- **Charging structure**
  Full and complete charging arrangements should be described in this section. Do not allow charging arrangements to be put elsewhere in the contract – ensure this by insisting that this schedule includes a provision that disallows charging details outside of this schedule. '
- **Master service level agreement (MSL6)**
  This schedule will outline the obligation to produce a MSLA after contract commencement and will describe its content.
- **Financial remedies**
  If required, this section will describe, in detail, the arrangements for financial remedies.
- **Standards**
  The quality of the service will depend on agreed standards. Standards may include not only technical standards but general standards that the customer conforms to as a matter of policy, e.g. workplace safety, environmental standards or ergonomics. The customer may also wish the supplier to conform to certified quality standards. The standards must be clearly articulated in a schedule.
- **Escalation procedure**
  A description of the contract escalation process.
- **Contract management procedures**
  A detailed description of the arrangements for performance monitoring; cost monitoring; performance improvements; administration; audit access; accommodation and other matters.
- **Prior documents**
  A copy (or reference to a copy) of a document that has significance to the

contract, e.g. a copy of agreements made with a trade union that the new supplier must honour under the terms of the agreement.

It is worth noting that while legal advisers will happily draft the contract terms and conditions, they will be less well equipped to draft the schedules. As part of the planning process, it would be highly beneficial to draw up the SoSR in a way that facilitates, in due course, the direct reproduction of text from the SoSR into the contract schedules, as appropriate.

GETTING TO A CONTRACT QUICKLY

Outsourcing contracts are complex and frequently cover circumstances for which, on the one hand, there is a substantial amount of detail and, on the other, very little information at all, for example undefined future requirements. The collection, collation and quality assurance of this information can cause significant project delay if it is deemed necessary for a contract to be wholly finalized in all respects before signature and contract commencement. There may, however, be some instances where some detailed information can be collected *after* the contract has started, possibly by the supplier, and consolidated into the appropriate contractual documents at a later date. Some examples follow.

SERVICE DEFINITION AND PERFORMANCE LEVELS

In circumstances where the outsourcing agreement leads to a complete transfer of an undertaking to the supplier, it may not be necessary for the service and its associated performance levels to be defined with very great precision before the agreement is signed provided that:

- the boundaries and broad components of the required service are described;
- the costs associated with those services residing within the boundaries can be calculated; and
- the new supplier is prepared to accept a commitment to provide services according to historical precedent – requirement and performance.

Under these circumstances it will be entirely reasonable to complete the detailed work after the agreement has been signed.

PRICE

In many outsourcing arrangements, the bulk of the cost base is transferred from customer to supplier. The supplier therefore relies on the customer's statement of costs, as presented in the SoSR, to construct its price. Many suppliers ask for a period of 'due diligence', immediately before contract signature, so that actual costs (and any other details of commercial significance) may be checked against the information provided in the SoSR. If the agreement is large and complex, this can delay contract commencement by a number of months. An alternative approach is to devise a 'post-contract verification process' which allows for a checking of facts, post-contract, and provides a strictly mechanical process for changing the price should any material errors be found.

DELAYED DECISIONS

There may be circumstances where mutual benefit can be derived by delaying a key decision. An example might be the assignment of accommodation to the supplier. Where the customer has alternative opportunities of disposal, it may be commercially beneficial if the supplier is allowed a period of grace before making a commitment to the assignment of accommodation. So long as the circumstances are properly documented in the schedules, for example timing of decision, effect on price, responsibilities of the parties, there is no reason why this issue has to be solved before signature.

These are just some examples of what can be done. Remember to consider each circumstance carefully and, where necessary, seek expert advice.

14 Evaluating the proposals

The evaluation of a conventional contract is relatively straightforward. The evaluation of a contract for the supply of services over a long period, during which requirements will change, is far from straightforward. The purpose of this chapter is to offer some insights and practical support regarding the evaluation of supplier proposals that are in the nature of 'strategic relationships'.

EVALUATION OVERVIEW

ORGANIZATION

Evaluation of proposals for large-scale procurements will be complex and, as a result, appropriate organizational arrangements must be put in place *as early as possible*. Figure 14.1 suggests a possible approach.

SELECTION PANEL

The selection panel will review all of the available evaluation material and make the final selection decision. It should be composed of senior executives, including representatives from the department(s) for whom the service is being procured and the users of its services.

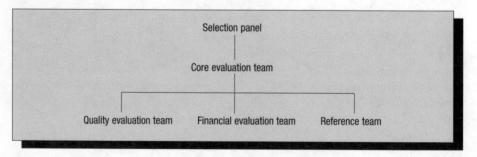

Figure 14.1 A structure for evaluation

CORE EVALUATION TEAM

The core evaluation team effectively runs and manages the procurement, develops the project deliverables and, depending on its terms of reference, may make recommendations to the selection panel. It should comprise a small multidisciplinary team of no more than six people and should be led by a senior executive of the department for whom the service is being procured. Depending upon the scale of the procurement, the core evaluation team may need to co-opt additional skills and manpower to facilitate a focus upon the three evaluation areas of quality, finance and references.

It is not uncommon for the procurement task to be delegated down the organization. In the case of large or complex procurements it is vitally important that this does not happen, for the following reasons:

- There will certainly be a need to develop policies that may have far-reaching implications for the organization as a whole.
- Senior executives across the business will need to be engaged and influenced throughout the procurement project.

Junior staff will not be effective since they are unlikely to have the breadth of vision or sufficient authority.

The senior executive appointed to be the core evaluation team leader should not be a member of the selection panel and should not, therefore, participate in selection panel decision making, although he or she would obviously attend all selection panel meetings as the representative of the core evaluation team. This approach provides an audit 'firebreak' between detailed evaluation work and the final decision.

The taking up of references, which is a key part of the evaluation, may be particularly time consuming. Therefore, set up a small team to provide a focus and continuity for the collection and analysis of reference material.

EVALUATION PROCESS

Figure 14.2 provides an evaluation process overview.

EVALUATION DOCUMENT FLOWS

A number of documents are used throughout the evaluation and Figure 14.3 illustrates their relationship. Each document will be described in detail later in this chapter.

GENERAL APPROACH TO EVALUATION

There are a number of facets to the evaluation of a complex agreement, the

103

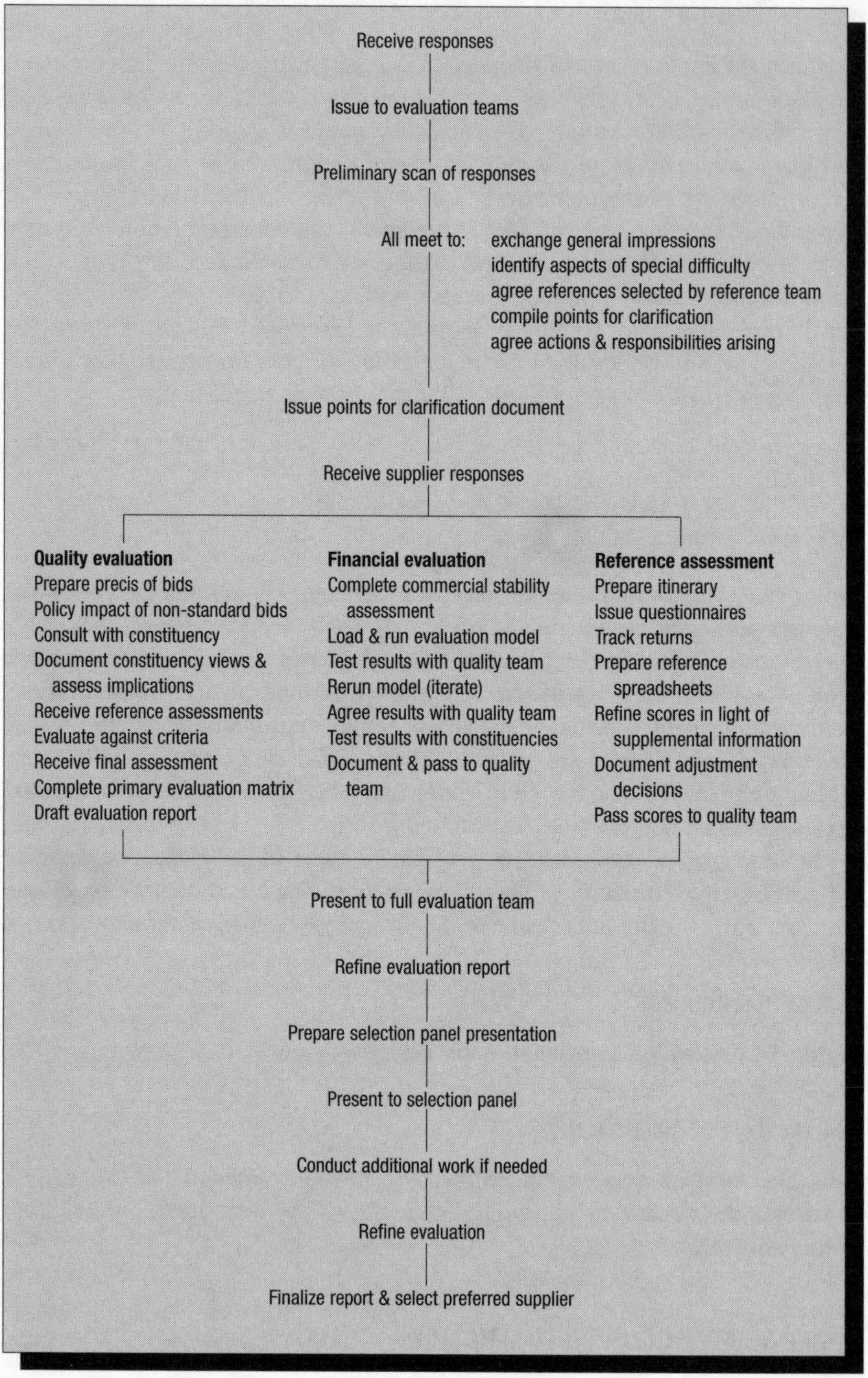

Receive responses

Issue to evaluation teams

Preliminary scan of responses

All meet to: exchange general impressions
identify aspects of special difficulty
agree references selected by reference team
compile points for clarification
agree actions & responsibilities arising

Issue points for clarification document

Receive supplier responses

Quality evaluation
Prepare precis of bids
Policy impact of non-standard bids
Consult with constituency
Document constituency views &
  assess implications
Receive reference assessments
Evaluate against criteria
Receive final assessment
Complete primary evaluation matrix
Draft evaluation report

Financial evaluation
Complete commercial stability
  assessment
Load & run evaluation model
Test results with quality team
Rerun model (iterate)
Agree results with quality team
Test results with constituencies
Document & pass to quality
  team

Reference assessment
Prepare itinerary
Issue questionnaires
Track returns
Prepare reference
  spreadsheets
Refine scores in light of
  supplemental information
Document adjustment
  decisions
Pass scores to quality team

Present to full evaluation team

Refine evaluation report

Prepare selection panel presentation

Present to selection panel

Conduct additional work if needed

Refine evaluation

Finalize report & select preferred supplier

Figure 14.2 An evaluation process

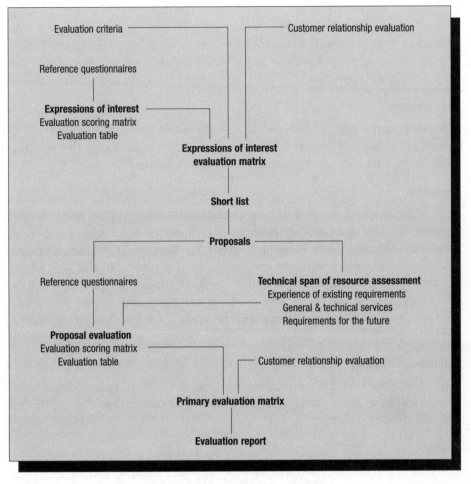

Figure 14.3 Evaluation document flows

primary components of which are identified below and discussed in greater detail later in this chapter.

Procurement objectives

Objectives for the agreement will have been set (see Chapter 1). The evaluation models must therefore be centred upon those objectives.

Short list and primary evaluations

Two evaluation models are usually required – one to arrive at a short list of possible suppliers and the other to determine the preferred supplier.

Dealing with innovation

The evaluation models must be positioned to compare proposals on a like for like basis. This may lead to an over prescription of requirements, which effectively disallows the presentation of innovative and potentially highly cost-effective solutions. Therefore it might be necessary to request two proposals – a 'standard' proposal that conforms to a prescriptive format suitable for accurate comparison and a 'non-standard' proposal that allows the introduction of innovation.

Relationships

Where an agreement is destined to run for many years, it is important to assess the ability of potential suppliers to form and maintain effective working relationships for extended periods of time (see Chapter 15).

Consortia

Where the service requirement is large and the resources of any one potential supplier are, by comparison, modest, it is common for suppliers to form consortia. Although there is nothing inherently wrong with consortia, ensure that there is a prime contractor who can be held accountable and with whom the customer will contract on behalf of the consortium. In addition, it will be necessary to test the legal and working arrangements within any given consortium and special provisions must be made for this within the evaluation models.

Commercial stability

When entering a long-term relationship that is likely to require significant investment from the supplier, it is essential to test their financial position and general stability.

Quality

The general capabilities and quality of service is, of course, a key component of any service and must be thoroughly tested within the evaluation process.

Cost

Cost will always be an important part of the evaluation but should not be the primary determinant. Given the empirical nature of cost evaluation, as distinct from the somewhat 'softer' aspects to do with quality, it is recommended that the criterion of cost not be assigned a weighting in the traditional sense but should be treated as a separate item to be considered alongside the broader evaluation picture.

Added value

In Chapter 8 the nature of added value was discussed and some ideas were presented as to how it might be achieved. It is difficult to evaluate added value within a single criterion, but, if the agreement is packaged correctly, the suggested approach to evaluation that follows will enable it to be assessed.

Standard proposals

Standard proposals are intended to follow closely the SoSR guidelines (see Chapter 16). As a consequence, proposals should comply with all matters of policy set out in the SoSR and establish a common base for assessment between the proposals.

Non-standard proposals

By implication, standard proposals must impose a range of constraints upon suppliers, the effect of which might be to prevent them from proposing a more innovative deployment of their resources and, as a consequence, inhibit the delivery of additional benefits for both parties.

The delivery of these additional benefits may require a sufficiently profound change to one or a number of policies as to make them unattainable. It may be, however, that significant additional benefit could be won with relatively minor policy adjustments. As a consequence, suppliers should be invited to submit proposals that are, in principle, free from policy constraints but comply with a minimum set of requirements, an example of which might be that the non-standard proposal must, as a minimum, include the same service elements as the standard bid.

The purpose of requesting non-standard proposals is therefore as follows:

- To ensure that the outer limits of all possible benefits have been identified.
- To ensure the proper consideration of the extent to which policies would have to change to acquire the benefits and to reach a clear judgement as to whether policies should change to facilitate delivery of additional benefits or, if policies are not to change, to document the reasons for not pursuing the additional benefits.
- To protect you from challenges by unsuccessful suppliers who believe that their proposals would have succeeded and money would have been saved if minor policy adjustments had been made.

Note:

- The SoSR should make it clear that you will not be compelled to accept non-standard bids. This is to offer protection against pressure to accept a low cost bid that demands unacceptable policy changes.
- Contract terms and conditions will be common to both types of proposals and therefore may not be varied within a non-standard bid.
- Standard and non-standard bids should be evaluated against the same criteria and evaluation process to assure comparability. Non-standard bids will, however, be subjected to an additional test that will identify the impact upon customer policies. The acceptability, or otherwise, of the policy changes may then be judged.

BASIS FOR EVALUATION

STANDARD AND NON-STANDARD PROPOSALS

Supplier responses to both standard and non-standard proposals should be examined under the following general headings:

- Cost.
- Potential for establishing and maintaining a good relationship with customers.
- Commercial stability.
- Policy impact (non-standard proposals only).
- A quality assessment designed to test the ability to deliver the required objectives.

PRIMARY EVALUATION MATRIX

A primary evaluation matrix should be prepared which brings together all of these factors in a manner designed to facilitate selection panel discussion and decision. Figure 14.4 shows a primary evaluation matrix for evaluation of SoSR responses.

The evaluation matrix should be used for evaluation of responses to both the expressions of interest advertisement and the SoSR, although its form and content will vary slightly between the two. The general heading of quality should be assessed by use of detailed weighted criteria. The general headings of cost, customer relationship, commercial stability and policy impact are not amenable to inclusion within the general quality assessment and, as a consequence, are assessed separately.

While every attempt should be made to identify objective and easily measurable criteria, inevitably many aspects of the evaluation will be judgemental. As a consequence, *all* markings should be tested, discussed and agreed by the evaluation team as a whole and judgements documented. As a final precaution for those organizations where it applies, it may be helpful to have representatives from internal audit functions present at every assessment meeting who will be able formally to audit the decisions made.

The SoSR should identify minimum requirements that the supplier response must address. Any responses that fail to conform should not be considered. The selection panel should then take into consideration all aspects of the primary evaluation matrix and any other issues that it judges to be of relevance when coming to a decision. Note that it is *not* intended that each heading be regarded as a hurdle to be cleared before moving to the next element of the matrix. Nor is it intended that the headings be aggregated to a single index of performance as such an aggregation would mix different currencies of performance to arrive at a misleading result.

	Rating	Suppliers																		Policy impact
		Standard						Non-standard												
		A		B		C		A₁		B₁		C₁								
		%	Score	%	Score	%	Score	%	Score	%	Score	%	Score							
Cost NPV % Reduction ASC % Reduction XXX																				
Customer relationship	Good																			
Commercial stability	Stable																			
Quality assessment																				
Outsourcing ability	Good																			
Objective 1	Good																			
Objective 2	Good																			
Caring for staff	Good																			
Total quality score																				

Figure 14.4 Primary evaluation matrix

The headings of relationship, commercial stability and quality have therefore quite deliberately been separated to allow the selection panel the scope to judge the individual effect of these topics when taken together.

PRIMARY EVALUATION MATRIX – GENERAL HEADINGS

Cost

The cost of supplier responses, taken over the life of the agreement, should be assessed under the following general categories:

- **NPV** (net present value)
  A standard analysis to arrive at the net present value for each proposal
- **% reduction**
  Suppliers will propose a price for the routine service or for each routine service strand (see Chapter 12). The proposed prices should be compared with current and planned customer costs, taking into account the potential for internal performance improvements, and the difference expressed as a percentage reduction (or increase) within the matrix. A reduction in cost should be shown as a positive number and an increase in cost should be shown in parentheses to denote a negative number.
- **% reduction ASC (additional services charge)**
  There will be charges for services in addition to those set out for the routine service – the additional services charge (abbreviated to ASC in Figure 14.4) (see Chapter 12). A list of these additional services together with their unit costs will be created and the average cost per service unit established. This will form a baseline against which supplier charges may be compared and the difference will be expressed as a percentage reduction (or increase) within the matrix. A reduction in cost should be shown as a positive number and an increase in cost should be shown in parentheses to denote a negative number.
- **% reduction XXX (other service components)**
  There may be different charging regimes for other service components and these should be dealt with along the lines discussed above but using different parameters.

Customer relationship

You will need to test the ability of each supplier to create and maintain a relationship of the type sought (see Chapter 15). Judgements must necessarily be subjective but should be based upon declared supplier objectives for entering the relationship (see Chapter 17), the results of reference visits and any other available information.

Suppliers should be assessed as poor, marginal, good or excellent. The minimum standard for a 'pass' should be 'good'. An assessment rated as 'poor' should result in automatic disqualification. A 'marginal' assessment should require discussion within, and a decision from, the selection panel where consideration should be given to all other assessment factors when coming to a decision.

Commercial stability

The commercial stability of suppliers and parent companies should be assessed by reference to the previous three years' financial performance together with other factors like market share and impact of industry trends. Suppliers should be assessed on a 'pass' or 'fail' basis, that is suppliers should be judged either to be stable or unstable. Those suppliers judged to be unstable would normally be disqualified.

Policy impact (non-standard proposals only)

The policy impact of non-standard proposals should be identified against each of the quality headings and given a designation of slight, significant or considerable. The selection panel should then judge the relative merits of each non-standard bid against the implications of the required policy change. The selection panel should consider all non-standard proposals but be under no obligation to accept a non-standard bid however apparently attractive.

Assessment of quality

The quality of proposals should be tested to determine the supplier's ability to deliver the objectives set. Detailed criteria and associated weightings should be developed for use in this assessment. In addition, actual performance data should be requested from supplier-nominated referees (see later in this chapter for a full reference questionnaire (p.120) and Appendix B).

The category of outsourcing ability is concerned with testing supplier service delivery infrastructures to assess the extent to which the business of outsourcing is understood by the supplier, together with the robustness of service delivery arrangements. Testing outsourcing ability should influence the scores for each of the objectives. This is because a supplier may, for example, be well equipped with the right tools and skills but lack a robust and sustainable means of delivering them. Some suggested criteria and weightings are provided at Figure 14.6 and 14.10 in this chapter.

An initial scoring assessment should be made by completing the evaluation scoring matrix at the end of this chapter (Figure 14.10, p. 126). The scores should then be decanted onto the evaluation table (Figure 14.11, p. 136), which provides an analysis by general heading and objective.

For the evaluation of expressions of interest, each general heading should be subject to a minimum score. Minimum scores should, if possible, be based upon an assessment of existing customer capability insofar as it can be compared with the requirements of the contractual relationship. It is likely that the minimum threshold below which suppliers should be disqualified will be in the order of 50 per cent although it could be higher.

The supplier scores should be brought together on the evaluation table. A supplier's total score may then be compared with the maximum score possible and the percentage score calculated. The percentage score will then indicate the assessment to be given on the following basis:

- **Poor**
  A percentage score less than 50 per cent will mean disqualification, although all aspects within the evaluation process should be considered before coming to a decision.
- **Marginal**
  A percentage score in the range 51–59 per cent should lead to disqualification but may need further sensitivity analyses and an explicit discussion within the selection panel. The selection panel should determine whether disqualification from the short list is appropriate.
- **Good**
  A percentage score in the range 60–89 per cent should mean a pass.
- **Excellent**
  A percentage score in excess of 90 per cent is an automatic pass and normally guarantees inclusion in the short list.

For the evaluation of SoSR responses, in order to complete the primary evaluation matrix, each general heading *should not* be subject to a minimum score. The supplier scores should be brought together on the evaluation table. A supplier's total score will then be compared with the maximum score possible and the percentage score calculated. The percentage score will then indicate the rating to be given on the following basis – poor, marginal, good or excellent.

The selection panel, when determining the preferred supplier, should take the following factors into account:

- The primary evaluation matrix scores, ratings and cost information.
- Any particular groups or subsets of the primary evaluation matrix scores that assist in differentiating between the proposals.
- Any other information contained within the proposals, or in the formal references taken up, that has not been reflected in the formal evaluation model.

EXPRESSIONS OF INTEREST EVALUATION

The matrix for evaluation of expressions of interest is shown in Figure 14.5 and is a subset of the primary evaluation matrix. Note, however, that no cost

	Min. Req.	Suppliers											
		A		B		C		D		E		F	
		%	Score	%	Score	%	Score		Score		Score		Score
Customer relationship	Good												
Commercial stability	Stable												
Quality assessment													
Outsourcing ability	Good												
Objective 1	Good												
Objective 2	Good												
Caring for staff	Good												
Total quality score													

Figure 14.5 Matrix for expressions of interest

113

information is requested at this stage since expressions of interest is concerned with testing general capability rather than proposals surrounding a specific requirement. In effect, the supplier's capability is tested on a general basis before it has to do any detailed costing work. This approach has the advantage of minimizing both supplier and customer bid costs and reduces the possibility of unhelpfully low priced submissions from unqualified suppliers.

CRITERIA FOR PRIMARY AND EXPRESSION OF INTEREST EVALUATION

Evaluation criteria will vary in line with specific requirements and it is, therefore, not possible to be prescriptive. In general, criteria for evaluation of expression of interest submissions will be a subset of those used to complete the primary evaluation matrix and the core evaluation team will need to decide which are relevant for their particular circumstance. Figure 14.6 gives some generic criteria which may need to be modified. The list should be augmented by more industry specific criteria.

GENERIC CRITERIA AMPLIFIED

Supplier's objectives for relationship

Designed to test the 'fit' between customer and supplier objectives for entering the relationship. Supplier objectives should be assessed for general compatibility with customer objectives, the ability of the customer to meet any of the implications associated with the supplier's objectives and their ability to be measured. In the case of consortia, the objectives for both consortia parties should be assessed.

Evidence of re-engineering capability by example with results

Designed to test the ability of suppliers to support the re-engineering of customer functional activities, if required. The extent to which suppliers are dependent upon one particular approach and the basis upon which appropriate tools and techniques are to be made available should be assessed. Up to five references should be taken up and empirical evidence should be sought to demonstrate the capability.

Technical span of resources

Designed to test supplier capabilities in terms of the range of their relevant products and skills, the technical span of resources will also be a primary factor in determining the ability of suppliers to respond rapidly and flexibly to changing customer requirements.

The range of technical capability should be tested in terms of the number

Supplier's objectives for relationship

Evidence of re-engineering capability by example with results

Technical span of resources

Consortia – nature of relationship – responsibilities of the parties

General approach to relationship

Experience of successfully creating a relationship on scale required

Integration experience

Scale of resources available

Provision for business development support

Management of large-scale operational environments

Evidence of managing change in own company & within absorbed organization

Provision for maintaining & developing the relationship

Service provision methodology

Contract implementation methodology

Implementation plan

General approach to staff transfer & pro forma terms & conditions

Staff training & development arrangements

Extent of ability to support multi-vendor environments

Extent of 'services'-oriented company philosophy

Pension arrangements

Growth & staff reduction record over last three years

Flexibility of proposed agreement

Specific industry experience

Outsourcing experience

Figure 14.6 Generic evaluation criteria

of products supported, the number of staff available to support each product and the skill level of those staff. A basis upon which technical capabilities could be assessed is provided later in this chapter.

Consortia – nature of relationship – responsibilities of the parties

Designed to reflect the additional problems that may occur between the consortium parties in terms of both maintaining their relationship over an extended period of time and delivering a coherent service. It should have a maximum positive score of zero and a maximum negative score of (x). It is important that the negative affects of consortia are assessed in this way since the positive aspects of a consortium, for example additional ability to absorb staff, wider skills, more tools, etc., will automatically emerge against the criteria designed to test those particular aspects.

General approach to relationship

Designed to test the organizational structure proposed for the relationship in terms of its clarity, simplicity and practicality.

Experience of successfully creating a relationship on the scale required

Designed to test the relative experience of creating and maintaining a strategic relationship in the style and on the scale envisaged. Suppliers should be asked to describe examples and include their duration, size, nature and objectives.

The intention is primarily to test supplier experience of creating and maintaining customer relationships in circumstances where the supplier has *direct responsibility* for operational management, on behalf of the customer, of those resources that have transferred from the customer to the supplier. Relationships based solely upon the simple provision of services should not qualify for scoring under this criterion. Agreements with a duration of less than five years should score lower than agreements with a duration of five years or more. Five references should be taken up.

Integration experience

Designed to test the ability and experience of suppliers to work with other suppliers to integrate a number of complex strands of activity. The assessment should be in terms of the number of years integration services have been provided, the number of agreements currently operating and the total number signed since services were first offered. Five references should be taken up and suppliers should be asked to provide details of the ten largest contracts (in terms of lifetime cost).

Scale of resources available

Designed to test the 'service' based resources available across the world, Europe and nationally. Scale of resources will be a key factor in determining both the ability of suppliers to absorb the customer requirement and their ability to respond rapidly and flexibly to changing needs.

Provision for business development support

Designed to test the sophistication of delivery infrastructures in terms of their ability to link supplier resources to the *business* requirements of the customer. More particularly, this category should assess the organization structure in terms of the extent to which it is directed towards both business and customer strategic requirements together with routine service support, the extent of dedicated supplier resources applied and the general approach adopted.

Management of large-scale operational environments

Designed to test the ability of suppliers to manage large-scale operational environments, if appropriate, by examining the number managed, the number of multi-site environments supported and the general level of performance attained. Five references should be taken up and suppliers should be asked to provide details of the ten largest contracts (in terms of lifetime cost).

Evidence of managing change in own company and within absorbed organization

Designed to test the ability of suppliers to manage large-scale programmes of change within their own companies and within those organizations acquired through strategic relationships. Evidence should be sought that demonstrates the number and scale of change programmes undertaken together with their objectives, deliverables and outcomes.

An outsourcing agreement alone does not, for the purposes of this criterion, constitute a change programme. Programmes of change must be properly constituted with clear terms of reference and formal deliverables. Suppliers should be asked to provide details of the ten largest contracts (in terms of lifetime cost) and five references should be taken up.

Provision for maintaining and developing the relationship

Designed to test proposals for maintaining and developing the relationship between the customer and supplier. More particularly, it should assess the proposed structure for maintaining and developing the relationship, the means by which the vitality of the relationship is to be maintained and the means by which the achievement of the objectives set for the relationship are to be assured.

Service provision methodology

Designed to test the service provision methodology in terms of both its fitness for purpose and the level of outsourcing sophistication attained by the supplier. More particularly, it should assess the organization structure for service provision, the arrangements for user support, the performance reporting arrangements and the service level agreement framework.

Contract implementation methodology

Designed to test the contract implementation methodology in terms of both its fitness for purpose and the level of outsourcing sophistication attained by the supplier. More particularly, it will assess the clarity with which implementation issues are identified, the extent of emphasis on main activities, the resources deployed against implementation issues and the timescale of the implementation phase.

Implementation plan

Designed to test the *application* of the contract implementation methodology. The detailed contract implementation plan, as it relates specifically to the customer, should be assessed in terms of both its fitness for purpose and the level of outsourcing sophistication attained by the supplier.

General approach to staff transfer and pro forma terms and conditions

Designed to test the sophistication of delivery infrastructures as they relate to staff transfer. More particularly, it will assess the extent to which transferred staff are integrated into the supplier organization, the means by which transfer is effected, the extent to which supplier staff terms and conditions compare with those of the customer, the degree of flexibility shown by suppliers when seeking to negotiate individual terms and conditions and the extent to which suppliers make use of secondment through the transfer process.

The use of secondment in the transfer process may earn a negative score because it increases staff uncertainty, prolongs the transfer period and delays the point at which staff and services stabilize. The use of secondment within the transfer process must not be confused with staff secondment post-transfer. Secondments post-transfer may be helpful in terms of building relationships and achieving a higher degree of staff flexibility and development.

Staff training and development arrangements

Designed to test the sophistication of delivery infrastructures as they relate to staff training and development. More particularly, it will assess the nature of schemes provided, the eligibility of transferred staff to participate, the timescale to full participation and the extent to which participation is monitored and assured.

Extent of ability to support multi-vendor environments

Designed to test the ability of suppliers to support, where appropriate, multi-vendor environments in terms of the number of different vendors supported and the number of multi-vendor environments currently supported. Five references should be taken up.

Extent of 'services'-oriented company philosophy

Designed specifically as a challenge to equipment manufacturers who believe that they can provide 'services' without understanding the differences between manufacturing and service provision. It will test the number of years that 'services', as opposed to manufacturing, have been a major business strand. It also establishes the total 'services' revenue and the extent of 'services' revenue as a percentage of total business turnover.

Pension arrangements

A comparison of pension arrangements offered by suppliers with those currently provided by the customer.

Growth and staff reduction record over last three years

Designed to test the ability of service delivery and organization development mechanisms to cope with both significant business growth and its implications for staff. The following should be assessed:

- 'Services' revenue and profit before tax figures for previous three years.
- Extent of 'services' revenue and profit growth year on year.
- Number of 'services' related staff year on year.
- Gross number of 'services' related staff released (for whatever reason) year on year.

Flexibility of proposed agreement

Designed to test the flexibility of supplier proposals in terms of the extent of any contractual constraints and the simplicity and flexibility of controlling formulae.

Specific industry experience

Designed to test experience of the specific industry or sector in which the customer is active in terms of the extent of involvement, the nature of experience gained and any other relevant experience.

Outsourcing experience

Designed to test the extent of supplier outsourcing experience by examining the number of clients of a similar profile to the customer requirement, the number of years during which outsourcing services have been provided, the number of outsourcing agreements currently operating and the total number of outsourcing agreements signed since the service was initially offered. Five references should be taken up and suppliers should be asked to provide details of the ten largest contracts (in terms of lifetime cost).

TAKING UP REFERENCES

Although the scoring of criteria related to quality is particularly subjective, it is, to some degree, possible to counter the effects of subjectivity by taking up a wide range of references, but in a highly structured way. A large number of references should be taken up for the following reasons:

- If structured in the right way, subjective views can be converted into scores.
- Responses will be statistically more valid.
- The effects of statistical outriders will be minimized.

By relating the reference approach to the evaluation criteria, it becomes possible to construct a reference questionnaire geared to the delivery of a more objective view of supplier performance. Appendix B contains a sample questionnaire, which includes the customer relationship questionnaire.

QUALITY EVALUATION SCORING

Two evaluation spreadsheets capture the scores for quality – the evaluation scoring matrix (Figure 14.10) and the evaluation table (Figure 14.11). Two sets of scores will exist – one each for expressions of interest and primary evaluation.

Although there will be some overlap of information between the sets, the evaluation for expressions of interest will necessarily be less rigorous than for primary evaluation. Primary evaluation sheets will contain some criteria not included in the expressions of interest sheets and a wider range of references should be taken up together with a deeper exploration of technical and performance issues. Ideally those references given for the expression of interest will not be those presented for the primary evaluation, although in some cases duplication may be necessary.

EVALUATION SCORING MATRIX

The evaluation scoring matrix is the spreadsheet that receives the base weighted scores for each supplier, as illustrated in Figure 14.10. Note that any numbers contained in the figure are indicative only.

EVALUATION TABLE

The evaluation table apportions, for each supplier and criterion, the base weighted scores across the objectives set for the relationship. Figure 14.11 provides an example of the evaluation table. Note that any numbers contained in the figure are indicative only.

TECHNICAL SPAN OF RESOURCES ASSESSMENT

The span of technical resources available to the supplier is critically important to the delivery of flexible future services. In general, a wide span gives greater flexibility. The technical span of resources should be assessed under the following headings:

- Experience of relevant products or services currently being used by the customer and which may be transferred to the supplier.
- General and technical services – the broad spread of technical expertise.
- Requirements for the future – in particular knowledge and expertise in known areas of interest.

EXPERIENCE OF EXISTING PRODUCTS AND SERVICES

Suppliers should be asked to complete the table 'Experience of existing products and services' (see Figure 14.7, p. 123) by indicating the number of staff who have at least two years' relevant experience. The number of staff should then be multiplied by the weighting. This table should list the primary products and services currently in use.

GENERAL AND TECHNICAL SERVICES

Suppliers should be asked to complete the table 'General and technical services' (see Figure 14.8, p. 124) by indicating the number of staff who have at least two years' relevant experience. The number of staff should then be multiplied by the weighting.

REQUIREMENTS FOR THE FUTURE

Suppliers should be asked to complete the table 'Requirements for the future' (see Figure 14.9, p. 125) by indicating the number of staff who have at least two years' relevant experience. The number of staff should then be multiplied by the weighting. This table should list those products, skills and services currently used and those thought likely to be needed in the future.

CONVERTING SCORES TO EVALUATION MATRIX

The criterion 'technical span of resources', within the evaluation scoring matrix, will have a maximum score of, say, 150. It will therefore be necessary to convert the actual scores from Figures 14.7, 14.8 and 14.9 to a score within the permitted limits for the evaluation scoring matrix (150). This can be done by applying a reduction factor for each section to bring the combined section scores within the limit of (150) as follows:

- Experience of existing products and services = (30 per cent).
- General and technical services = (40 per cent).
- Requirements for the future = (30 per cent).

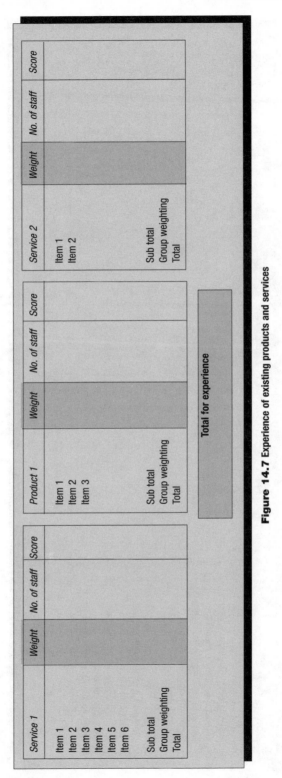

Figure 14.7 Experience of existing products and services

Functional capability	Weight	Trained practitioner	Fully trained practitioner	Experienced practitioner	Specialist practitioner	Principal practitioner	Director	Total score
Re-engineering, conversion & migration								
Laboratory facilities & capabilities								
Configuration & change management								
Project management								
Quality inspection								
Technical audit								
Evaluation of comparative products								
Strategic planning								
Technical research & development								
Feasibility appraisal								
Corporate & product data analysis								
Total								

Figure 14.8 General and technical services

Functional capability	Weight	Trained practitioner	Fully trained practitioner	Experienced practitioner	Specialist practitioner	Principal practitioner	Director	Total score
Total								

Figure 14.9 Requirements for the future

	Criteria totals			
	Maximum		**Actual**	
	%	Score	%	Score
Suppliers objectives for relationship	100	150		
General 'fit'	40	60		
Extent to which supplier commercial focus will assist objectives	100	60		
Extent to which supplier commercial focus may impede objectives – min. score (60)	0	0		
Ability to meet implications of partner objectives	30	45		
Performance implications	40	18		
Commercial implications	40	18		
Legal implications	20	9		
Ability to measure objectives	30	45		
Clearly defined deliverables	50	22.5		
Adequacy of measurement system provided	50	22.5		
Evidence of re-engineering capability	100	150		
Evidence of performance improvements achieved	40	60		
Extent to which supplier is dependent upon one approach/tools	30	45		
Basis upon which tools & techniques are to be made available	30	45		
Technical span of resources	100	150		
Experience of existing products, technical services and future requirements	100	150		
Sub total carried forward		450		

Figure 14.10 Evaluation scoring matrix

	Criteria totals			
	Maximum		Actual	
	%	Score	%	Score
Sub total brought forward		450		0
Consortia – nature of relationship	100	0		
Responsibilities of the parties – min. score (150)				
Ability successfully to work together – min. score (60)		0		
Evidence of successful completion of joint projects – min. score (18)		0		
Evidence of successful participation in outsourcing agreements – min. score (42)		0		
Responsibilities of the parties – min. score (45)				
Clarity of boundaries – min. score (29)		0		
Appropriate focus of capability – min. score (8)		0		
Overlap of capability – potential for conflict – min. score (8)		0		
Proposed organizational arrangements between the parties – min. score (45)		0		
Number of parties – 2 = 0, 3 = (5), >3 = (29)		0		
Clarity of structure – min. score (8)		0		
Simplicity of approach – min. score (8)		0		
General approach to relationship	100	120		
Nature & structure of legal entity	50	60		
Simplicity of approach	25	30		
Clarity of approach	25	30		
Sub total carried forward		570		

Figure 14.10 Evaluation scoring matrix (continued)

	Criteria totals			
	Maximum		Actual	
	%	Score	%	Score
Sub total brought forward		570		0
Experience of successfully creating a relationship on scale required	100	120		
Number of relationships created	30	36		
Duration of relationships	30	36		
More than 5 years old	66	24		
Less than 5 years old	33	12		
Nature & objectives of relationships	40	48		
Integration experience	100	100		
Extent to which projects have succeeded	60	60		
Achieved within timescale	30	18		
Achieved within budget	30	18		
Achieved to user satisfaction	40	24		
Number of years services offered	20	20		
Number of agreements currently operating	20	20		
Scale of resources available	100	100		
World services resource base	40	40		
European services resource base	30	30		
National services resource base	30	30		
Sub total carried forward		890		

Figure 14.10 Evaluation scoring matrix (continued)

	Criteria totals			
	Maximum		Actual	
	%	Score	%	Score
Sub total brought forward		890		0
Provision for business development support	100	100		
Structure for service support	50	50		
Business/customer strategic focus	50	25		
Focus on routine service strands	25	12.5		
Mechanisms for synthesising customer needs	25	12.5		
Extent of dedicated supplier resources applied	50	50		
Status of principals	60	30		
Number of dedicated staff	40	20		
Management of large-scale operational environments	100	100		
Performance against service agreements	50	50		
Number of multi-site environments managed	35	35		
Number of environments managed	15	15		
Sub total carried forward		1090		

Figure 14.10 Evaluation scoring matrix (continued)

	Criteria totals			
	Maximum		Actual	
	%	Score	%	Score
Sub total brought forward		1090		0
Evidence of managing change in own & absorbed companies	100	90		
Examples of change programmes with objectives & outturn	60	54		
Complexity of change programme	40	21.6		
Relevance of objectives	30	16.2		
Extent to which objectives were achieved	30	16.2		
Number & scale of change programmes undertaken & completed OK	40	36		
Number of programmes undertaken	40	14.4		
Scale of organizational change attempted indicated by number of staff affected	60	21.6		
Provision for maintaining & developing the relationship	100	90		
Structure for maintaining & developing the relationship	30	27		
Mean by which senior management attention will be focused on relationship issues	50	13.5		
Instruments & metrics for monitoring health of relationship	50	13.5		
Means by which the vitality of the relationship is to be maintained	30	27		
Level & nature of senior management relationships	30	8.1		
Extent to which specific provisions are made	50	13.5		
Adequacy of specific provisions	20	5.4		
Means by which delivery of relationship objectives are to be assured	40	36		
Provision of specific mechanisms to monitor progress	70	25.2		
Adequacy of progress mechanisms	30	10.8		
Sub total carried forward		1270		

Figure 14.10 Evaluation scoring matrix (continued)

	Criteria totals			
	Maximum		Actual	
	%	Score	%	Score
Sub total brought forward		1270		0
Service provision methodology	100	90		
Organization structure	60	54		
Outsourcing service delivery model & processes	40	21.6		
Technical support model & processes	30	16.2		
Quality assurance mechanisms	15	8.1		
Organization development interfaces	15	8.1		
User support arrangements	20	18		
Service management & help desk methods	50	9		
Performance against agreed service levels	50	9		
Performance reporting arrangements	10	9		
Routine reporting methods	50	4.5		
Quality of documentation	50	4.5		
Service level agreement framework	10	9		
Comprehensiveness, i.e. operations, development, maintenance simplicity	50	4.5		
Contract implementation methodology	100	90		
Clarity with which implementation issues are identified	50	45		
Extent of focus applied to main activities	40	36		
Template timescale of implementation phases	10	9		
Sub total carried forward		1450		

Figure 14.10 Evaluation scoring matrix (continued)

	Criteria totals			
	Maximum		Actual	
	%	Score	%	Score
Sub total brought forward		1450		0
Implementation plan	100	90		
Fitness for purpose	100	90		
Alignment of methodology to current circumstances	40	36		
Resources deployed against implementation activities	30	27		
Timetable & phasing	15	13.5		
Milestones	15	13.5		
General approach to staff transfer & pro forma terms & conditions	100	90		
Number of staff likely to be absorbed	40	36		
Extent to which staff are integrated into supplier organization	30	27		
Use of secondment in transfer process (max. negative score (50))	0	0		
Comparability of terms & conditions	10	9		
Flexibility when aligning individual terms & conditions	10	9		
Clarity with which transfer issues are identified	10	9		
Sub total carried forward		1630		

Figure 14.10 Evaluation scoring matrix (continued)

	Criteria totals			
	Maximum		Actual	
	%	Score	%	Score
Sub total brought forward		1630		0
Staff training & development arrangements	100	90		
Nature of scheme provided	25	22.5		
Integrated corporate scheme, i.e. departmental or whole company	40	9		
Clear staff development paths	40	9		
Quality of documentation	20	4.5		
Eligibility of staff to participate	25	22.5		
(i) automatic eligibility – maximum score	100			
(ii) Left to discretion of local managers – minimum score 0	0			
If not (i) or (ii) then score (iii)				
(iii) Probationary period – nature, duration & means of assessment	100			
Timescale to full participation	25	22.5		
Extent to which participation is monitored & assured	25	22.5		
(i) Automatic monitoring by senior management – maximum score	100			
(ii) Left to discretion of local managers – minimum score 0	0			
If not i or ii then score (iii)				
(iii) Ability of monitoring system to assure compliance	100			
Sub total carried forward		1720		

Figure 14.10 Evaluation scoring matrix (continued)

	Criteria totals			
	Maximum		Actual	
	%	Score	%	Score
Sub total brought forward		1720		0
Extent of ability to support multi-vendor environments	100	80		
General performance against service level agreements	50	40		
Numbers of vendors supported	25	20		
Number of multi-vendor environments supported	25	20		
Extent of 'services'-oriented company philosophy	100	80		
Per cent services revenue of total business earnings	50	40		
Total services revenue	25	20		
Number of years in which services have been leading business strand	25	20		
Pension arrangements	100	80		
Comparison of pension offered against current	100	80		
Growth & staff reduction record over last three years	100	70		
Services revenue & profit before tax year on year	25	17.5		
Services revenue & profit growth year on year	25	17.5		
Number of services staff year on year	25	17.5		
Gross number of services staff released year on year	25	17.5		
Sub total carried forward		2030		

Figure 14.10 Evaluation scoring matrix (continued)

	Criteria totals			
	Maximum		Actual	
	%	Score	%	Score
Sub total brought forward		2030		0
Flexibility of proposed agreement	100	60		
Extent of contractual constraints	50	30		
Simplicity & flexibility of controlling formulae	50	30		
Specific industry experience	100	50		
Extent of involvement	40	20		
Nature of involvement	40	20		
Other related experience	20	10		
Outsourcing experience	100	40		
Number of clients of similar profile	40	16		
Number of years services offered	20	8		
Number of agreements currently operating	20	8		
Total number of agreements signed	20	8		
Total	100	2180		

Figure 14.10 Evaluation scoring matrix (concluded)

Criteria	Outsourcing experience			
	Maximum		Actual	
	%	Score	%	Score
General approach to relationship	100	150		
Nature & structure of legal entity	50	75		
Simplicity of approach	25	38		
Clarity of approach	25	38		
Suppliers objectives for relationship	60	90		
General 'fit'	40	36		
Ability to meet implications of partner objectives	30	27		
Ability to measure objectives	30	27		
Consortia – nature of relationship – responsibilities of the parties	100	0		
Max score 0 – min score (150)				
Potential for fracture of the relationship	40	0		
Responsibilities of the parties	30	0		
Proposed organizational arrangements between the parties	30	0		
Experience of successfully creating a relationship on scale required	60	90		
Number of relationships created	25	23		
Duration of relationships	25	23		
Nature & objectives of relationships	25	23		
Reference visits	25	23		
Evidence of re-engineering capability	0	0		
Reference visits	50	0		
Extent to which supplier is dependent upon one approach/tools	25	0		
Basis upon which tools & techniques are to be made available	25	0		
Relevance & quality of alternative approach to requirement	40	60		
Extent to which developmental objectives are enhanced	40	24		
Extent to which charges are improved	30	18		
Extent to which charging profile is improved	15	9		
Extent to which staff retention opportunities are improved	15	9		
Extent to which risks are increased [max. negative score (150)]	0	0		
Sub total carried forward		390		0

Figure 14.11

Objective 1				Objective 2				Caring for staff					Criteria totals			
Maximum		Actual		Maximum		Actual		Maximum		Actual			Maximum		Actual	
%	Score	%	Score	%	Score	%	Score	%	Score	%	Score		%	Score	%	Score
0	0			0	0			0	0				100	150		
0	0			0	0			0	0				50	75		
0	0			0	0			0	0				25	37.5		
0	0			0	0			0	0				25	37.5		
15	23			15	23			10	15				100	150		
40	9			40	9			40	6				40	60		
30	6.8			30	6.8			30	4.5				30	45		
30	6.8			30	6.8			30	4.5				30	45		
0	0			0	0			0	0				100	0		
0	0			0	0			0	0				40	0		
0	0			0	0			0	0				30	0		
0	0			0	0			0	0				30	0		
15	23			15	23			10	15				100	150		
25	5.6			25	5.6			25	3.8				25	37.5		
25	5.6			25	5.6			25	3.8				25	37.5		
25	5.6			25	5.6			25	3.8				25	37.5		
25	5.6			25	5.6			25	3.8				25	37.5		
50	75			50	75			0	0				100	150		
50	38			50	38			50	75				50	75		
25	19			25	19			25	0				25	37.5		
25	19			25	19			25	0				25	37.5		
25	38			25	38			10	15				100	150		
40	15			40	15			40	6				40	60		
30	11			30	11			30	4.5				30	45		
15	5.6			15	5.6			15	2.3				15	22.5		
15	5.6			15	5.6			15	2.3				15	22.5		
0	0			0	0			0	0				0	0		

159	0	159	0	45	0	750	0

Evaluation table

137

Criteria	Outsourcing experience			
	Maximum		Actual	
	%	Score	%	Score
Sub total brought forward		**390**		**0**
Scale of resources available	**0**	**0**		
World services resource base	40	0		
European services resource base	30	0		
UK services resource base	30	0		
General approach to staff transfer & pro forma terms & conditions	**50**	**50**		
Number of staff likely to be absorbed	60	30		
Extent to which staff are integrated into supplier organization	20	10		
Use of secondment in transfer process [max negative score (50)]	0	0		
Comparability of terms & conditions	10	5		
Flexibility when aligning individual terms & conditions	10	5		
Provision for business & systems development support	**40**	**40**		
Structure for service support	30	12		
Extent of dedicated supplier resources applied	30	12		
Approach to be adopted	20	8		
Extent & range of flexibility	20	8		
Provision for maintaining & developing the relationship	**40**	**40**		
Structure for maintaining & developing the relationship	30	12		
Means by which the vitality of the relationship is to be maintained	30	12		
Means by which delivery of relationship objectives are to be assured	40	16		
Contract implementation methodology	**100**	**100**		
Clarity with which implementation issues are identified	50	50		
Extent of focus applied to main activities	30	30		
Resources deployed against implementation issues	10	10		
Timescale of implementation phase	10	10		
Sub total carried forward		**620**		**0**

Figure 14.1

Objective 1				Objective 2				Caring for staff				Criteria totals			
Maximum		Actual		Maximum		Actual		Maximum		Actual		Maximum		Actual	
%	Score	%	Score	%	Score	%	Score	%	Score	%	Score	%	Score	%	Score
158		**0**		**158**		**0**		**45**		**0**		**750**		**0**	
40	40			40	40			20	20			100	100		
40	16			40	16			40	8			40	40		
30	12			30	12			30	6			30	30		
30	12			30	12			30	6			30	30		
0	0			0	0			50	50			100	100		
60	0			60	0			60	30			60	60		
20	0			20	0			20	10			20	20		
0	0			0	0			0	0			0	0		
10	0			10	0			10	5			10	10		
10	0			10	0			10	5			10	10		
20	20			40	40			0	0			100	100		
30	6			30	12			30	0			30	30		
30	6			30	12			30	0			30	30		
20	4			20	8			20	0			20	20		
20	4			20	8			20	0			20	20		
15	15			30	30			15	15			100	100		
30	4.5			30	9			30	4.5			30	30		
30	4.5			30	9			30	4.5			30	30		
40	6			40	12			40	6			40	40		
0	0			0	0			0	0			100	100		
50	0			50	0			50	0			50	50		
30	0			30	0			30	0			30	30		
10	0			10	0			10	0			10	10		
10	0			10	0			10	0			10	10		
233		**0**		**268**		**0**		**130**		**0**		**1250**		**0**	

Evaluation table (continued)

Criteria	Outsourcing experience			
	Maximum		Actual	
	%	Score	%	Score
Sub total brought forward		620		0
Service provision methodology	50	50		
Organization structure	60	30		
User support arrangements	20	10		
Performance reporting arrangements	10	5		
Service level agreement framework	10	5		
Evidence of managing change in own & absorbed companies	40	36		
Reference visits	40	14		
Examples of change programmes with objectives & outturn	30	11		
Number & scale of change programmes undertaken & completed successfully	30	11		
Outsourcing experience	50	45		
Reference visits	40	18		
Number of clients of similar profile	30	14		
Number of years services offered	10	4.5		
Number of agreements currently operating	10	4.5		
Total number of agreements signed	10	4.5		
Integration experience	0	0		
Reference visits	60	0		
Number of years services offered	30	0		
Number of agreements currently operating	10	0		
Sub total carried forward		751		0

Figure 14.1

Objective 1				Objective 2				Caring for staff				Criteria totals			
Maximum		Actual		Maximum		Actual		Maximum		Actual		Maximum		Actual	
%	Score	%	Score	%	Score	%	Score	%	Score	%	Score	%	Score	%	Score
233		0		268		0		130		0		1250		0	
15	15			35	35			0	0			100	100		
60	9			60	21			60	0			60	60		
20	3			20	7			20	0			20	20		
10	1.5			10	3.5			10	0			10	10		
10	1.5			10	3.5			10	0			10	10		
0	0			30	27			30	27			100	90		
40	0			40	11			40	11			40	36		
30	0			30	8.1			30	8.1			30	27		
30	0			30	8.1			30	8.1			30	27		
0	0			25	23			25	23			100	90		
40	0			40	9			40	9			40	36		
30	0			30	6.8			30	6.8			30	27		
10	0			10	2.3			10	2.3			10	9		
10	0			10	2.3			10	2.3			10	9		
10	0			10	2.3			10	2.3			10	9		
50	45			50	45			0	0			100	90		
60	27			60	27			60	0			60	54		
30	14			30	14			30	0			30	27		
10	4.5			10	4.5			10	0			10	9		
293		0		398		0		180		0		1620		0	

Evaluation table (continued)

141

Criteria	Outsourcing experience			
	Maximum		Actual	
	%	Score	%	Score
Sub total brought forward		751		0
Extent & nature of supplier resources	0	0		
Supplier resources	60	0		
Equipment, accommodation & numbers of professional staff	40	0		
Technical span of resources	0	0		
Experience of existing products, technical services and future requirements	100	0		
Implementation plan	60	54		
Fitness for purpose	100	54		
Staff transfer methodology	25	23		
Clarity with which issues are identified	50	11		
Extent of focus applied to key activities	30	6.8		
Resources deployed against transfer issues	10	2.3		
Timescale of transfer phase	10	2.3		
Pension arrangements	0	0		
Comparison of pension offered against current	100	0		
Extent of ability to support multi-vendor environments	25	20		
Reference visits	50	10		
Number of vendors supported	25	5		
Number of multi-vendor environments supported	25	5		
Extent of 'services'-orientated company philosophy	50	40		
Percent services revenue of total business earnings	50	20		
Total services revenue	25	10		
Number of years in which services have been leading business strand	25	10		
Sub total carried forward		888		0

Figure 14.11

Objective 1				Objective 2				Caring for staff					Criteria totals			
Maximum		Actual		Maximum		Actual		Maximum		Actual			Maximum		Actual	
%	Score	%	Score	%	Score	%	Score	%	Score	%	Score		%	Score	%	Score
293		0		**397**		0		**180**		0			**1620**		0	
50	45			25	23			25	23				100	90		
60	27			60	14			60	14				60	54		
40	18			40	9			40	9				40	36		
75	113			75	113			0	0				100	150		
100	113			100	113			100	0				100	150		
0	0			0	0			40	36				100	90		
100	0			100	0			100	36				100	90		
0	0			0	0			75	68				100	90		
50	0			50	0			50	34				50	45		
30	0			30	0			30	20				30	27		
10	0			10	0			10	6.8				10	9		
10	0			10	0			10	6.8				10	9		
0	0			0	0			100	80				100	80		
100	0			100	0			100	80				100	80		
75	60			0	0			0	0				100	80		
50	30			50	0			50	0				50	40		
25	15			25	0			25	0				25	20		
25	15			25	0			25	0				25	20		
25	20			25	20			0	0				100	80		
50	10			50	10			50	0				50	40		
25	5			25	5			25	0				25	20		
25	5			25	5			25	0				25	20		
531		0		**553**		0		**387**		0			**2280**		0	

Evaluation table (continued)

Criteria	Outsourcing experience			
	Maximum		Actual	
	%	Score	%	Score
Sub total brought forward		888		0
Staff training & development arrangements	0	0		
Nature of scheme provided	25	0		
Eligibility of staff to participate	25	0		
Timescale to full participation	25	0		
Extent to which participation is monitored & assured	25	0		
Growth & staff reduction record over last three years	25	18		
Services revenue & profit before tax year on year	25	4.4		
Services revenue & profit growth year on year	25	4.4		
Number of services staff year on year	25	4.4		
Gross number of services staff released year on year	25	4.4		
Flexibility of proposed agreement	0	0		
Extent of contractual constraints	50	0		
Simplicity & flexibility of controlling formulae	50	0		
Specific industry experience	0	0		
Extent of involvement	40	0		
Nature of involvement	40	0		
Other related experience	20	0		
Total	36	906		0

Figure 14.1

Objective 1				Objective 2				Caring for staff					Criteria totals			
Maximum		Actual		Maximum		Actual		Maximum		Actual			Maximum		Actual	
%	Score	%	Score	%	Score	%	Score	%	Score	%	Score		%	Score	%	Score
	530		0		552		0		386		0			2280		0
0	0			0	0			100	70				100	70		
25	0			25	0			25	18				25	17.5		
25	0			25	0			25	18				25	17.5		
25	0			25	0			25	18				25	17.5		
25	0			25	0			25	18				25	17.5		
0	0			0	0			75	53				100	70		
25	0			25	0			25	13				25	17.5		
25	0			25	0			25	13				25	17.5		
25	0			25	0			25	13				25	17.5		
25	0			25	0			25	13				25	17.5		
0	0			100	60			0	0				100	60		
50	0			50	30			50	0				50	30		
50	0			50	30			50	0				50	30		
0	0			100	50			0	0				100	50		
40	0			40	20			40	0				40	20		
40	0			40	20			40	0				40	20		
20	0			20	10			20	0				20	10		
21	530		0	26	662		0	20	509		0		100	2530		0

Evaluation table (concluded)

145

15 Evaluating relationships

Outsourcing agreements are getting longer and can range up to ten years or more in duration. If the intention is to establish a long-term agreement, then it would seem prudent to assess the track record of potential suppliers in terms of their ability to forge and maintain good and trusting relationships with their customers.

Often, the first year of any reasonably complex outsourcing agreement will be difficult. For instance, if there are misunderstandings regarding the meaning or intentions of some contract clauses, they will be discovered very soon after the agreement has started. Resolution of these issues may strain the embryonic relationship. In addition, two disparate cultures are being thrown together with different styles of working and, perhaps, different expectations. If the relationship is to survive the first year, therefore, you need to know that your chosen supplier has previously demonstrated its integrity and can ultimately be trusted.

GENERAL APPROACH TO EVALUATION

Assessment of the ability of suppliers to relate effectively with their customers should be based principally upon the information collected from referees nominated by the supplier. The nature of the information to be assessed and the means by which it is collected necessarily gives rise to a subjective assessment and it is therefore better for those with real experience of individual suppliers to offer a view. For this reason, as many referees as possible should be consulted to minimize the potential for bias in the evaluation, and the final scores should be discussed and awarded by the evaluation team as a whole and not by any one individual.

Customer relationships may be examined under the following general headings:

Values

Those attributes of supplier organizations that guide the manner in which business is conducted and services are provided and that set the boundaries for

146

professional and principled behaviour.

Corporate emphasis

An indication of the focus of supplier priorities as they relate to the deployment of resources and management attention.

Responsiveness

The manner in which suppliers respond to the varying needs of customers.

Reliability

The extent to which supplier performance, in all its aspects, is assured without undue customer intervention.

Consistency

The extent to which all aspects of supplier behaviour and performance can be predicted with certainty.

EVALUATION CRITERIA

Taking the general headings as a guide, Figure 15.1 sets out the expanded criteria for evaluating customer relationships.

CUSTOMER RELATIONSHIP CRITERIA AMPLIFIED

Values

Trust/openness   The extent to which the supplier has, or has not, been shown to be open in its commercial dealings and dependable in conforming to its obligations and commitments.

Accommodating/flexible   The extent to which the supplier has, or has not, demonstrated a willingness to accommodate, without fuss, variations to plans, requirements or agreements of a non-commercial nature.

Commitment   The extent to which the supplier has, or has not, demonstrated an unequivocal commitment to, and emphasis on, the business and service objectives of its clients.

High standards of quality and service   The extent to which the supplier does, or does not, set for itself, and deliver, standards of service and quality above those likely to be required by its clients.

Ethical   The extent to which the supplier has, or has not, set standards of behaviour and codes of practice that regulate and police the ethical behaviour of the organization and its staff.

Criteria	Weight	Maximum score
Values		
Trust/openness	50	500
Accommodating/flexible	50	500
Commitment	50	500
High standards of quality & service	50	500
Ethical	40	400
Maintenance of reputation/pride in organization	30	300
Cultural maintenance	30	300
Corporate emphasis		
Customers	100	1000
Staff	50	500
Delivery	80	800
Innovation	50	500
Profit/shareholders (negative score max. minus 70)	(70)	0
Quality (supported by robust audit arrangements)	50	500
Responsiveness		
Speed of response	50	500
Willingness to adapt	50	500
Willingness to be inconvenienced	40	400
Reliability		
Need for supervision/management	80	800
Delivery against agreed timescales	80	800
Delivery to agreed costs	90	900
Delivery to quality standards	50	500
Consistency		
Stable values/emphasis/responsiveness/reliability	50	500
Low cycle time for key staff	40	400
Consistent service performance	50	500
Maximum total score	—	12100

Figure 15.1 Customer relationship evaluation criteria

Maintenance of reputation/pride in organization   The extent to which the supplier has, or has not, exhibited an awareness of its commercial reputation and a willingness to devote considerable effort to protect it.

Cultural maintenance   The extent to which the supplier has, or has not, a strong cultural identity and robust business processes for its maintenance and development.

Corporate emphasis

Customers   The extent to which the supplier has, or has not, focused its business processes and management thinking upon customer needs to the point where customers are conscious of the focus and feel its effects.

Staff The extent to which the supplier has, or has not, established policies that assure effective staff development in a way that supports both its business and customer needs.

Delivery The extent to which the supplier has, or has not, established a clear management emphasis on delivery of services or projects to the point where customers understand the delivery mechanisms and have confidence in the delivery assurance monitoring and escalation arrangements.

Innovation The extent to which the supplier has, or has not, demonstrated its ability and willingness to search for and provide innovative solutions even to the point where the solution proposed may fall outside the range of services offered by the supplier.

Profit/shareholders The extent to which the supplier has, or has not, demonstrated a willingness to put its requirements for profit ahead of customer needs rather than derive profit by meeting customer needs.

Quality (supported by robust audit arrangements) The extent to which the supplier has, or has not, committed itself to demonstrable quality standards and overt audit arrangements for their maintenance.

Responsiveness

Speed of response The extent to which the supplier does, or does not, respond to issues and requirements within agreed parameters and without fuss.

Willingness to adapt The extent to which the supplier is, or is not, able to react favourably to changes in circumstance or requirement.

Willingness to be inconvenienced The extent to which the supplier has, or has not, demonstrated an ability to absorb, with good grace, a reasonable amount of unplanned work or compensate for customer deficiencies.

Reliability

Need for supervision/management The extent to which the supplier does, or does not, require customer supervision or undue customer management input.

Delivery against agreed timescales The extent to which the supplier does, or does not, meet agreed service or project delivery timescales.

Delivery to agreed costs The extent to which the supplier does, or does not, meet agreed cost parameters.

Delivery to quality standards The extent to which the supplier does, or does not, meet agreed quality standards.

Consistency

Stable values/emphasis/responsiveness/reliability   The extent to which the supplier does, or does not, maintain a consistent performance in all attributes of values, corporate emphasis, responsiveness and reliability.

Low cycle time for key staff   The extent to which the supplier does, or does not, change senior customer facing managers within an [eighteen month*] cycle. * For some high technology industries, this is a long time. For more traditional industries, a longer period might be more appropriate.

Consistent service performance   The extent to which the supplier does, or does not, consistently maintain service performance within the agreed limits.

PROCESS

Base information should be collected from referees either during the reference visits or, for those referees where visits are not made, by telephone interview or post. The same number of references should be taken up for each supplier. The 'relationship with customer' section of the reference questionnaire (see Chapter 14) should be used to collect the information.

Referees should be asked to assess, on a scale of 1–10, supplier performance and behaviour against each of the criteria. In general, 0 indicates a poor assessment and 10 a good assessment. In the case of corporate emphasis – profit/shareholders, the scoring should be negative – the maximum score should, therefore, be zero – hence 0 equals good and minus 10 equals poor.

The scores from each questionnaire for a given supplier should be collated and recorded on the customer relationship assessment summary sheet (see Figure 15.2). This sheet brings together all the reference scores and adds the criteria weighting factors to give a total assessment score for the supplier. The supplier's scores are brought together for comparison on the customer relationship evaluation matrix (see Figure 15.3). A supplier's total score should then be compared with the maximum score possible and the percentage score calculated. The percentage score will indicate the assessment to be given on the following basis:

- **Poor**
  A percentage score less than 50 per cent – should lead to disqualification, but the final decision must be taken by the selection panel in the light of all other assessment factors.
- **Marginal**
  A percentage score in the range 51–59 per cent should lead to disqualification but may need further sensitivity analysis and an explicit discussion within the

Supplier:	Referees					Sub total	Weight	Total score
	Ref. 1	Ref. 2	Ref. 3	Ref. 4	Ref. 5			
Values								
Trust/openness								
Accommodating/flexible								
Commitment								
High standards of quality & service								
Ethical								
Maintenance of reputation								
Cultural maintenance								
Sub total								
Corporate emphasis								
Customer								
Staff								
Delivery								
Innovation								
etc.								

Figure 15.2 Customer relationship assessment summary sheet

selection panel. The selection panel will determine whether disqualification is appropriate in light of all other assessment factors.

- **Good**
  A percentage score in the range 60–89 per cent can be regarded as an acceptable score for an automatic pass.
- **Excellent**
  A percentage score in excess of 90 per cent is clearly acceptable.

In the case of consortia, each principal contributor to the consortium should be individually evaluated and the scores shown on the customer relationship evaluation matrix. The average score for the consortium should be used as the final basis of assessment.

The customer relationship evaluation matrix assessment will then be carried forward to the primary evaluation matrix (see Chapter 14).

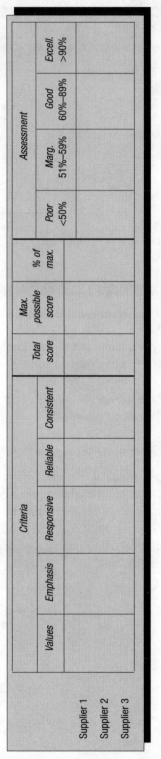

Figure 15.3 Customer relationship evaluation matrix

16 The Statement of Service Requirement (SoSR)

When seeking tender responses or proposals as part of an outsourcing procurement, you need to communicate your requirements to potential suppliers. This communication usually takes the form of a Statement of Service Requirement (SoSR). This chapter sets out the typical components of an SoSR.

The quality of the supplier responses will be significantly influenced by the quality of the SoSR. Furthermore, conducting the evaluation exercise itself will be markedly easier if the SoSR has been properly constructed and gives clear guidance, direction and sufficient information to the tendering suppliers. Deficiencies in the construction and content of the SoSR can lead to the following problems.

Evaluation

Evaluation may be difficult because supplier proposals may contain assumptions or misconceptions that arise through the provision of insufficient information, inadequate articulation or omission(s) of an issue or position in the SoSR. Thus, suppliers will arrive at different interpretations and assumptions to those intended. It will then be impossible to evaluate proposals on a like for like basis without some remedial action, which, in turn, will cost time, money and possibly some damage to the credibility of the outsourcing procurement team.

Negotiation

If there have been misunderstandings within the SoSR, these may not emerge until negotiations are underway, or worse, until after the agreement has been signed. Substantial delays to the procurement process may arise.

Increases in price

If misunderstandings exist and remain undetected until after the agreement has been signed, the successful supplier may be able to increase its price as a direct result of poor SoSR drafting.

Challenge

An unsuccessful supplier may believe there to be cause (or grounds if

EU/GATT provisions apply) for a challenge on the basis of misleading SoSR text. This is particularly relevant for central and local government organizations, although it is likely to occur more frequently in the commercial sector as competition grows. Most organizations have formal procedures for debriefing unsuccessful suppliers, which should help to minimize the possibility of a challenge. It is, therefore, worthwhile to assure that your procedures are known from the early stages of the procurement, are clearly understood by all parties and correctly implemented.

SoSR COMPONENTS

The precise composition of the SoSR will very much depend upon the nature of both the procuring organization and the function to be outsourced but, in general terms, a well-constructed SoSR will contain the following components.

DISCLAIMER NOTICES

As a frontispiece, the SoSR should post appropriate procurement disclaimers. These may include the following:

- Legal status of a partnership (see below).
- Confidentiality (see below).
- Representation of information/no liability arising from use of information.
- No guarantee of contract award resulting from a submission of tenders or proposals.
- Freedom to choose successful tender/proposal regardless of lowest price.

The nature of the procurement may suggest specific requirements and the customer's legal department will have standard phrases for different circumstances and a list of mandatory disclaimers. The following paragraphs provide illustrations for two such phrases.

Legal status of an arrangement base on 'partnership' principles

'Throughout this SoSR, references have been made to the project described herein as a "Strategic Partnership". This description reflects the customer's view of the close co-operation that will be needed between the customer and the successful supplier. Suppliers should note that the words "partner" and "partnership", within this document, are used to indicate the need for close co-operation and are *not* used in the strict legal definition of those terms as set out in the Partnership Act 1890 (UK) or other applicable statutes. The contracts negotiated will be arm's-length and will describe the basis of supply of services by the successful supplier. The successful supplier will be, and will remain, a third party independent contractor.'

Confidentiality

'The supplier is advised that all information which is contained in this SoSR or which is communicated in further correspondence or which is provided or obtained during any subsequent negotiations is confidential.'

'The supplier must not communicate, disclose or otherwise make available this information to any third party other than as set out below, nor use this information for any commercial or industrial purpose not connected with this procurement.'

'The supplier may communicate, disclose or otherwise make available this information to an employee, a professional adviser or a subcontractor who requires the information in connection with the preparation of the supplier's tender/proposal or to support any subsequent negotiation provided they are bound by equivalent conditions of confidentiality.'

'In view of the sensitive nature of some of the information contained in this SoSR, the customer requires the return of all SoSR documents and any copies made in whole or part immediately upon demand.'

TABLE OF CONTENTS

Obvious though it may be, a comprehensive and detailed table of contents will not only help suppliers produce effective and accurate proposals, but help the outsourcing procurement team navigate around the SoSR and proposal submissions during the evaluation and negotiation stages.

BACKGROUND INFORMATION

This section should describe the customer organization and include background information regarding the function or department to be outsourced. It will be helpful to describe any corporate policies that led to, or influenced, the outsourcing procurement decision.

THE USER COMMUNITY

This section should describe the user community of the function to be outsourced and particularly the nature of the interfaces between them. The relevance of this section will depend upon the nature of the procurement and any requirement for detailed information will be driven by its relative importance to the construction of suppliers' proposals.

PARALLEL ACTIVITY

Parallel work (e.g. projects/initiatives/changes) being undertaken either within the function to be outsourced or across the organization as a whole, may have a bearing on both supplier proposals and implementation of the intended contract. If relevant, it will be important to provide a description of the parallel activities and their potential impact on the procurement.

OVERVIEW OF REQUIRED AGREEMENT

As a prelude to providing potentially large volumes of detailed information relating to the services to be provided, suppliers will find it helpful to gain an overview of the requirement. The overview should, as a minimum, discuss the following issues.

Agreement principles

Agreement principles and the basis of evaluation will have been established as discussed in Chapters 8 to 15. This section should outline the high level principles associated with the requirement and may include the following information:

- Nature of agreement: partnership/arm's length contract.
- Nature of requirement: project based/ongoing service.
- Basis of payment: fixed/variable/fees/units, etc.
- The need for performance measures: service agreements/financial remedies.
- Basis for evaluation.

More detailed descriptions will need to be given later in the SoSR but a high level description at this point in the document will aid supplier understanding and, hopefully, avoid important issues being missed.

Objectives for relationship

Objectives for the relationship will have been prepared as discussed in Chapter 1. Those objectives and their associated measures should be set out at this point in the SoSR.

Broad service requirement

This section should, as discussed in Chapter 9, outline the operational service requirement in terms of the service boundaries to be imposed and the service elements that reside within those boundaries. The nature of any limits or constraints should be described, for example:

- Factors arising from the customer's risk assessment and management processes (see Chapter 5).
- Retained tasks or requirements that the customer believes it is better placed to provide, irrespective of the supplier's size or ability.
- Elements normally linked with the service requirement but specifically not

included (particularly when associated with the transfer of staff and assets).

- Technical characteristics, e.g. manufacturer specific engineering skills, particularly for circumstances where there is a distinct commercial effect, e.g. older or uncommon equipment for which experienced skills are rare or expensive.
- New and additional skills/attributes identified by technical innovation or performance improvement (see Chapter 2).

Procurement process and timetable

The procurement process will have been determined as discussed in Chapter 6 and, together with the agreed timetable, it should be set out at this point in the SoSR.

The preferred supplier will see a negotiating advantage if the customer, for legitimate operational reasons, declares an immovable implementation date. It is better to offer 'target' dates and leave the negotiation open-ended – even if an immovable implementation date actually exists.

Contract terms, duration and breakpoints

Describe, in outline, the required contract terms, its total duration and any requirement for breakpoints (see Chapter 13). A failure to specify minimum contract requirements may result in the following difficulties:

- A wide variation of supplier positions that will be impossible to evaluate on an equal basis.
- Invalidated supplier prices since changes to contract terms will, very often, result in changes to prices.

Therefore, ensure that the contract terms upon which proposals are to be based are clearly presented.

SERVICE REQUIREMENT

The service requirement will have been defined as discussed in Chapter 9 and should be set out at this point in the SoSR. A failure to articulate the complete requirement may well lead to the following problems:

- Inadequate evaluation.
- Delay to the completion of the negotiation.
- Additional charges.
- The risk of challenge from unsuccessful suppliers.

STAFF DETAILS

If the procurement involves the transfer of staff to the successful supplier, the bidders will need extensive information to enable their proposals to be constructed. The following information will, as a minimum, be required.

Size and organization of function

This section should provide the following information:

- Number of staff employed.
- Organizational structure.
- List of staff to be transferred, which gives, for each, the cost of their basic salary package, cost of employment, pension and any other benefits. Note that the names of individuals are not usually published in the SoSR.

External staff

The use of contract, consulting or casual staff should be clearly described in terms of numbers and cost. Suppliers regard external staff as a primary target for cost reduction or price improvement. Either way, suppliers will show a keen interest in external staff, and any deficiencies in the information relating to them will almost certainly impact upon the supplier's price.

Transfer of Undertakings (Protection of Employment) Regulations (TUPE)

The basis upon which staff are to transfer should be declared, as discussed in Chapter 10. Such transfers are normally conducted under the auspices of local legislation where it applies, for example TUPE regulations for the UK. The specific policy to be adopted should be set out in this section of the SoSR as it has commercial implications.

Redundancy and early retirement

Policies associated with the issues of redundancy and early retirement will have been formulated as discussed in Chapter 10 and should be set out at this point in the SoSR.

Pensions

Full details of the customer's existing pension plan will be needed to enable suppliers to prepare a comparison between it and their scheme. A failure to provide the details could result in either delays to the procurement timetable or the need for the outsourcing procurement team to prepare a comparison.

Trade unions

This section should include the policies and related information regarding trade union and staff representation as discussed in Chapter 10.

Staff development

Include here the policies and related information regarding staff development as discussed in Chapter 10.

THE STATEMENT OF SERVICE REQUIREMENT (SoSR)

Staff terms and conditions

Full details of staff terms and conditions should be provided. This may include, but is not limited to, the following:

- Grade structure.
- Current pay scales.
- Overtime arrangements.
- Meal, shift and on-call allowances.
- Shift working patterns or details of unsociable hours.
- Rules for flexible working hours.
- Notice of resignation.
- Smoking at work policy.
- Annual leave and special leave.
- Sick absence.
- Maternity leave arrangements.
- Official travel rules.
- Relocation rules.
- Trade union membership.
- Recognized trade union and staff associations.
- Career development opportunities.
- Car schemes.

ASSETS

The SoSR must provide clear guidance for dealing with all relevant assets, that is capital assets, property or accommodation, current assets or intangible assets. The policies formulated for assets as discussed in Chapter 11 should be set out at this point in the SoSR.

SERVICE COSTS

There is a widely held belief that providing suppliers with detailed cost information relating to the service to be transferred will disadvantage the purchaser. In fact, in circumstances where large and potentially complex services are to be transferred, the provision of detailed cost information, and particularly information relating to potential internal performance improvements (see Chapter 2) will sharpen the competition by ensuring that all tendering suppliers are aware of the bid threshold.

If suppliers are forced to guess at existing costs, then they will guess high to cover their perception of risk and error. This section of the SoSR should therefore contain all cost information relating to the services defined in the service requirement section of the SoSR (see Chapter 9). Where costs are to be transferred, a clear and unambiguous *cost base* must be declared based either on fact or, if the requirement is large or complicated, a detailed set of accounts that clearly indicate the composition of the costs.

A clearly delineated cost base will be an important input to either a due diligence exercise pre-contract signature or a post-contract signature costs verification process. It is almost certain that in the case of large and complex agreements, costs, and therefore prices, will be adjusted as a result of either genuine misunderstandings and omissions or deliberate attempts on the part of some suppliers to improve their commercial position having, say, bid low to beat the competition, subject to contract. There is therefore tangible value in a carefully structured base of costs against which any movements, both up and down, may be tracked and verified.

REQUIRED CHARGING ARRANGEMENTS

Set out at this point in the SoSR your requirements for charging as discussed in Chapter 12. Note that you will need to be reasonably prescriptive for the standard bid to enable a like for like evaluation. Remember though, that care should be taken to avoid a loss of innovation (see Chapter 14, pp. 105–6). A less prescriptive set of rules will therefore be needed for the non-standard bid.

REQUIRED SECURITY AND SPECIAL ARRANGEMENTS

Any special security requirements should be clearly described so that suppliers may take account of any commercial implications when preparing their proposals. Given the sensitive nature of security issues, separate documents describing the requirement are sometimes prepared either by a subset of the outsourcing procurement team or specialist security staff from within the customer organization. These documents are then dealt with by small groups of specialist staff from within supplier organizations to avoid a wider dispersal of sensitive information.

SERVICE AGREEMENTS

Where an existing operation is transferred or required to be replicated, it is important to describe current service and performance levels. If service agreements (sometimes known as service level agreements) exist between service departments and user departments, the terms associated with these should be stated.

CONTRACT MANAGEMENT ARRANGEMENTS

If real benefits are to be extracted from the outsourcing agreement, it will require careful management (see Chapter 19). Suppliers should be given an indication of the nature and extent of any intended contract management regimes and, as a minimum, the following information should be given.

Required contract management arrangements

This section should describe the interface requirements at various management levels, for example:

- Strategic interface.
- Contract management interface.
- User management interface.
- Operational interface.

Items of interest

There may be specific topics that are relevant and for which special attention will be warranted. Some examples follow:

- Performance reporting.
- Performance against objectives.
- Meetings hierarchy.
- Service agreements.
- Project control.
- Change control.
- Escalation procedures.
- Account management.
- Financial remedies.

SPECIFIC CONTRACTUAL REQUIREMENTS/NEGOTIABILITY

It is advisable to negotiate using draft contracts produced by your legal advisers. Where possible, draft contracts should be included in the SoSR (as an annex). This section of the SoSR should describe the draft contracts and indicate which clauses are non-negotiable. Additional legal requirements should be described in this section, for instance the need for a deed of guarantee from a parent company.

SPECIFIC OPERATIONAL REQUIREMENTS

There may be specific aspects of the operational service that the successful supplier will be required to provide. Some examples are described below:

Service contingency

A description of specific service contingency or disaster recovery arrangements as currently maintained by the customer, or potentially required in the future.

Change control

A description of specific arrangements, perhaps encompassing the use of existing procedures that the customer wishes to be maintained, or a specification for new procedures.

Audit access

Sometimes the customer has audit obligations that must be preserved even if the service is being provided by an outsourcing supplier. Other customers would wish to establish audit access facilities as part of the contract management regime. Either way, the requirement must be described in the SoSR.

Quality requirements

This is a statement of specific quality standards with which the supplier would be required to comply. Where possible, formal quality standards should be requested, for example ISO9000, European Foundation For Quality management (EFQM).

AGREEMENT IMPLEMENTATION REQUIREMENTS

Although responsibility for agreement implementation will rest with the supplier, it will be helpful to know, for evaluation purposes, how the supplier intends to tackle the task (see Chapter 20). In addition, you may have some specific implementation requirements. This section of the SoSR should specify your minimum requirements, which will normally include the following:

- The names and status of supplier staff who will be involved in the implementation and management of the agreement.
- The specific implementation obligations of the customer.
- The provision of pro forma implementation documentation and project plans.
- If appropriate, how the staff and asset transfers are to be conducted.
- The means by which the due diligence or post-contract verification review of transferred resources is to be conducted.

NOTICES TO TENDERERS

This section of the SoSR should offer suppliers some guidance regarding the formalities of the procurement process. Great care will be needed with this section since its quality will, to a large degree, determine the ease with which proposals may be evaluated on a like for like basis. The following elements should be included.

Pre-tender enquiries

Queries regarding the content of the SoSR should be channelled, in writing, through a nominated customer individual. The SoSR should indicate the date after which queries will not be answered. The SoSR should also indicate if questions and answers will be circulated to all tenderers.

Pre-tender discussions

This section should disallow any previous conversations between the customer and suppliers for the purposes of the evaluation and the construction of the contract.

Tender submission

This section should outline the details for tender submission including deadline date/delivery point etc. Sometimes, when the release date is uncertain, these details may be dealt with in a covering letter.

Rejection of bids

It is normal practice to state that tenders may be rejected if they do not meet conditions specified in the SoSR. This is designed to avoid bidders creating special terms or conditions that cannot be evaluated correctly. However, this should not prohibit suppliers from submitting one or more additional non-standard bids, if the SoSR makes such an invitation. It will be important to identify which conditions apply to *both* standard and non-standard bids.

Excluded costs

It is common practice among suppliers to 'exclude' costs from their bids, either through error or misunderstanding but sometimes deliberately to gain a commercial advantage. You should, therefore, make it clear to suppliers at this point in the SoSR that the price contained in their response is assumed to cover all aspects of service specified in the SoSR unless a list of 'excluded costs' is specifically provided.

Acceptance of tender

It is normal practice for the SoSR to declare that the customer shall not be bound to accept the lowest, or any, tender or to enter into negotiations.

INSTRUCTIONS TO TENDERERS

This section should provide suppliers with precise instructions regarding the format of their submission, a description of the proposal evaluation process and the basis upon which their proposals will be evaluated.

Tender format and information to be provided

No matter how hard you try, some suppliers will fail to meet the requirements specified in the SoSR and this makes evaluation much more difficult than it need be. It is worth, therefore, applying some effort in an attempt to minimize the scope for 'supplier deviation'. At its simplest, the more you can get the suppliers' responses to align with the requirements specified in the SoSR, the easier it will be to evaluate. The following example illustrates the required standard.

> The tenderer shall submit its tender in the following format and shall provide the information requested in each Part. Each response should have, at its head, the question, part number and section number/reference to which it refers. Tenderers shall not combine questions. A checklist identifying the page in the tender where the response to each requirement is given shall be provided together with references to any other relevant information.

Description of the tender evaluation process

This section should describe the remaining steps of the procurement.

Basis for evaluation

The basis upon which proposals are to be evaluated will have been prepared as discussed in Chapters 14 and 15. You will need to ensure that suppliers understand the broad basis upon which they are to be evaluated so that they can comply with both the proposal format requirements and the information requirements of the evaluation models, and the customer is able to assure the availability of information sufficient to feed the evaluation models. It will be necessary, therefore, to publish the criteria by which the suppliers are to be evaluated. We suggest that the evaluation scoring matrix (Figure 14.10) be set out at this point in the SoSR, but without declaring the scores and weightings to be used.

APPENDICES TO THE SoSR

The SoSR should be a compact and easily referenced document. It may help the structure of the SoSR if appendices are used for technical data, booklets and extracts from other documents or files. The following list illustrates some items that might be included in the SoSR as an appendix:

- Management cost accounts; annual accounts and other cost details.
- Copies of internal service records.
- Workload statements and service schedules.
- Inventories of plant and machinery.
- Inventories of 'soft' assets, e.g. intellectual property.

- Details regarding accommodation and property.
- Copies (extracts) of external contracts.
- Staff related memoranda, booklets and handbooks.
- Draft contracts.
- Publications, e.g. Annual Report/Operating Plan.
- List of publications or booklets not provided as part of the SoSR but available for inspection, e.g. staff handbooks, property plans, technical manuals.

Part III
Procuring the Agreement and Managing its Implementation

Introduction to Part III

Well, to have reached this far, you will have done much thinking, many jig-saw pieces will have been created and a good picture should be taking shape. The next problem is to test your thinking in the market and try to make a deal – and this is the point where you discover something about the quality of all that work done to date.

In Part III of this book, Chapter 17 'Making a market' provides some thoughts on how to engage suppliers in the procurement process in a manner that gains their confidence, assures their enthusiasm and, ultimately, has a positive commercial and performance impact on your deal. Chapter 18 'Negotiating the agreement' suggests an approach for delivering an effective agreement, notwithstanding all the complexities that stand in the way. And then, having sucessfully secured an outsourcing contract, Chapter 19 'Managing the contract' and Chapter 20 'Implementing the contract' discuss the difficult tasks of implementing and managing the contract to get the best from the relationship over the next few years.

17 Making a market

You would think, wouldn't you, that, were there a large service contract to be let for a significant number of years, a long queue of potential suppliers would be panting at the gate. Paradoxically, this may or may not be the case and, worse still, if there *is* a long queue, most are unlikely to be able to meet your needs notwithstanding the elegance of their glossy brochures and, sometimes, blandishments worthy of Pinocchio! Why should this be?

Some business functions like information technology or site maintenance are reasonably well served in terms of the number of outsourcing suppliers available whilst others like human resources are not. Where there *is* a ready availability of suppliers, it is probable that only a very small number will actually be mature and competent in both technical and outsourcing senses – some will, quite simply, be incompetent. The picture for those functions where there is *not* a ready availability of suppliers is not so good.

It is obvious, therefore, that you need to approach the 'market' with great care and, perhaps, a little shrewdness. Where there is a small number of competent suppliers who have the right amount of outsourcing experience, they will, on average, win more business than others. Two important implications flow from this:

- Competent suppliers are able to be more selective regarding the opportunities for which they bid and there are increasing signs that experienced suppliers will not bid if they do not like what they see. Worse still, they may withdraw from a procurement if they come to believe that the potential customer is either unreliable or insufficiently skilled to deliver contractual obligations.
- Their resources and management systems come under pressure as they rapidly expand.

When approaching sectors served by only a small number of competent outsourcing suppliers, it will be wise to have some idea of what suppliers will conclude when they assess you. You will need to present to the market an attractive business opportunity that both excites competent suppliers and signals you as an 'intelligent' customer, capable of creating and sustaining a good business relationship for a number of years. Of course, as an intelligent customer, you will look closely for any evidence of over-trading by those suppliers who impress you.

Where there are suppliers with the right amount of technical expertise but insufficient outsourcing experience, the approach requires a different emphasis. It is always possible to find sufficient companies to generate a competition. It may, however, be necessary to educate them in terms of the need for flexibility of thinking and service packaging. This is because outsourcing agreements quite often require 'imaginative' charging arrangements (see Chapter 12) and inexperienced suppliers sometimes find it difficult to come to terms with formulae that factor in a clear understanding of, for example, their actual costs. In extreme cases, inexperienced outsourcing suppliers have been known to withdraw from negotiations simply because they did not properly understand the dynamics of the outsourcing business. In addition to the need not to 'startle the horses' during negotiation, it will be necessary to test both their scale of resources and their quality of service delivery infrastructure to determine their capability to deliver an outsourced service.

Though the general approach to 'making a market' is the same for all circumstances, the emphasis will vary relative to sector maturity – mature sectors need enticement whilst immature sectors need education.

Since it is difficult to manage these issues effectively once the formal procurement process has begun, the whole point of 'making a market' is, therefore, as follows:

- To engage potential suppliers in *informal conversations*.
- To establish a clear understanding and lines of communication regarding your tactical and strategic needs.
- To articulate and control the process, including procurement, by which you intend to achieve your tactical and strategic objectives.
- To establish with each potential supplier a good working relationship, which may then be carried forward into a relationship with the winner.
- To establish your credentials as an 'intelligent' customer.

THE PROCESS OF MAKING A MARKET

There are a number of steps that should be taken if the market is to be correctly engaged. They are as follows:

- Prepare information pack.
- Select participant suppliers.
- Set meeting schedule, form and content.
- Conduct meeting 1 – handover and discuss information pack.
- Conduct meeting 2 – receive initial participant observations and questions.

- Conduct meeting 3 – agree refinements to approach and confirm understanding and objectives.
- Issue supplemental information pack, if needed.

PREPARE INFORMATION PACK

The information pack is a useful device that will help to guarantee consistent messages to the market, minimize misunderstandings and assist discussions within the customer and supplier organizations. It will be helpful to circulate the information pack to those internal people with a direct interest (see Chapter 4) and, in so doing, achieve, insofar as is possible, an agreed document for presentation to potential suppliers.

The information pack brings together the various strands of activity and thinking into a single set of documents, which may then be used as a basis for discussion and communication with suppliers. It will, in effect, become the agenda for the first meeting and should, as a minimum, contain the following information:

- The making a market process.
- Schedule of participant meetings.
- Your objectives and measures.
- Broad outline of requirement.
- Likely supplier capabilities.
- Evaluation criteria.
- Limits of supplier involvement.
- Procurement process and timetable.

The making a market process

A description of the process to be followed for this first stage of the procurement, offering a preamble perhaps in the following style:

The making a market process is designed to lay the foundations for a lasting relationship. It seeks to establish the clearest possible understanding, for both parties, regarding their respective objectives, measures, anxieties and limits. The main steps in the process are as follows:

- Set meeting schedule, form and content.
- Meeting 1 – handover and discuss information pack.
- Meeting 2 – receive initial participant observations and questions.
- Meeting 3 – agree refinements to approach and confirm understanding and objectives.
- Issue supplemental information pack, if needed.

Schedule of participant meetings

A description of the meetings to be held in this phase and the objectives to be achieved at each meeting. The schedule of participant meetings provides participants with the following information, offering some suggested drafting for inclusion in the relevant documents.

The names of other participants   Not only does this list have the effect of establishing an openness in the relationship, but it should stimulate the competition.

The basis of selection   This section offers a basis for their selection at this stage and could take the following form:

> Participants have been selected on a superficial assessment of their size and capacity relative to the size of [your company name] and the likely future requirement. It should be noted that in drawing up the participant list, it is not the intention to exclude any supplier from responding to the 'expression of interest' advertisement if or when placed.

Meetings structure, form and content   This section describes the meeting structure, form and content and could take the following form:

> The style and tone of meetings must be open and relaxed. Each party must feel free to articulate any and all anxieties regarding the other party. It will be a closed conversation and therefore held in the strictest confidence and without prejudice to any subsequent procurement. The objective is to lay the foundations for a true relationship, which will flourish only if completely open. Discussions must, therefore, transcend what might be regarded as a normal 'sales' conversation.
>
> Three meetings will be held with each participant. The first will be introductory in nature and an information pack will be delivered and discussed. The following principles will be discussed:

- Both parties will have their own objectives and deliverables for the relationship. They must be set out and clearly understood by the other party as a first step.
- Both parties must agree that, in principle, both sets of objectives are capable of being met and are generally complimentary.
- The primary focus of service requirements will be indicated by [your company name], i.e. the maintenance of reliable routine services or the attainment of longer term objectives or both.
- [your company name] will signal its clear intention to achieve a high degree of value for money to ensure that participant expectations are correctly set.
- [your company name] will also signal its clear understanding that the participant must make a reasonable return.
- Participants should be asked to define the term 'reasonable return' to ensure that the [your company name] expectation is correctly set.
- The two sides should discuss the feasibility of, and potential need for, 'open book' tendering.

- [your company name] will signal its intention to minimize the burden and cost that will fall to the participant as a consequence of bidding for the contract. Observations should be invited from participants as to how current [your company name] thoughts on the procurement process might be improved.
- [your company name] will signal its clear understanding of the obligations and commitments it will undertake as a party to the relationship. It must also demonstrate its determination to fulfil its obligations.
- [your company name] will openly share any concerns it might have regarding the disposition, performance or perception of a particular participant.
- It should be emphasized that any 'negative' observations advanced by [your company name] are offered in a spirit designed to provide each participant with an opportunity either to correct any misunderstandings on the part of [your company name], or to react to the observations in any way it sees fit prior to commencement of the formal procurement process.
- The participant should openly share any concerns it might have regarding [your company name] and its ability to deliver its obligations and commitments to the relationship.

The second meeting will receive the participant's considered response. The third will confirm the understanding of each party to the other's requirements, concerns and limits of involvement after which all informal communication will cease prior to commencement of the formal procurement process [if there is to be one] subject only to the issuing of a supplemental document, which updates the initial information pack in light of the preceding discussions.

When all meetings have been concluded, a paper may be produced, for [your company name] consumption only, which describes the boundaries of potential participant involvement and will inform the overall agreement packaging process [see Chapter 8], the structure and content of the SoSR [see Chapter 16] and wording of the 'expressions of interest' advertisement where appropriate.

Objectives and measures

A written articulation of the business/corporate/project objectives to provide a point of reference for the discussions. The objectives and measures will be those derived from Chapter 1.

Broad outline of requirement

A description of the service requirement to provide a context for the planned discussions. This will be a *broad* outline of the services, will avoid any real detail and will be derived from work discussed in Chapter 9.

Likely supplier capabilities

A description of your expectations, the discussion of which allows the supplier to update, and if necessary correct, your perceptions. This section will offer participants an overview of the capabilities thought by the customer to be necessary to deliver the service requirements. If prepared carefully, it can be used to regulate responses without alienating the market-place, that is the capability statement can be made more or less demanding depending upon the general condition of potential suppliers.

Evaluation criteria

A description of the basis by which you will judge the competition. It provides a high level view of likely evaluation criteria but without offering a view of weighting (see Chapters 14 and 15).

Limits of supplier involvement

This description of the boundaries around the likely service requirement can be helpful in identifying those aspects of service that will *not* pass to the supplier, that is the retention of strategic control (see Chapter 8).

Procurement process and timetable

A description of the procurement process to be followed and the broad timetable of events (see Chapters 6 and 7).

SELECT PARTICIPANTS

It is likely that participants will be chosen from well established service suppliers and, as such, they must clearly understand that an invitation to the making a market meetings does not confer any privileges or preferred status. The following issues are relevant:

- Participants must be made to understand that the informal discussions are not intended to provide an opportunity for an early sales discussion. It must be recognized that, although the process does present them with an opportunity to create a good impression, its primary purpose is to promote a clear understanding and for them to influence the thinking and approach.
- Suppliers of existing, related, services will be acutely sensitive to their position and the possibility of the loss of business. Since their services are likely to be required up to the start of an outsourcing arrangement and, perhaps beyond, they will need to be handled with care. Exclusion from this process may send unhelpful signals and create adverse reactions. Inclusion of existing, relevant, suppliers in the process at this time, even if there is little prospect of continued business, may be helpful to the conduct of the procurement exercise and maintenance of existing services.

SET MEETINGS SCHEDULE, FORM AND CONTENT

The approach to making a market suggests a series of three meetings. In certain instances, it may be more important for there to be, perhaps, four meetings. The point here is that the meetings must be planned and once set, they must be scheduled within the scope of the complete project. Declaration of a schedule of meetings, with dates and times, provides everybody with a clear understanding of the pace at which the process will be conducted.

A word of caution, however. Since the meetings will be on an individual basis, the more organizations selected, the more meetings to be held. Four half-day meetings with six organizations add up to 12 days' work – a hefty commitment for busy managers. Undoubtedly there will be a balance between the number of organizations to be involved and the commitment of time.

MEETING 1 – HANDOVER AND DISCUSS INFORMATION PACK

The purpose of the first meeting is to discuss the content of the information pack and the pack should be used as the agenda. Limit the meeting to this agenda. If there is need for a broader discussion, then the information pack is probably incomplete. Allow the receiving parties to listen, absorb and take the issues and comments away – you are looking for considered observations, not instant reactions.

MEETING 2 – RECEIVE PROSPECTIVE SUPPLIER OBSERVATIONS AND QUESTIONS

The various organizations return with their considered comments and observations. This is the opportunity for the customer to listen while the supplier attempts to influence and educate. Inevitably some bias will apply as each supplier couches their comments in terms that suit their resource and commercial disposition. However, their comments, taken as whole, will provide valuable input to the thinking associated with the procurement. Although some supplier questions may allow an immediate answer, where this is not obviously the case, avoid a quick response and take the issue away for further reflection and discussion at Meeting 3.

MEETING 3 – AGREE REFINEMENTS TO APPROACH AND CONFIRM UNDERSTANDING AND OBJECTIVES

Having considered the comments made in Meeting 2, you can now air and debate the issues and the parties can come to some conclusions. Ideally the suppliers should leave this meeting with a clear intention to bid for the business when the procurement is initiated. The customer should leave the meeting with a heightened perception of requirement and an enhanced view of how to conduct the procurement.

ISSUE SUPPLEMENTAL INFORMATION PACK

Depending on the discussions that have gone on, you may feel the need to update the information pack. Certainly where policies have been refined, there is a strong argument for updating the information pack for circulation to colleagues and the suppliers.

18 Negotiating the agreement

This chapter deals with the basics of negotiating an outsourcing agreement that the outsourcing procurement team will need to understand if a satisfactory and balanced agreement is to be delivered. Note that the potential for failure is higher in outsourcing agreements because of their scale and duration. If the supplier is unhappy with the agreement at the outset of the deal, the risk of failure increases dramatically.

Negotiation issues are discussed under the following general headings:

- The negotiating team.
- The negotiating process.
- General issues.

THE NEGOTIATING TEAM

The size and composition of your negotiation team will depend on the scope and complexity of the required agreement but, in general, it should display the following characteristics:

- The team must have a blend of skills appropriate to the subject matter of the negotiation.
- The team should be capable of sustaining a clear negotiating focus and provide a strong thread of continuity across the entire procurement.
- The team must be able to maintain an overview of how the entire transaction is shaping and how the various components interrelate.

The negotiation team must maintain an interface between itself and the emerging contract management team (see Chapter 19). It is also important that the negotiation team maintains appropriate interfaces with all interested parties (see Chapter 4).

ROLES OF THE NEGOTIATING TEAM MEMBERS

The negotiation team will comprise a number of roles both full-time and part-time.

All negotiation team members will need to understand the demands that will be placed upon them by the negotiation and must commit to that level of effort. They must also understand the need for a high degree of personal discipline and be prepared for careful and comprehensive planning for each negotiation session.

All or some of the following roles will be required.

Negotiation leader

The negotiation leader has responsibility for the conduct of the negotiation as a whole. He or she will direct the activities of the negotiation team and, as chairperson and spokesperson, will lead direct negotiations with the supplier's negotiation team. He or she will be responsible for reporting progress and clearing issues of principle, policy or business direction with directors or the appropriate authority. *Most important of all, he or she will be empowered to conclude the negotiation.*

During negotiating sessions, the negotiation leader should direct, by invitation, who responds or speaks during negotiation so that members of the team never talk across each other, interrupt or contradict. The negotiation leader must never ask someone to speak at the negotiating table if it has not been established, at the earlier internal planning meeting, what that person is to say.

Deputy negotiation team leader

For some negotiations it may be prudent to appoint a deputy negotiation leader who will monitor adherence to agreed policy and negotiation decisions. If the negotiation is time critical, the deputy must be prepared to step in to cover the negotiation leader's absence or to chair parallel negotiations.

Negotiation manager

The negotiation manager is responsible for administration of the negotiation, e.g. agenda, minutes, adherence to agreed policies, etc. He or she will maintain an overview of the transaction to ensure that the negotiation team is still operating in line with policy and procurement objectives.

Although the negotiation manager does not take a speaking role, he or she will attend all negotiation meetings and adopt a policing role, watching for potential problems with negotiation points, which, because of the hurly-burly of debate, are not readily noticeable by other members of the team.

More particularly, he or she will maintain a 'map' of each of the primary negotiation issues relating to both sides so that as the commercial position of each party ebbs and flows, the customer's commercial position can be tracked, compared with that of the potential supplier, and an appropriate response formulated for the next negotiating session.

Commercial advisers

The negotiation leader may wish to appoint specialist advisers as full-time members of the negotiation team to provide support or commercial advice associated with the proposed agreement.

Legal adviser

A legal representative should be present on the negotiation team. Legal representation can take two forms:

- A senior legal adviser who will be able to negotiate directly on legal points.
- A junior legal adviser who will be able to take appropriate notes so that the draft contracts can be updated.

Some negotiation leaders may deliberately choose not to have a senior legal adviser present at meetings with the supplier so that difficult negotiation points can be 'agreed, subject to legal advice'. The point in question may then be considered away from the negotiating table where all team skills may be brought to bear in the formulation of a response.

If one side elects to include a senior legal adviser on their team, then the other side will be forced to do the same. It may be considered an advantage not to allow the attendance of senior legal advisers so that discussions between the two parties are concentrated on the contract principles and business issues rather than legal technicalities. Should this be the preferred approach, however, appropriate legal expertise must always be available in support of all internal planning meetings. A senior legal adviser will almost certainly be needed towards the end of the negotiating round to facilitate final contract drafting.

Experts

Experts on specific parts of the service requirements may be needed for relevant parts of the negotiation. However, care must be taken regarding the manner in which experts are introduced to the team. Their team role must be clearly understood and monitored and they must be thoroughly briefed regarding the disciplines of negotiation. The negotiation leader must, of course, know beforehand what the expert is going to say.

Administration/secretariat

The extent of administration will largely depend on the approach taken for legal documentation and the audit trail. Do not underestimate the time and resource required for these activities.

Legal documentation   Control of drafting the legal documents should be retained by the customer team. Draft contracts will need to be updated and circulated on a timely basis. (Solicitors often include such facilities as part of their service.)

Audit trail   If a detailed audit trail is required, including minutes of all meetings, the administrative effort required will be considerable – remember that the person concerned has to attend all meetings, write up the notes, circulate papers and probably maintain a document library.

THE NEGOTIATING PROCESS

THE IMPORTANCE OF PLANNING

For a negotiation team to be well prepared for a meeting with the supplier, it must spend sufficient time planning. Effective plans will take 4 to 6 hours to prepare for each hour at the negotiation table. Planning matters will include, but will not be limited to, the following:

- Preparing the agenda – see below.
- A review of environment.
- Preparing an opening statement – see below.
- Checking which documents are required for each session and arranging for sufficient copies.
- Identifying the supplier's decision makers and key players, which may change from meeting to meeting.
- Reviewing draft and updated contracts.
- Ensuring that key points have been correctly (re-)drafted.
- Testing the team's understanding of key points.
- Identifying potentially contentious areas and deciding on what line to take.
- Checking figures and relevant calculations.
- Preparing stance on main issues/identifying thresholds for agreement.
- Identifying an escalation route above the most senior member of the supplier negotiation team.
- Planning how to deal with any attempt by the supplier to escalate above your negotiating team.
- Identifying the points that cannot be conceded.
- Reviewing the constituency management list.

DRAFT CONTRACTS

The drafting and updating of contract documentation is a heavy commitment. However, control of the documentation is a significant negotiation advantage. It is inevitable that the first draft of a contract will have a bias towards the drafting party. The opposing party is left to find the bias and negotiate it out. Your negotiation team should therefore take on the responsibility for drafting the contract and its associated schedules.

The project manager must allow sufficient time in the project plan, between appointment of the preferred supplier and the first negotiation meeting, for drafting the contract and schedules. Under no circumstances accept the supplier's standard draft contract, even if project time is tight.

THE AGENDA

The meeting agenda (for both planning meetings and negotiation meetings) is an important planning aid and has a number of purposes as follows:

- It sets the content of the negotiation meeting.
- It sets the order of discussion.
- It ensures that items are not missed or forgotten.
- It instils discipline into the planning process.
- It conditions attitudes and responses from others.
- It provides a basis for time management.

The following checklist will assist with its formulation:

- Identify subjects to be discussed.
- Predict other parties' objectives for the meeting.
- Rank subjects in order of priority to suit your team.
- Determine time needed for meeting/allocate time for each subject.
- Identify secondary issues that may be deferred if time runs out.
- Programme recesses and breaks.

OPENING STATEMENT

The negotiation leader should prepare an opening statement for the first meeting. This statement will condition the atmosphere and negotiations that follow. The statement will include a reminder of the benefits of the proposed contract to the supplier, a summary of the contract and its intended operation and any requirements in the conduct of the negotiations.

If appropriate, prepare opening statements for any subsequent meetings where a particular atmosphere, tone or objective is to be achieved. Each opening statement must be written down and rehearsed to ensure that the agreed text is presented correctly.

PROGRAMME

Where possible, define a formal and cyclical negotiation programme, an example of which follows:

- Day 1 – internal planning meeting.
- Day 2 – negotiation meeting with supplier.
- Day 3 – internal review meeting to discuss the previous day's negotiation and instruct drafting lawyer.

- Day 4 – update draft contract.
- Day 5 – release updated draft to supplier.

Where possible, construct the negotiation programme around a fixed weekly or fortnightly cycle – this makes setting diaries much easier and minimizes unnecessary loss of progress due to other commitments.

ACCOMMODATION

Prepare negotiation accommodation carefully. Since it is possible to dictate mood by creating a hostile or relaxed environment, the customer should invariably host the negotiations unless there are obvious reasons for meeting at the supplier's premises, for example access to information.

Plan seating arrangements to suit the composition of the negotiation team. In later stages of the negotiation, always provide the supplier with a room nearby for private discussions during a recess.

GENERAL ISSUES

Negotiation is a skilled activity. Should the size, scope or value of the procurement warrant it, arrange specialist negotiation training beforehand. One or two days of training for the negotiation team will almost certainly pay for itself. Even seasoned negotiators can benefit from having their experience and knowledge refreshed.

Some general negotiation points are described below.

DECISION MAKERS

Ensure that the supplier's decision maker is known. Note if he or she is an attendee at the negotiation meetings. Ideally, both negotiators should be empowered to make binding decisions.

If negotiations reach a sticking point, do not allow the supplier's negotiator or higher level executives to bypass the negotiation table. This might lead to concessions being made by the customer's senior executives without full understanding of some potentially complex issues.

OBJECTIONS/COMPLAINTS

A common defence against difficult negotiation questions is complaint or objection. Counter such tactics by using logical persuasion and explanations in a businesslike manner. Your position should always be logically unassailable if sufficient planning has been done!

SILENCE

When faced with an awkward question or unhelpful line of argument, the supplier may remain silent to avoid a reply. A prolonged silence is designed to be embarrassing and force the other side to divert the issue. The negotiation leader should not break the silence except to repeat the question or argument.

INTELLIGENCE

A skilled negotiation team will take every opportunity to gather intelligence and pass it back to the negotiation leader. If there is a need for the supplier to talk to your 'experts' who are not part of the negotiation team, your negotiation leader should:

1. Ensure that the expert is fully briefed and that he or she knows what is going to be said.
2. Ensure that the expert is accompanied by a member of the negotiation team during the discussions.

BODY LANGUAGE

Posture and mannerisms can give important information to the supplier's negotiation team. All members of your negotiation team should be aware of their own particular mannerisms – negotiation training will help with this – and, where appropriate, avoid passing unconscious information to the opposing team.

In particular, make sure that the negotiation team refrains from nodding to points with which they agree. If the supplier makes an acceptable point which, for the moment, the negotiation leader does not wish to concede, a verbal rejection of the point may mean little if the rest of his or her team are quietly nodding their agreement.

The negotiation manager should make a point of tracking body language from both sides. A report of the supplier's body language should then be offered to the negotiation team in the debriefing session and reminders given to your team about their own mannerisms if important positions are being weakened.

NUMBERS

Never let the other side do your calculations. Always re-check figures that are offered in negotiation. Keep a running total of the value of the contract and refresh the view regularly. Most particularly, always maintain, as best you can, a view of the other side's commercial position so that you may judge when to press for an improved position or when to stop pressing because a balanced agreement has been reached.

19 Managing the contract

Any outsourcing agreement of substance will require consistent and robust management if the objectives and benefits set for it are to be delivered. Although each agreement will differ in detail, the principles that govern good practice are common to all. This chapter offers some insight into the general principles, high level processes and organizational structures that will guide development of the contract management arrangements.

The ultimate size and shape of the contract management function will be determined by a core set of activities, which are geared to the maintenance of contractual propriety and delivery of the agreement objectives. The precise form of the contract management team cannot be determined without some view of what those core activities are, the general principles that they serve, and their relationship to wider contract issues.

GENERAL PRINCIPLES

Activities required to manage the contract can, conceptually, be said to operate at four levels:

- **Level 1**
  Proactive customer interfacing – the mechanism by which continually changing user requirements are understood by the contract management team and outsourcing supplier.
- **Level 2**
  Translation of user requirements into acquisition of resources and services in a manner that maximizes value for money from the contract.
- **Level 3**
  Performance monitoring – assuring operational performance and commercial/technical compliance.
- **Level 4**
  Facilitating delivery of the outsourcing agreement objectives.

Levels 1, 2 and 3 might be regarded as routine and will deal with the day-to-day operation of the relationship. 'Routine' does not, however, mean 'simple' and some difficult issues must be overcome if effectiveness is to be assured. Level 4 might be regarded as a higher level function in the sense that the contract has no purpose if it does not deliver the objectives set for it, and yet it is not immediately obvious how one might give effect to Level 4 activities. The position becomes more difficult since the complexities inherent in Levels 1, 2 and 3 will further obscure Level 4 issues and distract from delivery of the agreement objectives.

The contention is, therefore, that contract management arrangements should have at their centre mechanisms that are *specifically* designed to facilitate attainment of the agreement objectives and, on the way, deliver the requirements of Levels 1, 2 and 3. Without such a determined emphasis on Level 4 issues, the complexities and sheer volume of day-to-day activity will at best slow down, and at worst, defeat the delivery of the agreement objectives. The contract management function must, therefore, be multi-layered with Level 4 activities firmly directed towards the effective delivery of agreement objectives, and ensuring that Levels 1, 2 and 3 contract management mechanisms maintain their effectiveness over time.

GENERAL SKILL REQUIREMENTS

LEVEL 1 – PROACTIVE CUSTOMER INTERFACING

This level is primarily customer/business facing and will form the primary interface between the customer/business and the provision of service. Since the contract manager must be aware of, and sympathetic to, end user requirements, this level will also be concerned with business planning and, where appropriate, the conversion of business requirements into technical requirements.

The contract management team will need:

- good inter-personal skills;
- appropriate technical awareness and/or technical skills;
- an expert understanding of relevant internal planning and administrative mechanisms; and
- a conviction that success is measured by the extent of satisfaction, in service terms, from your end users.

LEVEL 2 – TRANSLATION OF USER REQUIREMENTS

Level 2 is concerned with ensuring that the user requirements identified at Level 1 are correctly translated into appropriate services but in a manner that maximizes value for money from the contract. In other words, the contract management team will ensure that supplier estimates for the resources required by the new services are both reasonable and purchased in line with the agreed charging formulae. Any lack of rigour at this point will allow costs to escalate over time.

LEVEL 3 – PERFORMANCE MONITORING

Level 3 deals with supplier performance as measured against contract terms and will require a sound understanding of the operational and primary contract mechanisms. An ability to operate sophisticated monitoring processes in a consistently meticulous manner will be essential, since it will be necessary to interpret early warning signs and react effectively to negative performance situations.

LEVEL 4 – DELIVERY OF STRATEGIC OBJECTIVES

Level 4 activities must be firmly directed towards delivery of the contractual objectives (for both parties) and the effectiveness of the Level 1 and 2 processes. Level 4 demands a clear understanding of the cultures and *modus operandi* of the various parties and the ability to apply commercial considerations and techniques.

CORE CONTRACT MANAGEMENT PROCESSES

CORE ACTIVITY AREAS

To support the central objectives within the contract management function the following core activity areas will require robust processes, which, depending upon the complexity of the agreement, may need to be computerized. These are necessary both to manage the contract and to de-skill the tasks in order to give the management team some resilience over time as staff come and go. The core activities are as follows:

- Maintenance of service levels and performance reporting.
- Management of resource based contracts.
- Change control.
- Response to performance reporting and escalation.
- Performance improvement.
- General administration.

The cost of establishing and operating these processes will need to be balanced against the contract benefits and risks to their delivery. If the contract is reasonably simple, and every effort should be made to make it so, then the contract management arrangements can also be simplified. If, however, the potential benefits are large and require a complex service to achieve them, more complex contract management arrangements will, unfortunately, be needed.

Maintenance of service levels

The primary activity of any contract management function is to ensure that the supplier is meeting satisfactory performance standards. The details of the required performance standards should be listed and described in a contract schedule and, if necessary, further described in a master service level agreement (MSLA). Alternatively the service details can be defined in a number of separate contractual agreements – user related service level agreements (SLA) – the scope and format of which will be described in one of the contract schedules. This latter arrangement may be particularly appropriate where the contracting department has its own users or clients, for example a maintenance department that provides maintenance services to a number of locations or departments – each location being a user in its own right with specific service requirements described in the SLA.

Contract schedule/service level agreement　The contract schedule/service level agreement defines, in qualitative and quantitative terms, the primary service components, constraints on demand for the service, the charges and the method by which performance will be measured and reported over the life of the agreement.

Where the service provision is complex, a master service level agreement (MSLA) can be used specifically to cover contract arrangements and provides an umbrella for the service components as a whole. Typically a MSLA will exist for each principal type of service to be provided. Service level agreements exist within the framework of the MSLA and may provide variations applicable to a specific service component. In situations where no SLA exists, the elements of the MSLA will become the default minimum service level.

A service level agreement will include the following:

- Delivery and acceptance dates.
- Availability.
- Reliability.
- Performance.
- Functionality.
- Security.
- SLA processes.

Processes concerned with the creation and maintenance of service level agreements include the following:

- Sanction of new services and projects.
- Specification and creation of service agreements for new services and projects.

- Securing of appropriate approvals.
- Sanction of amendments to existing services (change control).
- Maintenance and refinement of existing customer service agreements.
- Update of service level agreements in line with efficiency impacts/ technological improvements.

Clearly a number of these processes will interact with the procurement/contract negotiation activities as the SLA will form part of the contract and may materially affect the costs.

Special requirements   In certain instances additional processes may be required to monitor conformance to specialist requirements, for example:

- Confidentiality.
- Maintenance of satisfactory records for audit purposes.
- Specific technical requirements.
- Environmental specifications.
- Contingency/system resilience.
- Quality systems.

Performance levels and standards for these must be enshrined, to varying degrees of detail, in the service contract, MSLA and service level agreements.

Performance reporting   These processes manage the routine performance reports which flow from operational sources. Performance and progress statements will be collected by operational departments and passed to contract management for collation and onward presentation on a daily, weekly, monthly and quarterly basis as appropriate. These reports will cover both quantitative performance and compliance with the contracted service level agreements. Some reports will date from before the outsourcing agreement started, while others will have been specially devised, perhaps by the supplier, following agreement commencement.

Performance reporting should facilitate responses and feedback from users and contract management through the meeting regime, escalation procedures and exception reporting processes.

The main elements of performance reporting are as follows:

- The timing, manner, format and presentation of performance information that is defined within the master service level agreement and (where applicable) service level agreements.
- The regular reporting and maintenance of performance records on a daily, weekly, monthly and quarterly basis, concluding every 12 months with an annual report.
- The input of quantitative data from operational performance, project progress and incidents.

● The speedy assimilation of issues, problems and observations to be enabled by the supplier, with the provision of a help desk (if appropriate) and an effective information dissemination process.

Management of resource based contracts

There is a continuing trend towards contracts based upon a resource demand forecast. Such contracts offer significant potential for cost saving as suppliers are able to offer beneficial rates for a known committed workload (see Chapter 12). Typically this type of contract would be based upon a minimum resource profile for which a charge would be levied (even if it is not used) and provision to take additional resources with the charge level dependent upon the amount of prior notice given of the requirement. Utilization of this resource pool would be taken up by the various services/projects to be provided to the user community.

Management of the resource utilization and forward planning processes are central to achieving the following:

● Maximum utilization of the contracted resource pool.
● Purchase of resources at the most advantageous rate.
● Warning of potential failure to purchase at the most advantageous rate.
● Calculation and reporting of cumulative effect of missed opportunities.

Changes to service provision, whether this be downsizing or expansion, must consider the impact upon any forward plan resource contracts. The timing of delivery of the service may be important given the possibility of lower charges for early notification of requirements.

Change control

Occasionally an amendment will be required to a service contract necessitating a simple process of review which will lead to discussion and agreement. The main elements of the process will be as follows:

● Review of the contractual change, to include impact upon the SLA.
● Formulation of proposal for change.
● Obtain agreement for proposal.
● Initiate change.
● Monitor and report on implementation.

Response to performance reporting and escalation

Performance reporting must facilitate responses and feedback through the meetings regime, exception processes and escalation procedures. These processes must perform the following functions:

● Respond to reported poor performance.
● Ensure that remedial action is initiated.
● Ensure that necessary escalation is timely.

- Monitor and report progress through to completion of remedial action.

The existence of poor service achievement must be identified and recorded (by a help desk, if available) in response to input from the users or contract management. The appropriate management and users should be advised of an incident regardless of the source.

Processes are required to cover the evaluation and authorization of remedial action. Contract management must consider the contractual implications of the options for remedial action in conjunction with the operational departments and service supplier. However, the detailed technicalities of the remedial action are likely to be outside the remit of the contract management function. Further, the scope of any remedial action may be of such magnitude as to constitute a project (and contract) in its own right, in which case it may be necessary to intercept the normal service provision/project request process.

The progress of remedial action must be monitored and reported and if necessary escalation procedures invoked. In the event of remedial action failing to provide the required result the process must be restarted and will be subject to escalation within the appropriate management hierarchy.

Performance improvement

Where specific performance improvement programmes have been put in place processes will be required to perform the following functions:

- Monitor progress.
- Predict the likelihood of successful completion at each monitoring point.
- Routinely report on progress.
- Capture outturn.
- Match outturn to target benefits and project costs.
- Report upon performance of the programme and impact upon delivery of relationship objectives.

General administration

Non-technical processes will be required for administering the contract. For example:

- To check and pay supplier invoices. Inevitably this process will interface with existing financial processes.
- Contract management personnel must record and distribute meeting minutes and telephone conversation notes.
- A document library will be needed to hold the latest versions of all documents relating to the relationship and agreement. It is good practice to ensure that the conduct of all meetings is recorded by your contract management team to assure a proper 'balance' in the audit trail.

WIDER CONTRACT MANAGEMENT ISSUES

In some circumstances there may be a number of wider contract management issues that need consideration and for which processes may be required. These include, but are not limited to, the issues discussed below.

FEASIBILITY APPRAISAL

From time to time, workload changes (enhancements, new projects) may require some technical verification of the resources being offered by the supplier. Ensure that you have either retained a specialist capability or identified a suitable source, possibly external, of appropriate expertise.

FINANCE AND PLANNING

Specialist finance skills may be needed for such aspects of contract management as 'open book' and other audit requirements.

CUSTOMER/USER LIAISON

Where a number of your departments or functions (users) are receiving a service, it is important to represent each department's interests satisfactorily. The contract management function should ensure that the contract management processes are sensitive to user department perceptions.

Contract management processes will have failed if they fail to detect user dissatisfaction.

MANAGEMENT OF SUPPLIERS

There may be circumstances where complementary or linked services are provided by two or more different sources or suppliers. Special processes will be required to measure primary performance indicators in a way that ensures that fault or service failure can be correctly attributed.

SECURITY AND QUALITY MANAGEMENT

Contract management processes may be needed for the monitoring of special contractual security arrangements or especially critical quality requirements.

A high-level overview of contract management processes can be found in Appendix C.

20 Implementing the contract

If the right amount of effort has been applied to preparing and negotiating the agreement, you will, no doubt, be feeling that, after your second glass of champagne at the signing ceremony, the mountain has been well and truly climbed! Well, by all means enjoy your champagne while you can because, now you have the most difficult task to face – making it all work! The contract must now be implemented, and the skill with which the implementation task is conducted will determine the long-term success of the contract.

Implementation management is the central activity at the beginning of the contractual arrangement. The conduct and attitude of both parties at this time will set the tone for the ongoing relationship between you and your supplier. Be aware of the effect of a particular approach or style. Ideally implementation is an opportunity to establish the framework for an agreement characterized by trust, support and attention to each other's objectives. At the same time, however, decisions will be made that will affect the agreement for its whole duration. Therefore take extreme care to ensure that the supplier, who may also appreciate the importance of this period, does not use the implementation phase to improve the commercial standing of the agreement to your financial disadvantage. Your negotiation manager must ensure that he or she understands the long-term implications of any and all requests from the supplier, and must let none past that are not clearly understood and judged to be reasonable.

The procurement process itself should ensure that suppliers are obliged to provide draft implementation plans as part of their bid submissions (see Chapter 14). You must develop your own implementation plan for the period running up to operational commencement, using proposed implementation plans from the supplier, any previous plans from other outsourcing procurements and the perceptions of the outsourcing procurement team. The supplier will produce its own implementation plan, based on the contract terms, which will be initiated once the contract is signed. There are three stages of implementation:

● Pre-contract, i.e. activities before the agreement is signed.
● Post-contract, i.e. activities after the contract has been signed and *before* the agreed contract commences operationally.

- Post-commencement, i.e. activities after the contract has operationally commenced.

PRE-CONTRACT IMPLEMENTATION

Pre-contract implementation activities are those to be conducted before the contractual documents have been finalized between the parties. It is good practice to prepare for implementation, so far as you can, but to remain circumspect about actually doing anything that might undermine your negotiating position until contracts are finalized (see 'Undermining the negotiation' below).

EARLY PLANNING

The most important pre-contract implementation message is that good, early planning will not only facilitate a smooth and successful implementation of the contract, but create a means by which potential difficulties from third parties can be identified. A comprehensive implementation plan must be in place, and agreed with the supplier, before the contract is signed. Appendix D provides an illustrative implementation plan. In reality, of course, the actual content is dependent upon the function to be outsourced and the general approach of the outsourcing supplier.

THIRD PARTIES

In most agreements, third parties will need to be consulted if they are affected by the planned contractual arrangement. Establish early on whether any of the third parties will react unhelpfully to the planned agreement or specific implementation issues. Some companies may object to what you are proposing, for example novation of an agreement to a primary competitor, and cause difficulty or delay. Other companies may not object to the plan but may not react particularly quickly to requests.

Some caution will be needed here because some third parties will see an opportunity to secure from you additional revenue by asking for 'transfer fees' for the novation of contracts. Frankly this is a 'try on' and all that is required is some firmness. However, particularly in the information technology arena, third party contracts increasingly contain specific clauses relating to outsourcing. The outsourcing procurement team should therefore review third party contracts and licences, identify relevant clauses (i.e. no re-assignment) and formulate an appropriate approach.

UNDERMINING THE NEGOTIATION

When thinking about undertaking pre-contract implementation activities, you should be aware that, by definition, the contract is not signed, negotiations will be continuing and, by this time, will have reached their most sensitive and difficult stage. No activity should be allowed to undermine your negotiating position. For example, where staff are to transfer, the supplier may suggest that it commence the business of meeting staff and their induction. Once the supplier has engaged with your staff and perhaps set some expectations, it becomes more difficult to consider withdrawing from the negotiation if there is a sticking point. In effect the contact with staff will have weakened your negotiating position. Since the outstanding issues at the end of a negotiation will always be the most difficult and contentious, care must be taken to maintain the strongest possible negotiating position.

SUPPLIER CONTRACT LIAISON

It is useful at this time to ask the supplier, before you commit, for the names of the supplier's implementation team and the responsible managers. It is also worthwhile establishing on what basis the supplier implementation team will report progress and the regularity of intercompany progress meetings.

POST-CONTRACT IMPLEMENTATION

Post-contract implementation refers to implementation activities to be conducted after the contract is finalized and signed, but before the contract has commenced operationally. The length of time between contract signature and contract commencement will be affected by many factors, including the following:

- Operational convenience.
- Opportune timing for change.
- Staff matters, including the need for consultation.
- Novation of agreements with third parties.

Ideally there should not be a period between signature and commencement, but if unavoidable, it should be as short as reasonably possible. A delayed start may increase unrest especially if staff transfer is involved. You should seek to get the supplier into place and operationally responsible for the service as quickly as possible.

The negotiation manager should take careful account of the tasks that must be completed before contract commencement. For example, some might argue that payroll data for transferring staff must be handed over before the contract commences. In reality, the deadline date needs to be the latest date by which the receiving payroll department can receive data to be in a position to pay transferred staff. The deadline date for large numbers of staff who are paid weekly may well be before contract commencement, whereas the data for a few monthly paid staff is generally after commencement.

POST-COMMENCEMENT IMPLEMENTATION

Post-commencement implementation refers to implementation activities to be conducted after the contract has commenced operationally.

Once an agreement has commenced, the emphasis of an implementation plan passes to the supplier. Much of the customer's involvement will be in response to the supplier's work. For this reason, it is essential that the supplier's implementation plan is visible to the parties and that its validity has been formally agreed between the parties. Remember that, as part of the procurement and evaluation processes, you have already seen an outline implementation plan (see Chapter 14). Make sure that this plan is used as the basis for refinement into the actual plan. Once the plan is agreed, demand regular progress reports and monitor the effect on service provision until implementation is complete. Also remember that there will be tasks for the customer, even if they are restricted to signing off project deliverables. Failure to meet such obligations will provide the supplier with excuses not to meet planned objectives.

Frequently, implementation projects do not formally conclude but wither away through disinterest. There is a very wise saying that the last 20 per cent of any project takes 80 per cent of the time. *Sometimes the last 20 per cent never gets done.* It is strongly recommended that you establish three significant elements of supplier contract management:

- The clear delineation of deliverables from activities on the implementation project plan.
- A maintained library of implementation deliverables.
- Formal progress reporting for the implementation project with regular minuted meetings.

Ideally every implementation programme will be formally concluded by a sign off report to your management, even if some activities have not actually finished. Legitimately overdue activities can be finished late – make sure that the contract management function keeps such tasks in sight. If the task is not important then take it out of the plan at the beginning and do not cause the supplier nugatory work.

An illustrative implementation plan can be found in Appendix D.

Part IV
The Suppliers' Perspective: Three Case Studies

Introduction to Part IV

Inevitably, when getting to know a potential new supplier, potential new customers will remain 'on guard' against the threat of being misled, let down or overcharged. This lack of trust constitutes a real barrier to effective communication between the two parties. The trouble is that, on many occasions, the customer is right to behave in this way as, sadly, there are too many suppliers that are unable to be trusted. In a conventional customer/supplier relationship, the world, over thousands of years, has developed strategies for managing the risks associated with a lack of trust.

In the case of outsourcing, however, a lack of trust is more problematic. An outsourcing agreement will usually run for a number of years and will therefore require a good working relationship between the parties if maximum mutual benefits are to be delivered. In the early stages of 'getting to know' each other, a mature and competent outsourcing supplier will, by definition, have a much greater understanding and practical experience of the issues surrounding outsourcing. The supplier will therefore seek to pass on some of this knowledge to the potential customer in an attempt to help the customer avoid the more obvious pitfalls, which, in the longer term, will give both parties a problem. If, however, the customer is 'on guard', much of what the supplier has to say may be discounted to the ultimate long-term detriment of the relationship.

In an attempt to circumvent this barrier to effective communication, we invited three of the world's leading providers of outsourcing services to offer some advice to potential customers in the hope that, through the medium of this book, we may all take what they say at face value. We wrote to all three in the following terms:

> I attach an outline structure where you will see that Part IV is intended to offer the suppliers' perspective. What I have in mind here is a section which highlights the unnecessary problems faced by suppliers resulting from, on the one hand, poor preparation and understanding from customers and, on the other, over zealousness in their anxieties to avoid being 'ripped off'.
>
> … it is for you to offer any messages you wish along the lines of what not to do when procuring and operating an outsourcing agreement.

What follows is their unedited response the value of which we leave you to judge.

CSC Computer Sciences Ltd

Meyrick Williams, Director of Public Services, and Dr Tom Williams

OUTSOURCING: THE BASICS

STRATEGY

In today's competitive business environment, organizations are driven by the need continually to improve the delivery of goods and services to customers who demand individual treatment. And while the rapid evolution of information technology (IT) has increased the potential for greater efficiency and productivity, it is increasingly prohibitive to maximize capabilities without dedicating vast in-house resources to IT. In essence, that which stimulated productivity now threatens to stall future growth by its own complexities.

For many organizations, this challenge has prompted a new look at business objectives and the processes that support them. To increase or sustain market share, they must make sure that every business activity is directly supportive of their real business – that of delivering a product or service capable of attracting buyers.

With this in mind, many executives are taking steps to realign their organizations by identifying what they do best, relocating resources accordingly, and delegating all else to those who are best at their respective functions – often to outside providers who can execute non-core processes more efficiently.

This strategy – outsourcing – can provide access to more advanced technologies, better cost structures and greater expertise of industry specialists, while freeing more personnel and resources to concentrate on core competencies – giving the business an immediate edge over less-focused competitors.

Successful outsourcing requires a clear understanding of business objectives, as well as the tasks and processes that deliver them. How well these tasks and processes support objectives will help determine outsourcing tactics. This evaluation process is the essence of business re-engineering. Business re-engineering has become a key strategy for increasing performance in today's market-place, and outsourcing has emerged as a principal means of implementing this strategy. CSC is a world leader in both areas.

VALUE

The decision to outsource IT should be based on the deliverable return – or value – the move would offer. And a good measure of this value is in terms of technological leverage. Approaching an outsourcing agreement as a strategic technological alliance, where industry best practices meet world-class technology, fosters a partnership environment in which shared resources work continually to improve the quality and reduce the cost of IT processes. This relationship inspires performance gains in the core processes of both parties – and ensures a high degree of business value. Accordingly, the choice of an outsourcing partner should be determined by the ability to provide such value.

When you outsource IT processes you should choose a partner whose core business is IT. You then leverage the vast resources of a pre-eminent global information systems partner with the capability to support multinational clients. The partner should have deep technological know-how and proven management consulting expertise able to deliver integrated solutions that focus on business results. In addition, the outsourcing partner should be able instantly to access a vast knowledge base through a proprietary data communications network, designed to promote the sharing of technologies, methodologies, tools, and techniques throughout the entire organization.

The outsourcing vision is to enable business leaders to optimize consulting, technology and systems investments for overall business gain. This includes converting fixed costs to variable ones, providing an immediate infusion of cash, and offering access to leading edge systems and technologies that can be acquired through economies of scale unavailable to most companies. Outsourcing needs should also relate to business objectives, and implement solutions that can improve productivity, reduce time to market, and above all, offer a means to reassign internal resources to what the organization does best – thereby creating growth, profitability, quality and value.

PEOPLE

Outsourcing, by nature, involves the transfer of people and resources from an organization to its outsourcing partner. People are a critical component of any organization and, to outsource successfully, must be simultaneously aligned with transitioning technology and business processes. The approach must address all aspects of the personnel transition – organizational structure, job content, career development, leadership style and performance management.

At CSC, we attribute much of our own success to the collective mindpower of our people – many of whom joined our staff through outsourcing agreements. And since no one understands the human side of outsourcing better than those who have experienced it first hand, these CSC staff members are well qualified to understand the transfer of people and equipment.

This insight consistently demonstrates that incumbent mindpower is a prerequisite for a successful, uninterrupted transition of services. Accordingly, great emphasis should be placed on transitional strategies that are not only attractive to existing staff, but actively involve and embrace them. Outsourcing strategies should therefore provide an appealing environment of expanding career opportunities and personal growth for transitioning staff.

Clearly, a successful transition demands the simultaneous alignment of technology, business processes and people, all of which support the overall business objectives of exponential increases in productivity. The approach to the people transfer process involves a transition team composed of experienced managerial and support staff dedicated to establishing early and effective working relationships with client representatives. The end result is a transitional environment that emphasizes open and frequent communication.

RESULTS

Outsourcing must be a partnership of shared success achieving high levels of customer satisfaction. At CSC, our success depends on the success of our clients and our relationships with them. Past experience should be leveraged, proposals always unique to each client, addressing specific and individual needs as they relate to re-engineering, consulting, systems integration and outsourcing. Furthermore, contracts should be flexible enough to manage change – incorporating price structures that reflect a declining unit cost based on price, performance and productivity, and terms that support the clients' strategic goals.

An independent service provider should draw on the best components from any source and approach each new challenge with complete objectivity and bias-free commitment to engineering the best overall solution. A diverse network of global partnerships provides a conduit for exchanging knowledge, expertise and skills with which to support and enhance service delivery. Moreover, a team-oriented approach to outsourcing fosters a healthy atmosphere conducive to achieving the clients' established business objectives.

CASE HISTORY: THE BAe AND CSC PARTNERSHIP: ONE YEAR LATER

Dr Tom Williams

The internal computing resource of British Aerospace is formidable: 11 000 pcs, 1600 workstations, 400 mid-range computers and some 15 000 employees across 14 diverse business units. Data centres using large mainframe computers and facilities equipped with huge number-crunching machines are the backbone of this information technology empire. In April 1994, all of these valuable resources joined the Computer Sciences Corporation (CSC).

BAe hived off its entire internal computing function to CSC in a ten-year $1.5 billion deal. That decision is part of a growing trend known as outsourcing. The theory is simple. A company takes the essential IT operation, transfers it to a third party, allowing it to concentrate on its primary or core business. This emphasis enables key internal staff to concentrate on the strategic aspects of running the business, rather than deal with the problems involved in keeping up with new IT, or with the day-to-day management of data centres, systems development and maintenance.

Successful outsourcing vendors are characterized by strong capabilities in systems integration, data centre and distributed network operations, software development and maintenance, facilities management and strategic planning. Vendors such as CSC have recognized the business opportunities associated with the needs of the emerging outsourcing market-place.

Most outsourcing contracts are large enough to warrant the investment necessary to promote the relationship, understand the requirement and compete for the business. As a result, outsourcing has been established as a viable business strategy with clear advantages for both client and vendor. This is the basis for growth of an outsourcing market projected by Dataquest to reach $51 billion in 1998, with a growth rate of about 17 per cent a year.

At BAe, CSC has rationalized its 20 data centres running expensive mainframe computers, down to just six operating at four locations. The company's internal data network has been redesigned and the current data centres have been upgraded with more reliable and economical equipment. Information resident on old legacy systems is now held in brand-new devices that deliver more MIPS for the buck. As a dedicated services provider, CSC is totally independent of the IT industry's hardware and software vendors. This is no accident. We guard this independence jealously because we know it dramatically helps our total objectivity when replacing and installing equipment and systems.

All of these developments are contained in a legal service level agreement between BAe and CSC, which establishes a clear responsibility for CSC to deliver a first-rate product. Although it wasn't called outsourcing at the time, we won our first deal of this kind at NASA's Marshall Space Flight Center back in 1966 during the days of the Apollo 6 man on the moon programme. I was a computer scientist at Huntsville at the time and can still recall the pride and excitement we all shared in that vision. I sense that same kind of excitement today as we seek to create similar breakthroughs for BAe.

In my first year at CSC, we recorded annual revenues of $100 million. Today, that figure has mushroomed to $3.4 billion, reflecting a compounded annual growth rate of 24 per cent. Outsourcing partnerships have played a leading role in this phenomenal growth; specifically with BAe, a $3 billion contract with General Dynamics and, most recently, a $1 billion contract with Hughes Aircraft Company. At the heart of this growth is the CSC culture and our ability to partner with our clients. That is reflected in our growth as well as in our people.

CSC has also been instrumental in completely overhauling BAe's telephone service so employees can now pick up a phone and speak directly to any other company operation in any part of the UK. At the same time, we are helping BAe to move into the world of multimedia as we supervise the installation of technology that will allow voice, data and video images to flow within the company.

Staff morale is a huge consideration in any successful outsourcing enterprise. We realized this early on in our dialogue with BAe and placed a high priority on the feelings and fears of migrating BAe personnel. These highly-skilled people had to be sold – and sold is the operative word – that their future lay with CSC. From my perspective, this effort was just as serious and important as the contractual relationship.

Initial economies have come from reductions in technology spending rather than redundancies. As a result, BAe costs have been cut by 10 to 20 per cent in most areas. By implementing a new way of designing computer software, CSC has boosted the skills of its BAe staff while replacing previous disparate techniques with one coherent process. Known as the catalyst methodology, this approach has helped computer personnel to identify with their new employer. As a result, they now regard their former employer, i.e. BAe, as a valued client, a remarkable and laudatory transition for a loyal and dedicated workforce to make.

The true role of IT is to underpin a broad spectrum of business functions. CSC's duties embrace management consultancy and the development of new systems that will deliver the products that BAe wants. It is a policy of support from cradle to grave.

BAe and CSC have come a long way in only 12 months. The aerospace contractor has entered into a strategic partnership with an IT specialist and the resulting outsourcing group has grasped the challenges and opportunities of a vast enterprise. Together, we apply the strength of fast-moving technology to the far-sighted world of aerospace.

PARTNERSHIP OVERVIEW

Expectations

In choosing CSC as its outsourcing partner, BAe sought not only single-point accountability for the provision of its IT services, but also a partner whose management of the service would add real value to BAe's business. This relationship with CSC was envisaged as a full and open partnership, based on trust and common goals, which would yield financial savings and a competitive boost for BAe.

BAe saw in CSC a partner who would:

- Enable BAe to enhance its focus on its core business in defence and aerospace.

- Provide access to the best, most up-to-date information technology in the world.
- Reduce fixed asset costs.
- Convert *fixed* data processing costs to controlled variable costs according to changing business needs.
- Improve the business effectiveness and efficiency of IT operations.
- Provide IT services that would improve business flexibility, responsiveness and productivity.
- Yield significant savings in projected annual IT costs.

Early benefits

The realization of the key requirements sought by BAe yielded immediate financial benefit. On an ongoing basis it guarantees continuing operational and financial benefit over the term of the contract. There were a number of prime areas of benefit to BAe:

- The sale of IT assets to CSC provided BAe with a cash injection.
- Some 1500 BAe IT staff transferred to CSC with minimal disruption to the ongoing service.
- Administration of over 800 software licences, over 1000 leases, purchases of distributed equipment worth over £10 million, and the processing of over 15 000 associated invoices were transferred to CSC.
- Pricing structures and productivity commitments were undertaken to provide:
  - Significant annual improvement in the service delivery as defined in the service level agreements.
  - Significant annual productivity savings in the development and maintenance of applications software.
  - Substantial reductions in the cost of mainframe processing services.

The year in review

In the first year of the partnership CSC focused effort on the parallel tasks of stabilization and reduction of the baseline service costs, and progressive infusion of CSC's management and technological expertise. The execution of these tasks – and as a step towards the realization of BAe expectations of service delivery improvements – included certain achievements:

- CSC has invested in upgrading the infrastructure serving BAe.
- Data centre and network consolidation programmes have underpinned cost reduction commitments and established a new level of technical capability for future exploitation.
- A software metrics process has been implemented and a productivity baseline established to manage the delivery of application development and maintenance improvements.

- Investments have been made and are being accelerated in training staff in CSC's advanced methodologies, project management, legacy systems re-engineering and rapid applications development.
- Initial imports of CSC best practice and leading-edge capabilities are being applied at a number of BAe business units.
- BAe managers have attended CSC seminars and visited CSC clients in the USA and elsewhere to evaluate business solutions employing advanced information technologies.
- BAe managers are participating in CSC Research and Advisory Services programmes.
- Productivity and cost avoidance schemes have been firmly established.
- The organization has been restructured to improve service delivery and to facilitate generating 'added value' at a business level.

On the evidence of these activities, we believe that sound steps have been taken to deliver the promised benefits of partnership. Immediate and ongoing cost benefits have been realized. The transition of the total IT service provision to CSC management has been achieved, thus relieving BAe of these non-core activities.

This process has been complex. CSC experienced initial difficulties in service delivery in some areas; many of these difficulties have been resolved. Those difficulties outstanding are receiving serious management attention. In general a sound base is being established from which to deliver added value. CSC's pre-eminence in the deployment of world-class information technology to achieve client business objectives underpins this delivery.

EDS

David Thorpe, Managing Director, EDS UK

INTRODUCTION

TRUST

Trust is perhaps the most significant, and sometimes most elusive, factor when developing and sustaining any long-term business relationship that is truly based on partnership. When both parties trust one another, they can start to share fully the risks and rewards inherent in the given business venture, they can tie their business goals more closely together and they can respect each other's capabilities so that each can concentrate on what they do best in order to achieve synergistic results.

At EDS, our most successful business partnerships are built on trust. We are involved in many of the world's most significant outsourcing contracts, not only in terms of size, but in terms of the ground-breaking nature of the relationships – based on principles that extend far beyond traditional customer-supplier values.

In this chapter, I'd like to share some of these principles through the definition of a series of 'Don'ts'. These thoughts are not pitched as autocratic lessons that must be employed by all those considering the outsourcing decision, but they have been developed from almost 35 years of involvement in the outsourcing business. The rest of this book gives a tremendous insight into the process and detail of outsourcing, but we'd like to take the opportunity to highlight some of the potential pitfalls.

By and large, most of our customers, such as the Inland Revenue, General Motors, the Driver and Vehicle Licensing Agency (DVLA), and Rolls-Royce Aerospace Group to name but a few, have approached the decision to outsource in the context of their overall business, rather than in 'simple' IT terms. They have looked for a business partner. In many ways, the EDS focus on its customers' business and its desire to work together towards shared business goals, demands this approach. So, let's start with the first question we ask a prospective customer.

WHAT ARE YOU TRYING TO ACHIEVE?

Outsourcing is *not* about information technology (IT). It is a business decision to work with an external service provider to develop the most effective means of achieving a specific business goal. It is about understanding the competitive and environmental forces affecting your business, so that you can leverage technologies, new business processes and human resources to stay one step ahead of the pack. The real challenges facing you are not whether you can shave an extra £1.0 million off the IT budget, but whether you can make your whole organization more cost-effective, whether you can add increased value to your own products and services and whether you can satisfy a demand to improve customer satisfaction.

In today's business world, effecting any of these changes will inevitably have implications for your organization's IT strategy, but there will more probably be greater implications for the way in which you manage your business processes. In understanding what you are trying to achieve, never forget that you have an opportunity to challenge the norm and even re-engineer parts of your traditional business model.

WHAT ARE THE ISSUES YOU FACE IN TRYING TO ACHIEVE YOUR BUSINESS GOAL?

Having established clear business goals, now you must understand the issues that have to be managed in order to achieve these goals. Let me summarize just a few of these:

- Evaluating and choosing hardware and software is a costly and potentially risky business. There are, as the saying has it, many ways to crack a nut. Some are more efficient than others. Some will cost more than others. Some will render the kernel inside inedible. Deciding which is the best way for your organization can waste you much time and money, when all you want to do is eat the kernel. To extend the analogy even further, employing a nut-cracking expert to work with you can be a more cost-effective, lower risk strategy.
- Do you have access to the capability you need? Many organizations do not have the necessary skills or technologies within their organization to effect change. More often than not, they have too many people with exactly the wrong skills. Working with an external organization that specializes in the management of change delivers instant access to the capability you need. Further, EDS is seeing an ever growing demand from its customers for a complete service 'continuum'. This means that they are looking for a partner capable of delivering initial strategic consultancy and planning through systems development and integration to ongoing systems management and business process management. To the customer there are obvious benefits from using one service provider for each stage in the 'continuum'. Both cost and time savings can be had from eliminating the extra learning curves

required by using more than one company. Continuity of staff and ideas is guaranteed. The service provider will be more reliable, security will be greater. Above all, the customer gains greater stability and minimises risk. You know you need to get to market more quickly, but you know that you don't have the time or capital to invest in new capabilities and technology. Again, working with a specialist can afford you the guarantee that the necessary level of resources is brought to bear to guarantee the changes you need to make will be delivered in the timescales you demand.

Having read this far, you will have hopefully decided that to work with an external organization is a valid way of achieving your business goals, and you will also understand the general principles of making the outsourcing decision. Let me now take the opportunity to offer some advice, based on the assumption that you wish to achieve your business goals through the development of a close working partnership. The rest of this book has covered many of the 'Dos' of outsourcing, so let me suggest a few of the 'Don'ts'.

DON'T HIDE ANYTHING FROM YOUR PARTNER

I started this chapter by defining trust as one of the key components of a successful partnership. If I achieve nothing else with these words, I would hope that I reinforce the importance of partnership and associated principles such as honesty and openness in the development of a successful business relationship. It is a recurring theme in this chapter and underlies all of the most successful relationships we have with our customers. Indeed, EDS is often referred to not simply as a supplier, or even a service provider, but, as with the Inland Revenue and General Motors, as a true strategic partner. Working as a true partner, EDS recommended to the CAA that it did not require additional technology; the requirement could be met by revising operating procedures.

DON'T OUTSOURCE THE PROCESS WHILE RETAINING ALL OF THE RISK

Often, organizations believe that they can obtain a better price by breaking up the services they wish to outsource and placing these with a number of different service providers. The belief is that the inherent competition among the service providers will deliver a lower cost. While this may be true, the real issue comes when there is a problem with service delivery, as responsibility will not lie with any one, individual supplier. Thus, the risk is retained by the customer having to manage many suppliers. By choosing a single prime contractor the customer ensures liability is manageable and outsources much of the risk.

Nearly all EDS outsourcing contracts provide a single point of control for the customer. With the Inland Revenue contract, for example, any specialist requirements that lie outside EDS' capability, such as the provision of wide area networking services, are managed directly by EDS and remain 'transparent' to the customer.

DON'T EXPECT TO SHARE THE RISK, BUT NOT THE REWARD

Partnerships grow from shared motivation – profit, growth, technological superiority and so on. I would not be so naive as to expect a service provider such as EDS and its customers to have all of their corporate goals in exact alignment – effectively we would be either the same company or extremely fierce competitors! However, in respecting each organization's individual capabilities, certain goals can be shared. For instance, the refinement of business processes and the introduction of new technologies to take 2 per cent of total manufacturing costs off the bottom line.

It has to be recognized that the most effective service can be provided by establishing a true strategic partnership with a customer – sharing risk and reward and developing a relationship based on co-operation and collaboration. EDS refers to this concept of strategic partnership as CoSourcing. For the customer, control is retained over the services EDS provides, while the risk inherent in investing in new technologies is minimized. For EDS, staff develop an even deeper understanding of the customer's business and thus provide higher quality, more focused services that have a tangible impact on the customer's bottom line.

CoSourcing is effected by tying the value of a contract to a measurable target that produces a benefit to the customer. This may be the performance of a particular system and its relationship to the profitability of the customer (this may be relatively simple for City-based dealing systems, for example), or an independently assessed measure, such as a change in customer perceptions or a positive impact on stock levels.

CoSourcing is not yet as widespread as we would like. In the UK, we have established a number of the world's most significant deals of this kind, notably with Girobank and Rolls-Royce Aerospace Group. For Girobank, our technological expertise and investment capability will allow us to deliver a technical infrastructure that will take the bank into a whole new market, that of 'merchant acquiring' services in the world of electronic commerce. As Girobank grows more successful, so we will be motivated and rewarded to deliver ever more effective systems.

Although we are in only the early stages of our relationship with Rolls-Royce as I write this chapter, we have already defined a strategy by which we will deliver design, manufacturing and other technologies that guarantee the aero-engine manufacturer a quicker time to market for new engines than it was capable of before. When we achieve this goal, EDS will be rewarded in accordance with the actual effect we have on Rolls-Royce's profitability.

DON'T OVERESTIMATE THE CAPABILITY OF YOUR CHOSEN SERVICE PROVIDER

Before you even begin to estimate contract value, ensure that the service providers under consideration are capable of delivering the service you require to meet your business goal. There are a wide variety of systems integrators, facilities management houses, outsourcing specialists and consultancies all desperate for your business and all prepared to promise the earth. Look very closely not only at their technical capability, but also at the state of their business. Will they have the investment capital required to deliver new services? Do they have a strong track record in the management of third parties? Do they have the human and technical resources to guarantee delivery? The answers to these type of questions will soon enable you to differentiate between companies that will be able to act as true strategic partners, adding real value and those that can only 'mind' your technology infrastructure. Visiting existing customers will help you differentiate.

DON'T IGNORE THE CULTURAL SIMILARITIES, AND DIFFERENCES, OF SERVICE PROVIDERS

Not only should you well understand the differences in capability between the different types of service providers, you should also look closely at the corporate culture of those organizations within the chosen category. In line with the desire to achieve a particular goal, you may want to partner with a company with a specific type of culture.

Ask yourself whether you want to work with a company with a similar culture to your own organisation's, or whether you deliberately want to work with an organization that challenges your own in the belief that this will stimulate creativity and deliver a more 'complete' combined face to the rest of the market. Whichever culture you feel is best, traditional or youthful, acquisitive or conservative, always look to partner with an organization that is results-focused, achievement-driven and flexible.

DON'T DELEGATE THE RESPONSIBILITY

The decision to outsource and the focus for the implementation must begin and remain at board level and preferably at the highest level. Outsourcing typically involves both a significant business investment and a substantial change in the organization – at a human resources level if nothing else. In order to push through this kind of change and ensure that the focus remains on the strategic objective, the drive must come from the very top of the organization. That is not to say that members of the board should be the only ones involved in the decision. Supporting them should be a strategic management team spanning all the areas of the organization that will be affected – IT, human resources, business managers and so on. This team can take responsibility for researching and defining the business model and for advising the board on appropriate directions. However, to succeed, this team must have the full backing of the executive. Control remains with the customer. Control is the ability to get what you want done, when you want it done, for an agreed price, with the opportunity to change your mind.

DON'T BELIEVE THAT IT'S JUST ABOUT PRICE

More often than not, organizations that outsource non-key processes may not spend any less on technology solutions. Let me qualify that, they will spend less on processes that are exactly replicated – companies like EDS guarantee this – but they should be looking to gain greater value from IT and a more direct impact on the bottom line. You must consider the entire financial status of your organization and the capability of service providers when leveraging technology and external expertise to achieve your goals. For example, with our new strategic partner, Rolls-Royce Aerospace Group, we are guaranteeing cost-savings on the ongoing delivery of their 'basic' IT requirements, but we are also committed to developing new programmes that will help the Group bring new aero-engine technologies to the aerospace market more quickly than its US rivals. No matter how attractive a proposal may look, if it does not bring you closer to your end goal then it is not a wise use of capital. In the worst case, a failure to take advantage of the capabilities available in the market may ultimately put you out of business.

DON'T GET FOOLED INTO A FALSE ECONOMY

Often, when an organization announces that it is to outsource, the board is approached by the incumbent management team with a management buyout option. Almost without exception, this option will be the least costly – the level of overheads is much lower than for an external organization and large research and development operations do not have to be funded. However, the real challenge for the MBO comes when its former parent demands innovation and programme development that require significant investment. Already highly leveraged, the level of capital available to the management team can never be enough to guarantee success. There are no further resources to bring to bear, no new skills available. The specialist outsourcing service provider, on the other hand, can call on global resources and specialist skills from throughout the organization. The typical end result of an MBO is that the fledgling private company will be acquired by a larger specialist – the customer will have lost not only time in that it now has to deal with a new service provider, but it may also lose money, having 'sold off' its asset at a low cost.

DON'T MICRO-MANAGE YOUR SERVICE PROVIDER

If your service provider is to be able to find the best solutions to the challenges facing your organization, it must be given the freedom to choose and develop the architecture and organization structure that it believes is most appropriate. Sometimes, an organization fears that it may lose too much control over service delivery and becomes embroiled in the technical detail, trying to direct the process and challenge decisions. The key to success lies in retaining a sufficient level of technology-literate staff in order to remain aware of the implications of the service provider's chosen route, but not so many as to duplicate management and, more dangerously, confuse decisions such that they become compromises and thus less effective.

Too many organizations retain two to three times too many people in order to fulfil the contract management function. This only creates an extra headache when the customer realizes some time later that these people are not required. The benevolent service provider may incorporate them into the contract, or the customer may be left with an embarrassing and difficult human resources problem. Drafted correctly, the service contract defines the level of control and outlines the responsibilities and expectations of each side.

DON'T FORGET THE PEOPLE

Of course, no management team either forgets or ignores the human resource implications of an outsourcing decision. A cynic might say that outsourcing the technology also outsources the responsibility for the people – and when costs have to be saved, jobs will go. This does not have to be the case. Your service provider should always look to redeploy and retrain staff that make the transition to its workforce as it should realize the industry knowledge and skill base this workforce represents. Even in areas where job prospects are not high generally, positive moves can be made. In Swansea, for example, almost 100 former DVLA staff, who would have been out of work once efficiency measures had been put in place, were retrained in a new genre of computing technology known as client/server computing. The Swansea site is now established as a centre of excellence whose skills and resources can be drawn on by EDS project teams worldwide. Communication is vital. The rationale for the outsourcing must be communicated to all levels in the company.

DON'T UNDERESTIMATE THE REAL COSTS OF YOUR CURRENT IT ORGANIZATION

Ask a person how much it takes to run a computer and they will almost always underestimate. Try it. How much do you believe it costs each year to run a single PC in a typical business. Allowing for the amortization of the initial hardware and software costs of, say £1500, over three to five years and annual support costs, is it £1000? £2000? Even £3000? The current estimate is actually around £10 000 each year for every PC in your organization. Not only must you factor in the easily identifiable costs, such as how much the machine cost to buy and the maintenance bill that comes in each quarter, there are a raft of other costs – support staff, general office staff providing human resources and finance support, rent, heating and ventilation, opportunity costs caused by power outages and down time and so on. Is it a hard or soft asset? Is it expendable or a capital item? The first three parts of this book help in assessing these costs, such that you can determine a realistic proposal from potential service providers. I would just like to reinforce the importance of rooting out all delegated and departmental IT budgets. More often than not, these hidden costs, which should be included if the true added value of the external service provider is to be brought to bear, can represent a significant sum. EDS always works closely with its customers to assess these costs before contracts are finalized.

DON'T EXPECT MIRACLES OVERNIGHT

Is this just the cry of a service provider who does not want to face up to the challenge of providing a quality service? No, but it is a word of warning, aimed at setting realistic expectations on both sides. The customer always expects and demands a higher quality service from an external service provider than its previous internal organization – that is a fact of life that we in the industry well understand. However, we work with our customers to help them understand and define the exact improvements over current activities they want and then set a realistic plan and approach for achieving those improvements. Sometimes, we have to help them clearly understand what level of service they previously achieved, as the definition and recording of measurable levels has not always been clearly thought out.

It is important to agree problem management in the contract. For the Inland

Revenue contract EDS agreed an 'expert procedure' for problem resolution. In effect, if the two organizations could not resolve a problem, both would accept the ruling of a pre-identified and agreed third party.

DON'T UNDERESTIMATE THE RESISTANCE TO CHANGE WITHIN THE COMPANY

What may seem like a series of well-researched and sound business decisions in the boardroom, can lead to a very personal, potentially traumatic time for the staff involved. It is crucial to quantify properly the social impact of outsourcing – both real and perceived. At EDS, we attach great importance to that well-known 'FUD factor' – Fear, uncertainty and doubt. Each employee will have particular needs and circumstances that must be considered and addressed. To smooth out the transition process a system must be put in place that will let staff know that they are being considered, and not just told. The process is enhanced by trained personnel who are available to listen to staff and answer concerns, and who also have established communication channels to relay feedback directly to the management team. Suppliers must pay attention to the people affected as this is often where resistance lies.

DON'T FORGET TO AGREE MEASURABLE TARGETS

Finally, and perhaps most importantly, work very closely with your service provider to define measurable and agreeable targets that form the basis of contract verification. As I mentioned before, it is not the delivery of specific inputs that should be measured, nor the process itself, but rather the outputs of the process. Yes, you should be aware of how those outputs are being delivered, but do not try to impose.

One of EDS UK's most successful contracts is with the Parking Committee for London, a 'greenfield site' organization set up by the London Boroughs to adjudicate and manage parking tickets and fines throughout Greater London. The organization was set up with extremely strict budgetary limits that necessitated the introduction of an external service provider that would be able to bring its own level of investment to the relationship. Out of an organization of almost 50 people, less than 20 per cent are actually employed by PCFL, all the rest are EDS employees. The director of PCFL has no real interest in how EDS manages to cope with several thousand letters and calls each day, but he takes a very great interest in the level of service that is being delivered to the general public and the speed and efficiency with which queries are handled.

CONCLUSION

This chapter was billed as a 'supplier's' perspective and yet you may have noticed that throughout I have hardly used the word 'supplier'. Rather, the generic term I have used is 'service provider', reflecting the ongoing nature of an outsourcing relationship. Outsourcing an organization's non-core business processes cannot be achieved simply by buying a solution 'off the shelf'. However, I would be happier if I could replace all the occurrences of 'service provider' with the term 'business partner'.

At EDS, we believe that the future of our industry is in the development of measurable partnerships based on mutual respect for each other's abilities and the sharing of goals founded on a sound and clear business vision. There are indications that more and more contracts will use this approach and, in our own experience, this is where the greatest success comes. Customers such as General Motors, the Inland Revenue and Rolls-Royce view us as a strategic business partner, and not just a faceless service provider.

By bearing in mind some of the thoughts I have expressed, look to demand more of the external organizations with which you work and leverage their capabilities to make your own organization even more successful. Manage them through the service they deliver and not the way in which they deliver it. Choose an organization that can grow with your requirements and that can adapt to the changes that will inevitably effect your own market. Only when you choose a reliable partner who delivers what is promised, will it be easy to develop that most precious of commodities – trust.

Serco: Achieving change and continuous improvement through competition and outsourcing – a supplier's view

Richard Nicholls of the Serco Institute

Serco is an international task management contractor providing technical and support services to leading public and private sector organizations. The Serco Institute undertakes applied research in the field of outsourcing and service delivery and facilitates the exchange of best practice in this field for the benefit of Serco businesses and customer organizations. The Institute is a non-profit making organization and operates independently of Serco's direct business interests.

INTRODUCTION

For many organizations, competition and outsourcing have become key techniques for managing change. For others, the skills and techniques associated with these processes are relatively new. Serco welcomes the opportunity to present a supplier's view based on three decades' experience of operating outsourced services in a wide range of markets.

Serco's origins as a task management contractor lie with a contract that the Company has held for over thirty years to operate and maintain the UK Ballistic Missile Early Warning System at RAF Fylingdales in North Yorkshire. This contract provided a model for later contracting out initiatives during the 1980s and 1990s, when UK public authorities and private sector organizations embarked upon management programmes designed to introduce competition into the provision of first their support services and, increasingly, their primary areas of business activity.

Much has been learned in the intervening years about the use of competition and outsourcing as a means of introducing change and promoting innovation and continuous improvement. The benefits are now undisputed. Successive studies and government reports consistently put savings from competition for the provision of services in the range of 10–30 per cent – without taking account of the significant non-cost benefits that normally accrue, or allowing for indirect savings within the customer's residual organization.

In this chapter, we offer, first, our view of current trends in the market for outsourced services, and, second, some suggestions for avoiding the most common pitfalls that face organizations embarking on a strategy of outsourcing. We conclude with a suggested planning framework that addresses the central issues and considerations.

MARKET TRENDS

Few corporate observers can fail to have recognized the rapidly developing market for outsourced services, as evidenced by the introduction in 1994 of a separate business classification for support services in UK share listings. Since then the number of companies in this category, and the range of activities they represent, have grown substantially. At the same time there has been an increase in the demand for consultancy and advisory services associated with outsourcing, and most prominent management consultancies now have departments specializing in this area.

The growth in outsourcing activity during the 1980s and 1990s has reflected a trend in the private sector towards more open, networked organizational structures based on contractual rather than hierarchical relationships and on concepts of branding and supply chain management as a means of controlling the service supplied to the end customer. These moves are paralleled in the public sector where initiatives such as privatization, market testing and the introduction of private finance to fund capital assets are increasing the role played by the private sector in the provision of public services.

DIFFERENT VIEWS OF 'CORE' BUSINESS

Much has been written about the benefits to organizations of concentrating management effort and other resources on 'core' business activities and outsourcing the 'non-core' tasks. The definition of what is 'core' and 'non-core' is, however, very much a matter of corporate perception and management style. To some large concerns the operation of support activities upon which their business processes depend is, by virtue of their criticality, a core task. Yet others have a long tradition of contracting out tasks that form an integral part of the service they provide to their customers and that are vital to their business success.

Increasingly, organizations striving for world-class performance are adopting a radical view of the way in which different elements of their business processes are resourced. Instead of dividing activities into 'core' and 'non-core', they examine the management competencies they are best able to sustain and seek relationships with others in areas where they are less able to compete against world best practice. This results in a variety of relationships, ranging from relatively straightforward contracts to perform defined tasks for a fixed price to conprehensive agreements taking the form of franchises, strategic alliances and joint ventures and involving more sophisticated arrangements for sharing risks and rewards.

The approach adopted by a number of Australian public utilities and transport authorities to the definition of their 'core' business illustrates this trend. Figure 1 shows the planned contractual structure for managing the infrastructure and services provided by the South Australian Passenger Transport Board. The Board's senior management has defined the Board's 'core' business as being the planning and overall control of an integrated public transport system for the Adelaide metropolitan area. The model involves separate contracts for the delivery of services by type and by geographic area, together with functional contracts for the provision of central services, such as travel information and ticketing, which maintain overall integrity of the network. Having devolved responsibility for the day-to-day operation of the network, the senior management team is able to concentrate on strategic initiatives to improve the performance of the network and develop the services it provides to the public.

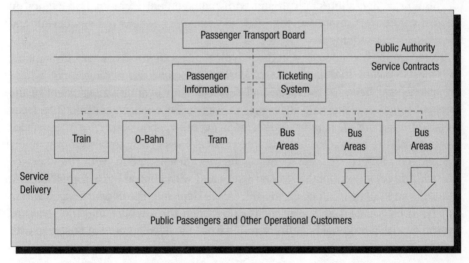

Figure 1 Illustrative arrangement of South Australian Passenger Transport Board operating structure

INCREASING SCALE AND PACE OF PROJECTS

As confidence grows in the ability of corporate managers to exercise strategic control over outsourced functions so the size and scale of projects is increasing, with greater reliance being placed on high level performance indicators and quality assurance systems to measure the level and quality of service supplied to the end customer. Outsourcing deals involving entire service operations with annual turnovers of £30–50m and employing up to 1000 staff are no longer uncommon, and projects of this magnitude are being implemented in similar timescales to smaller projects involving more conventional packages of support services. By their nature, large-scale outsourcing projects result in the transfer to the contractor of expertise that is essential for the overall planning and development of the service. With more suppliers in the field capable of tackling projects of this magnitude, few organizations take the view that they must retain the technical expertise to step in to recover an operation in the event of failure.

With contracts for more comprehensive tasks comes the involvement of end users in both the definition of the service and in measuring how well it is performed. This trend may show up in the arrangements for financial control, with the transfer of budgets to user departments who place orders for services, or in terms of user representation on evaluation and review panels, or through the commissioning of user surveys (or a combination of these measures). In all cases, the emphasis is on moving from the measurement of process outputs to evaluating policy outcomes, with end customer satisfaction emerging as a central factor in the evaluation and development of the service. This aligns with trends in large organizations towards the centralization of strategic planning and devolution of operation control, and with management techniques designed to secure continuous improvement, such as business process re-engineering and total quality management.

These trends are illustrated in three typical generations of contract for support services depicted in Figures 2a–c. Figure 2a shows an arrangement where contracts have been let for individual services with overall management of the support function remaining in-house. In Figure 2b a single contract has been awarded covering all support tasks, with overall responsibility for the service resting with the contractor but with the vertical lines of accountability essentially unchanged. Figure 2c represents a further development, with the service provider directly accountable to end users and with central control restricted to strategic and policy matters. In the third case depicted, the support organization has been established as a joint venture between the supplier and the strategic customer with additional benefits deriving from the development of business with external users.

KEY ISSUES AND CONSIDERATIONS

Whether the task to be outsourced represents a complete activity of strategic importance or a minor support task, similar issues and considerations will arise. These range from the way in which the scope of the task and associated success criteria are defined to the way in which the project is managed and staff issues handled. In addressing these issues, it should be remembered that outsourcing represents a change process that will have implications falling outside of the areas directly involved. If outsourcing is handled well, the effects of the process can be harnessed as part of a wider strategy of cultural change. If the process is not handled well, the wider negative effects may outweigh the direct benefits sought.

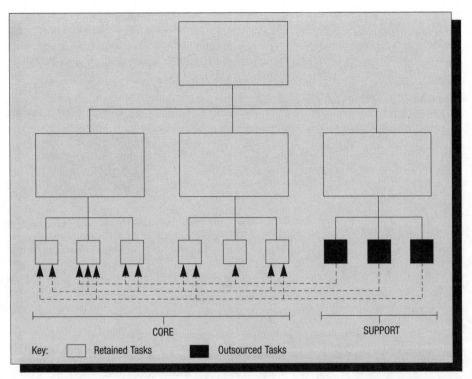

Figure 2a Single task support service contracts (overall management retained)

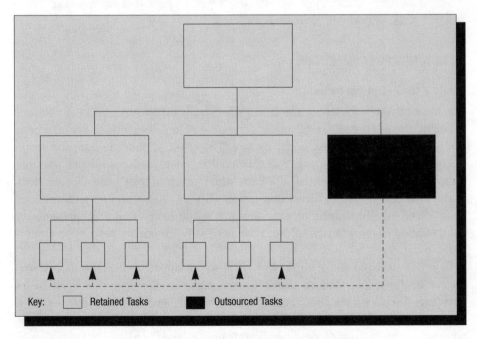

Figure 2b Comprehensive multiple task support contract

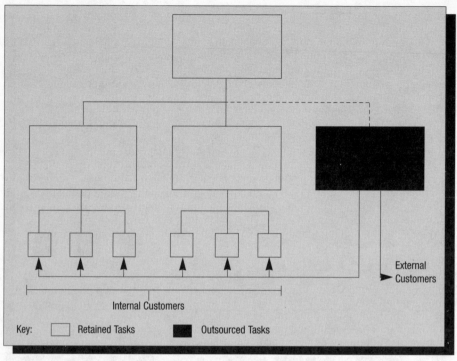

Figure 2c Establishment of support services as an outsourced business unit

The following paragraphs identify the main factors to be considered and suggest some underlying principles.

STRUCTURING FOR COMPETITION

Create a clear strategic focus

The most common reason for the failure of centrally driven outsourcing initiatives to realize the full benefits available is delegation of key decisions to a level where vested interests begin to enter the picture. The effect of this is to limit the scope of the contract before a proper evaluation has been made of all the possible options. It also places potential suppliers, who may already be providing services in the area concerned, in direct discussion with managers who may themselves be affected by the award of a contract. The difficulty that this presents is compounded if the activity selected for review is known to have been under-performing.

In order to avoid these difficulties it is important to undertake a strategic review of the activity before decisions are made on the scope of work to be outsourced. This review should report at the highest level and be conducted by a team of people who are able to determine the success criteria for the project but who are personally unaffected by the outcome of the review. The team should examine every option for delivering the service and evaluate the cost benefits available from each. The team also provides an essential point of contact for potential suppliers who can present alternatives to the present methods of service delivery without alienating people in the customer organization with whom they have long-established working relationships.

Sort out the buyers and the sellers

The strategic review is made simpler if the organization is already structured in a way that distinguishes between those responsible for purchasing or commissioning services and those responsible for their delivery. This implies the existence of a clear customer/supplier relationship with defined service levels and readily identifiable costs. If this essential separation of functions is not already present then it will be the first task of the review to establish the baseline of performance and costs against which the success of the project can be measured.

Fund outputs not organizations

Whatever the outcome of the strategic review, the introduction of a clear focus on performance and costs will contribute to the future direction and management of the service. By shifting the basis of funding from organizations and inputs to process outputs and service outcomes, the review will move the balance of presumption away from the status quo and create a climate in which change is the norm. The result will be a service delivery system that is better able to respond to changes in the nature and volume of the requirement and more open to innovation and new working methods.

Define the role of end users

It is important at this point to consider the role to be played by end users in determining the arrangements for providing the service and in its ongoing management.

Often a balance must be struck between control over capital investment and other strategic factors and decisions that affect the way in which the service is delivered to operational units in the business. Taking asset maintenance as an example, it may be appropriate for operational departments to decide on the levels and frequency of routine maintenance and whether or not work should be carried out during normal hours (and to account for the cost implications of their decisions), but there is no point in delegating responsibility for initiating substantial upgrades with a payback of several years if operational units are working to annual budgets.

These decisions about who controls the quality, volume and timing of the services will determine the role to be played by end users in the management of the outsourcing project, the way in which interfaces are drawn and the arrangements for ongoing direction and review of the service. It is common for the interests of end users to be neglected during the early stages of outsourcing projects, costing valuable time and effort during the implementation phase while operational managers or other key interests are brought on board.

ESTABLISH CLEAR OBJECTIVES

Before detailed work begins on any outsourcing project it is essential to clarify the aim of the exercise and the nature of the improvements sought. To embark upon a costly and time-consuming procurement process without having first established the basis upon which eventual decisions will be made opens the way to delay and confusion at critical stages in the project. And without clear aims and success criteria, communication of the plan to key interests such as end users, staff and unions is much more difficult.

This is not to say that every aspect of the evaluation criteria that will be used to select the supplier must be agreed in advance of the procurement process. But senior managers responsible for acquiring the service must state clearly what it is they want to accomplish and provide broad guidelines on the way possible solutions will be judged. This provides a basis for dialogue with potential suppliers and, when the time comes, for communicating details of the project to those who may be affected by the outcome.

Some of the key questions to be addressed in formulating this management strategy are as follows:

- How efficient is the present operation? In what areas can improvements be made? How does the operation compare with industry norms and other benchmarks?
- Are we looking for short-term cost savings or do we seek long-term value for money? If value for money is the objective, how will this be measured? Over what period must the project show a return, and how will this be calculated.
- Do we want to secure a step change in performance or are we seeking progressive improvement (or a combination of these)? If the objective is continuous improvement, how will this be measured and what incentives arrangements should apply?
- Does the present operation represent an asset or a liability? Are there under-utilized assets that could be exploited (capital assets, skills and know-how, intellectual property)?
- What are our intentions regarding staff currently employed to provide the service? Does their future lie with the existing organization or with the contractor? What are the implications of each course for both continuity of expertise and employment prospects for staff?
- How do we expect the service to develop in the future? What effect will this have on current skills and capacity? How will these changes be accommodated in our relationship with a supplier?

- How does this outsourcing project fit into the corporate strategy of the organization as a whole? Must decisions be co-ordinated with other developments for technical, planning or change management reasons?

INVOLVE POTENTIAL SUPPLIERS

The outputs from the key activities described above – the strategic review of the service and development of a clear management strategy for outsourcing – provide the basis for consultation with potential suppliers whose views should be sought before decisions are made on the scope and nature of the detailed requirement or the manner in which the service will be procured. While it may seem obvious to seek views from those who will be asked to develop proposals for providing the service, it is surprising how often organizations embark upon outsourcing projects without a clear view of how potential suppliers would approach the task.

In order to gain maximum benefit from the dialogue with potential suppliers it should be established as a formal stage in the project and supported with appropriate information and resources – a series of unstructured discussions can be as unhelpful as no consultation at all. In most cases, it will be appropriate to prepare a briefing document setting out the broad scope of service, the nature of the improvements sought and the success criteria to be applied. This provides a sound basis on which to identify potential suppliers and obtain their inputs to the project.

The brief should identify the key questions to which answers are sought and indicate the extent to which the customer is open to alternative methods of service provision. Wherever possible, it should include an assessment of the strengths and weaknesses of the present arrangements and identify the competencies that the customer believes are required in order to improve the service. Areas of critical concern to the customer should also be identified.

For some requirements, preparing a list of potential suppliers to be consulted may seem straightforward, based upon the organization's previous experience of outsourcing and its knowledge of the market. For projects involving new areas or where substantial changes are sought in the way the service is to be performed, it will be necessary actively to *market the requirement* so as to encourage organizations with the right competencies to take an interest. In any event, it is easy to be complacent about the merits of an existing supplier base and to miss the opportunity to introduce a new player who may bring fresh ideas to the table.

Remember, even with suppliers with whom there is a long established relationship, the project needs to be packaged and 'sold' so as to secure the best ideas and thinking available. In some cases suppliers will need to form an alliance or joint venture in order to satisfy the requirement. Establishing these arrangements takes time, and suppliers need time to develop an understanding of the skills and capabilities they will need to mount a successful bid.

DEFINE ROLES, RESPONSIBILITIES AND INTERFACES

When the views of potential suppliers have been obtained, the project team can begin to define in detail the scope of the service to be supplied, to determine the respective roles and responsibilities of the customer and supplier organizations and to design the key management interfaces and arrangements for controlling and monitoring the contract. This requires clear thinking if the new structure is not to replicate inefficiencies that exist in the existing arrangements, and care should be taken to avoid premature assumptions about the solutions likely to be offered by suppliers or about the residual organization that will be needed to manage the contract.

A useful approach to determining the role to be played by each party is to prepare a high level process chart identifying the principal activities involved in the delivery of the service, and to define for each stage in the process the key variables and risks to be managed. Figure 3 shows a typical high level chart for an asset maintenance activity, starting with asset creation and upkeep policy and extending through the formulation of maintenance programmes and specification of tasks to the assessment of work and payment of bills. The chart provides a useful framework for determining the skills and experience needed for successful performance and hence the involvement of each party in the process stages.

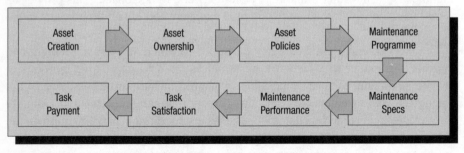

Figure 3 Asset maintenance sequence

Once roles and responsibilities have been defined, and before deciding finally on structures and interfaces, it is important to consider the way in which the contract will be controlled and monitored. A typical structure for a task contract is shown in Figure 4. The customer's strategic management team (or client unit) is shown at the top with the contractor reporting to the client unit and taking full responsibility for the delivery of specified services to the end customers shown at the foot of the diagram. Direct monitoring of service performance should be the responsibility of the contractor, who demonstrates the quality and levels of service provided by means of regular management reports and reviews. This should be the primary means by which the contractor's day-to-day performance is judged.

226

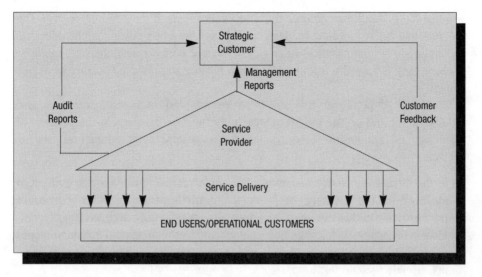

Figure 4 Control and monitoring arrangements

The client unit will also wish to be satisfied that the operation conforms to specific requirements in terms of technical standards, financial accounting, legal obligations, and so on, but the emphasis should be on joint, post-event audit and not on direct, real-time monitoring of the service. The client unit should, however, obtain an unbiased view of the *overall effect of the service* by means of regular feedback from end customers. This can be obtained in conjunction with the contractor, but it should be done in a way that is independent of the day-to-day operation of the service.

Structures such as that depicted in Figure 4 have been used to control activities involving substantial operating costs with minimum duplication of effort across the customer/supplier interface. As a guide to what can be achieved, one service operation involving an annual spend of £50m is operated in this way with a permanent client unit of five full-time staff, supported on a part-time basis by specialist and consultancy resources as required.

The key to achieving these levels of efficiency is to examine the total cost of the service, including related management costs incurred within the customer organization, and to set targets for the total cost of operating the service (i.e. the *total acquisition cost*). Organizations that do not keep track of the total acquisition cost of the service generally miss an opportunity to secure an element of available cost benefits.

REMEMBER THE HUMAN DIMENSION

Having defined the interfaces between the customer and supplier, the project team can assess the impact of the new structure on the existing staff and begin to prepare the ground for changes that are likely to result. Depending on how the process has been handled to date, staff may already be feeling considerable uncertainty over their future. In any case, a clear communications plan must be in place by the time the intention to invite bids or to award a contract becomes known.

Much will depend on the policy to be adopted over staff transfers and redeployment and on the extent to which staff will be involved in the process of selecting and appointing a contractor. Some points to be considered are as follows:

● Is the business case for improving the performance of the service evident to staff? Will outsourcing be seen to contribute to broader corporate performance and is the need for improvement generally accepted?
● How is the rationale for selecting outsourcing as the preferred option to be put across? Does the process relate to wider corporate initiatives whose objectives are already well understood?
● What are the immediate concerns of staff in the area to be outsourced and in the residual organization? To what extent can assurances be given in advance of the appointment of the selected contractor?
● What rights and obligations exist under the relevant employment laws (such as those arising from the EC Acquired Rights Directive) and how will these be accommodated?
● What obligations arise under trade union or other collective agreements and what arrangements are planned for consultation with staff and their elected representatives?

It is important that potential suppliers are given an opportunity to comment on aspects of the communications/consultation plan that anticipate the selected contractors' approach on staff matters, and care must be taken to ensure that information provided to staff during the consultation stage does not conflict with other requirements that are placed on the contractor.

SELECT THE RIGHT CONTRACTOR

The important thing to remember about choosing a contractor to provide an ongoing service is the long-term nature of the relationship. Task contracts of five years duration are no longer uncommon, but even if a contract runs for three years there is much that can change in this timescale that cannot fully be anticipated at the time the contract is let. A service contract must therefore by its nature represent a partnership between the customer and supplier, and care should be taken to select a supplier who will fit in with the culture of the organization and who can meet the customers' long-term needs as well as satisfy short-term requirements.

In addition to the normal technical and financial criteria, the following points should be considered when assessing how well a supplier will meet the longer term needs of the organization:

- How well do they understood our corporate aims and objectives? Do they appreciate the trends and pressures that will drive our business over the coming years, and will they have the foresight, innovation and flexibility to work with us to achieve our corporate goals?
- Have they understood the wider issues surrounding the task to be outsourced? Has the bid team explored the upstream and downstream effects of their proposal and does it reflect a systematic approach to meeting our requirements? Does the proposed solution add value to our processes or simply meet the defined tasks?
- Who are the driving forces behind the supplier's proposals and will they still be around once the contract has been let? Are they people with whom we can develop a long-term strategy for the services? What structures and mechanisms do they propose to put in place to ensure that long-term issues are addressed?
- What skills and capabilities is the supplier able to draw upon in meeting future needs that are not reflected in the current requirement? How will these be accessed and on what basis will they be made available? Does the supplier have management competencies that will substantially strengthen our business position?

The weighting placed upon these factors will vary from organization to organization, but assessing suppliers on their potential to contribute to the business in the longer term will, at the very least, provide valuable information about the quality and depth of their management.

MAINTAIN COMPETITIVE PRESSURE

Last, but perhaps above all, it is essential no matter how close the working relationship with the supplier to ensure that competitive pressure is applied to every part of the service delivery system. There are different ways of achieving this. Competitive tendering is one method, and this has proved highly successful in delivering cost benefits over successive retendering exercises, but it is not necessarily the only answer. The following approaches might also be considered:

- Continuous performance comparisons between parallel contracts covering similar requirements in, for example, different geographic areas.
- Untying of end users from the service (wholly or in part) to introduce customer choice and place the contractor in continuous competition with other sources of supply.
- Different forms of benchmarking to demonstrate the cost-effectiveness of the service in relation to corporate, national and world standards.

These approaches are not mutually exclusive, and a combination of ongoing competition with periodic retendering will be appropriate for many organizations. The only rule is that competition must be real, it must be sustained, and it must reach every aspect of the service.

CONCLUSION

The market for outsourced services is developing rapidly in most countries of the developed world. Traditionally distinctions between 'core' and 'non-core' services are being challenged as many organizations pass to suppliers the responsibility for performing tasks that form an essential part of their business processes. The question today is not so much 'what functions must we retain?' but 'where can we gain competitive advantage by engaging the skills and capabilities of others?'.

This competency-based approach gives rise to networked organizations founded on contractual relationships rather than ownership and vertical control, and on strategic alliance and partnership rather than detailed specification and tight contract enforcement. But at the end of the day a supplier must deliver a sound and responsive operational performance before attention can be turned to the longer term needs of the customer.

The key is to strike the right balance between short-term objectives and long-term goals. This requires a clear strategic focus coupled with thorough preparation and meticulous planning, with arrangements for periodic review of the resulting outsourced operation and for re-competition of the service at appropriate intervals. This approach is summarized in Figure 5. Potential suppliers can play an important role in both the strategic review and the detailed planning stages. They are able to draw on a wide experience of outsourcing projects and their views should always be sought before key decisions are made.

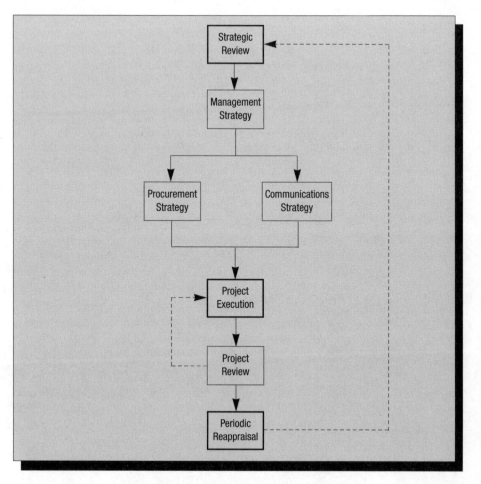

Figure 5 Framework for strategic planning and review

Appendix A: Illustrative project plan

This extract from a real project shows the breadth and depth required for a large procurement. It is not the complete plan and will include some elements not appropriate to all such projects. More to the point it will not cover all aspects of procurement projects due to the varied circumstances.

Note that:

- The first column indicates the activity, event or milestone.
- The second column indicates likely elapsed time. The example comes from a very large procurement and the elapsed times shown here indicate a great deal of work that may not be necessary for less complex or valuable procurements. Note that 'elapsed time' is a function of inputs and delivery dates and does not reflect the effort needed to do the task.
- The last column indicates the identified deliverables.
- Explanatory comments or observations are shown in square brackets.

Task	Elapsed time	Deliverables
Co-ordinating team		
Establish co-ordinating team	6 days	Publish team names in Project Newsletter
Establish working protocols	5 days	File protocol descriptions in Project Handbook
Scope project	4 days	Policy paper – file in project library
Confirm bid principles	1 day	Policy paper – file in project library
Strategy test		
Brief selected suppliers for informal response	18 days	No formal deliverable required
Receive supplier informal responses	11 days	File responses in project library
Visit to referees	11 days	Visit reports – file in project library
Review supplier informal responses	10 days	Report – review of supplier responses
Determine viability of strategy	4 days	Report – viability of strategy
Determine number of likely partners	milestone	No formal deliverable required
Project planning		
Develop project plan	10 days	Project plan – circulate/file in project library
Refine and agree plan	9 days	Project plan – circulate/file in project library
Agree resource requirements	9 days	No formal deliverable required
Commit to agreed resource requirements	6 days	Minutes of senior management meeting
Commit to agreed plan	18 days	Minutes of senior management meeting
Supplier capabilities		
Supplier capabilities	8 days	No formal deliverable required
Compare capabilities with deliverables	4 days	No formal deliverable required
Report on supplier capabilities	4 days	Report – supplier capabilities
Develop paper re. internal bids	11 days	Report – internal bids
Data collection – establish working protocol		
Assign responsibilities	7 days	File names in Project Handbook
Set individual terms of reference	7 days	File terms of reference in Project Handbook
Set reporting arrangements	4 days	File reporting arrangements in Project Handbook
Corporate policies – establish working protocol		
Assign responsibilities	7 days	File names in Project Handbook
Set individual terms of reference	6 days	File terms of reference in Project Handbook
Set reporting arrangements	6 days	File reporting arrangements in Project Handbook
Communications		
Develop strategy to manage staff communications	5 days	Policy paper – circulate management team/file in project library
Prepare trade union policy	7 days	Policy paper – file in project library
Prepare defensive management initiative	44 days	Policy paper – circulate management team/file in project library
Develop strategy to manage press and supplier communications	33 days	Policy paper – circulate management team/file in project library
Objectives and deliverables		
Determine objectives and deliverables for suppliers	6 days	No formal deliverable required
Document deliverables and objectives	4 days	Policy paper – file in project library

Task	Elapsed time	Deliverables
Principal working mechanisms		
Determine supplier/management interfaces	8 days	Policy paper – file in project library
Research existing performance reporting mechanisms	21 days	No formal deliverable required
Evaluate existing performance reporting mechanisms	15 days	No formal deliverable required
Develop required performance reporting mechanisms	0 days	Policy paper – file in project library
Research existing change control mechanisms	11 days	No formal deliverable required
Evaluate existing change control mechanisms	2 days	No formal deliverable required
Develop required change control mechanisms	5 days	Policy paper – file in project library
Future skill set		
Develop future skill set requirements	milestone	Policy paper – file in project library
Research performance improvements initiatives		
Identify internal performance improvement initiatives	3 days	No formal deliverable required
Quantify targeted benefits for IPI initiatives	8 days	Policy paper – file in project library
Assess impact of supplier involvement on initiatives, projects and procurements	milestone	Policy paper – file in project library
Research projects		
Identify current and planned projects	4 days	No formal deliverable required
Identify key cost components and value	12 days	No formal deliverable required
Report circumstances – current and future projects	milestone	Policy paper – file in project library
Research procurements		
Identify current and planned procurements	8 days	No formal deliverable required
Identify key cost components and value	14 days	No formal deliverable required
Report circumstances – current and future procurements	milestone	Policy paper – file in project library
Management of staff briefings		
Devise process for attitude counselling managers	3 days	Policy paper – file in project library
Agree annual conference theme	3 days	No formal deliverable required
Invite internal delegates for conference	8 days	No formal deliverable required
Formulate agenda for conference (speakers and schedule)	milestone	Publish agenda in Project Newsletter
Obtain speaker scripts for conference	2 days	No formal deliverable required
Key milestone – confirm to proceed	1 day	No formal deliverable required
Produce speaker visual support for conference	1 day	No formal deliverable required
Rehearse speakers for conference	1 day	No formal deliverable required
Annual conference	1 day	No formal deliverable required
Key milestone – data collection	milestone	No formal deliverable required
Key milestone – policies and principles	milestone	No formal deliverable required
Key milestone – tenders selected	milestone	No formal deliverable required
Key milestone – preferred supplier selected	milestone	No formal deliverable required
Key milestone – contract agreed	milestone	No formal deliverable required

Task	Elapsed time	Deliverables
Key milestone – contract signed	milestone	No formal deliverable required
Key milestone – partnership start date	milestone	No formal deliverable required
Staff expectation and anxiety		
Devise monitoring and reporting process	5 days	Policy paper – file in project library
Month 1 – monitor and report staff condition	5 days	Report of results – circulate to management team
Counsel managers to respond	milestone	No formal deliverable required
Month 2 – monitor and report staff condition	5 days	Report of results – circulate to management team
Counsel managers to respond	milestone	No formal deliverable required
Month 3 – monitor and report staff condition	5 days	Report of results – circulate to management team
Counsel managers to respond	milestone	No formal deliverable required
Month 4 – monitor and report staff condition	5 days	Report of results – circulate to management team
Counsel managers to respond	milestone	No formal deliverable required
Month 5 – monitor and report staff condition	5 days	Report of results – circulate to management team
Counsel managers to respond	milestone	No formal deliverable required
Month 6 – monitor and report staff condition	5 days	Report of results – circulate to management team
Counsel managers to respond	milestone	No formal deliverable required
Month 7 – monitor and report staff condition	5 days	Report of results – circulate to management team
Counsel managers to respond	milestone	No formal deliverable required
Month 8 – monitor and report staff condition	5 days	Report of results – circulate to management team
Counsel managers to respond	milestone	No formal deliverable required [The management in this procurement decided to canvass the views of staff regularly to gauge morale – the above activities show a cyclical process of review and report.]
Constituency management		
August review	milestone	Minutes of meeting/file in project library
September review	milestone	Minutes of meeting/file in project library
October review	milestone	Minutes of meeting/file in project library
November review	milestone	Minutes of meeting/file in project library
December review	milestone	Minutes of meeting/file in project library
January review	milestone	Minutes of meeting/file in project library
February review	milestone	Minutes of meeting/file in project library
March review	milestone	Minutes of meeting/file in project library
April review	milestone	Minutes of meeting/file in project library
May review	milestone	Minutes of meeting/file in project library
June review	milestone	Minutes of meeting/file in project library [Elsewhere we suggest that constituency management is part of any regular meeting. In this project, special meetings were convened to consider constituency management.]

Task	Elapsed time	Deliverables
Data collection – training dept		
Identify current costs	39 days	Draft schedule for service requirement
Identify current workload	13 days	Draft schedule for service requirement
Identify current service schedules	13 days	Draft schedule for service requirement
Identify future costs	13 days	Draft schedule for service requirement
Identify future workload	13 days	Draft schedule for service requirement
Identify scale of internal performance improvement	9 days	Draft schedule for service requirement
Establish hardware inventory	11 days	Draft schedule for service requirement
Establish software inventory	11 days	Draft schedule for service requirement
Establish inventory of proprietary 'products'	11 days	Draft schedule for service requirement
Establish inventory of training materials	11 days	Draft schedule for service requirement
Establish communications inventory	34 days	Draft schedule for service requirement
Establish inventory of accommodation	11 days	Draft schedule for service requirement
Establish inventory of environmental equipment	11 days	Draft schedule for service requirement
Establish inventory of fixtures and office equipment	11 days	Draft schedule for service requirement
Establish inventory of consumables and stocks	11 days	Draft schedule for service requirement
Establish staff register	10 days	Draft schedule for service requirement
Establish inventory of third party agreements	11 days	Draft schedule for service requirement
Establish inventory of internal agreements	11 days	Draft schedule for service requirement
Bring together all work schedules	milestone	Finalized schedules for service requirement
Data collection – data preparation dept		
Identify current costs	80 days	Draft schedule for service requirement
Identify current workload	88 days	Draft schedule for service requirement
Identify current service schedules	88 days	Draft schedule for service requirement
Identify future costs	11 days	Draft schedule for service requirement
Identify future workload	11 days	Draft schedule for service requirement
Identify software maintenance requirement	76 days	Draft schedule for service requirement
Identify scale of internal performance improvement	11 days	Draft schedule for service requirement
Establish hardware inventory	93 days	Draft schedule for service requirement
Establish software inventory	14 days	Draft schedule for service requirement
Establish inventory of proprietary products	14 days	Draft schedule for service requirement
Establish communications inventory	72 days	Draft schedule for service requirement
Establish inventory of accommodation	72 days	Draft schedule for service requirement
Establish inventory of environmental equipment	72 days	Draft schedule for service requirement
Establish inventory of fixtures and office equipment	72 days	Draft schedule for service requirement
Establish inventory of consumables and stocks	72 days	Draft schedule for service requirement
Establish staff register	11 days	Draft schedule for service requirement
Establish inventory of third party agreements	72 days	Draft schedule for service requirement
Establish inventory of internal agreements	72 days	Draft schedule for service requirement
Bring together all work schedules	milestone	Finalized schedules for service requirement

237

Task	Elapsed time	Deliverables
Data collection – computer services dept		
Identify current costs	15 days	Draft schedule for service requirement
Identify current workload	15 days	Draft schedule for service requirement
Identify current service schedules	15 days	Draft schedule for service requirement
Identify future costs	11 days	Draft schedule for service requirement
Identify future workload	11 days	Draft schedule for service requirement
Identify scale of internal performance improvement	11 days	Draft schedule for service requirement
Establish hardware inventory	14 days	Draft schedule for service requirement
Establish software inventory	14 days	Draft schedule for service requirement
Establish inventory of proprietary 'products'	14 days	Draft schedule for service requirement
Establish communications inventory	14 days	Draft schedule for service requirement
Establish inventory of accommodation	14 days	Draft schedule for service requirement
Establish inventory of environmental equipment	14 days	Draft schedule for service requirement
Establish inventory of fixtures and office equipment	14 days	Draft schedule for service requirement
Establish inventory of consumables and stocks	14 days	Draft schedule for service requirement
Establish staff register	11 days	Draft schedule for service requirement
Establish inventory of third party agreements	24 days	Draft schedule for service requirement
Establish inventory of internal agreements	14 days	Draft schedule for service requirement
Establish historical profile of hardware usage	11 days	Draft schedule for service requirement
Establish profile of future hardware requirements	11 days	Draft schedule for service requirement
Bring together all work schedules	milestone	Finalized schedules for service requirement
Data collection – external sites		
Identify current costs	82 days	Draft schedule for service requirement
Identify current workload	83 days	Draft schedule for service requirement
Identify current service schedules	83 days	Draft schedule for service requirement
Identify future costs	1 day	Draft schedule for service requirement
Identify future workload	1 day	Draft schedule for service requirement
Identify scale of internal performance improvement	1 day	Draft schedule for service requirement
Establish hardware inventory	72 days	Draft schedule for service requirement
Establish software inventory	72 days	Draft schedule for service requirement
Establish inventory of proprietary 'products'	72 days	Draft schedule for service requirement
Establish communications inventory	72 days	Draft schedule for service requirement
Establish inventory of accommodation	1 day	Draft schedule for service requirement
Establish inventory of environmental equipment	1 day	Draft schedule for service requirement
Establish inventory of fixtures and office equipment	1 day	Draft schedule for service requirement
Establish inventory of consumables and stocks	1 day	Draft schedule for service requirement
Establish staff register	1 day	Draft schedule for service requirement
Establish inventory of third party agreements	1 day	Draft schedule for service requirement
Establish inventory of internal agreements	1 day	Draft schedule for service requirement

Task	Elapsed time	Deliverables
Establish historical profile of hardware usage	1 day	Draft schedule for service requirement
Establish profile of future hardware requirements	1 day	Draft schedule for service requirement
Bring together all work schedules	milestone	Finalized schedules for service requirement
Formulate policy		
Determine charging approach	10 days	Policy paper – file in project library
Termination and indemnity requirements	10 days	Policy paper – file in project library
Penalty/performance reward clauses	10 days	Policy paper – file in project library
Determine legal obligations/constraints	10 days	Policy paper – file in project library
Supplier/board representation	58 days	Policy paper – file in project library
Nature of supplier funding requirements	10 days	Policy paper – file in project library
Guidance document re. conflicts of interest	19 days	Policy paper – file in project library
Security requirements		
Determine security requirements	9 days	Policy paper – file in project library
Draft contract terms	9 days	Policy paper – file in project library
Service agreements		
Background statement on service agreements	milestone	Policy paper – file in project library
Collect copies of existing service agreements	17 days	File copies
Review existing service agreements	21 days	No formal deliverables
Produce pro forma service agreements	7 days	Draft schedule for service requirement
Redundancy policy		
Generate full staff lists, by cost centre	24 days	Draft schedule for service requirement
Identify current redundancy rules	28 days	No formal deliverable required
Identify current redundancy costs	1 day	No formal deliverable required
Consider redundancy circumstances	23 days	No formal deliverable required
Develop outsourcing rules and policy statement	milestone	Policy paper – file in project library
The tender process – expression of interest		
Develop advert (to minimize inappropriate responses)	17 days	File copy of advertisement
Prepare press statement for release prior to advert	1 day	File copy of press statement
Advertise for expressions of interest	24 days	No formal deliverable required
Develop process for dealing with excluded suppliers	44 days	Policy paper – file in project library
Identify issues for clarification with suppliers	3 days	No formal deliverable required
Meet suppliers to clarify issues	6 days	No formal deliverable required
Prepare for supplier/reference site visits/reference visit packs	15 days	Visiting briefing pack
Evaluation visits (supplier/references)	15 days	No formal deliverable required
Finalize evaluation/write evaluation report	22 days	Report – file in project library
Selection panel meeting 1	1 day	Minutes of meeting/file in project library
Selection panel meeting 2	1 day	Minutes of meeting/file in project library
Finalize ITT timetable	31 days	Finalized timetable
Short-list recommendation to board	1 day	Report – recommendation
Refer recommendation to ministers	23 days	No formal deliverable required

Task	Elapsed time	Deliverables
Prepare process for announcing shortlist	22 days	Policy paper – file in project library
Notify suppliers	1 day	No formal deliverable required
Debrief unsuccessful suppliers	20 days	Minutes of meeting/file in project library
QA review of project library	43 days	Report – file in project library

The tender process – issue ITT

Task	Elapsed time	Deliverables
Release ITT to selected suppliers	milestone	No formal deliverable required
Brief suppliers on ITT	1 day	No formal deliverable required
Receive supplier's written questions	27 days	No formal deliverable required
Respond in writing to questions	27 days	File copies of response in project library
Prepare library pack of Qs & As	28 days	File copies of response in project library
Receive tender responses	milestone	File copies of response in project library

The tender process – prepare financial model

Task	Elapsed time	Deliverables
Prepare timetable	8 days	Timetable – for review by management
Contact external audit authority – define requirements	8 days	File record
Contact internal audit – define requirements	8 days	File record
Establish external interest in financial model	8 days	File record
Develop [conceptual/generic] financial model	10 days	File record
Circulate description of financial model	1 day	No formal deliverable required
Formal review (meeting) of financial model	1 day	Minutes of meeting/file in project library
Prepare paper – Skill mix/method of costing future workload	27 days	Policy paper – file in project library
Prepare paper – 10 year forecast workload scenarios	22 days	Policy paper – file in project library
Prepare paper – Superannuation	42 days	Policy paper – file in project library
Prepare paper – Tax effects – CT and VAT	27 days	Policy paper – file in project library
Prepare paper – Cash flow impact/retained capital forecasts	42 days	Policy paper – file in project library
Prepare paper – Cost of retained functions	42 days	Policy paper – file in project library
Prepare paper – Baseline severance costs	42 days	Policy paper – file in project library
Prepare paper – Profit sharing	4 days	Policy paper – file in project library
Prepare paper – Central overheads	13 days	Policy paper – file in project library
Prepare paper – Notional insurance	13 days	Policy paper – file in project library
Prepare paper – Estimate of variable costs	29 days	Policy paper – file in project library
Prepare paper – Base costs/allocation to tranches	13 days	Policy paper – file in project library
Prepare paper – Funding effect	13 days	Policy paper – file in project library
Prepare paper – Indexation	9 days	Policy paper – file in project library
Prepare paper for selection panel – Final evaluation overview	10 days	Policy paper – file in project library
Presentation of prototype model	6 days	File record/minutes of meeting
QA by finance division (certification of model)	18 days	File certificate in project library
Agree financial model with review group	milestone	Minutes of meeting/file in project library
Agree financial model with selection panel	8 days	Minutes of meeting/file in project library
Devise financial evaluation process (FEP)	10 days	Process description – circulate to management
Agree FEP with review group	6 days	Minutes of meeting/file in project library
Apply tender responses (under controlled conditions)	95 days	File record

Task	Elapsed time	Deliverables
Modelling team project plan	82 days	Append to Project Handbook
Update support files common to bids	10 days	Policy paper – file in project library
Retained function costs	8 days	Policy paper – file in project library
Future capital	8 days	Policy paper – file in project library
Redundancy costs – policy paper delivered	10 days	Policy paper – file in project library
Other adjustments – policy paper delivered	10 days	Policy paper – file in project library
Separation of capital – policy paper delivered	10 days	Policy paper – file in project library
Allocation to tranches – policy paper delivered	10 days	Policy paper – file in project library
Estimation of efficiency ratios	5 days	Report – copy to project library
Collect formulae	15 days	No formal deliverable required
Man year requirements	5 days	Policy paper – file in project library
Link between staff numbers and accommodation	7 days	Policy paper – file in project library
Hardware capital acquisition and disposal costs	7 days	Policy paper – file in project library
Maintenance and support costs	6 days	File record
Estimate of network costs	5 days	File record
Profile of variable costs	7 days	File record
Profile of other variable baseline costs	7 days	File record
Sharing performance gains	4 days	Policy paper – file in project library
Supplier 1 – core model/base bid: ASC/FSC/SCR components	5 days	File record
Supplier 1 – re. model/base bid: indexation	5 days	File record
Supplier 1 – detailed model: scenarios	9 days	File record
Supplier 1 – detailed model: amortization formulae	6 days	File record
Supplier 1 – detailed model: minimum charges	10 days	File record
Supplier 1 – detailed model: adjustments (following PfCs response)	6 days	File record
Supplier 1 – analyse Supplier 1 bid against ITT costs	6 days	File record
Supplier 1 – non-standard bid: re-align ITT costs	20 days	File record
Supplier 1 – non-standard bid: detailed model	6 days	File record
Supplier 1 – present initial results to financial evaluation team	1 day	File record
Supplier 1 – prepare report (Supplier 1 only) for core evaluation team	6 days	File record
Supplier 2 – return of PfCs	milestone	File record
Detailed model: adjustments (with PfCs response)	16 days	File record
Present initial results to financial evaluation team	25 days	Report – circulate to management
Adjust results	6 days	No formal deliverable required
Prepare report for core evaluation team	25 days	Report – circulate to management
Present results to core evaluation team	milestone	Minutes of meeting/file in project library
Funding effect estimates	6 days	Report – circulate to management
Model documentation	28 days	File record
Internal audit verification of model	68 days	Report – copy to project library

241

Task	Elapsed time	Deliverables
Final QA to confirm fitness for purpose	14 days	Report – copy to project library
The tender process – review third party agreements		
Finalize initial review of major third party agreements	48 days	No formal deliverable required
Identify full list of third party agreements	57 days	No formal deliverable required
Identify third party agreements to be assigned	86 days	No formal deliverable required
Establish plan of action	57 days	Timetable for circulation
Execute plan of action	105 days	No formal deliverable required
Finalize review of all third party agreements	12 days	Report – circulate to management
The tender process – evaluation management		
Release draft score and table evaluation spreadsheets	2 days	File record
Check construction of score and table evaluation spreadsheets	61 days	No formal deliverable required
Finalize score and table evaluation spreadsheets	17 days	No formal deliverable required
Release draft reference questionnaire spreadsheets	2 days	No formal deliverable required
Review draft reference questionnaire spreadsheets	30 days	No formal deliverable required
Develop process for selecting referees	4 days	Policy paper
Finalize reference questionnaire spreadsheets	2 days	No formal deliverable required
Release draft of span of technical resource spreadsheets	2 days	No formal deliverable required
Validate and check construction of span of technical resource spreadsheet	66 days	No formal deliverable required
Finalize span of technical resource spreadsheet	10.5 days	File record
Release draft primary reference questionnaire	13 days	File record
Finalize primary reference questionnaire	4 days	File record
Finalize supplemental reference questionnaire	13 days	File record
Finalize supplemental reference questionnaire process	13 days	File record
Finalize reference team conventions	13 days	File record
Devise composition of reference selection team	10 days	File record
Finalize composition of reference selection team	2 days	File record
Devise process for key negotiating issues	13 days	File record
Finalize process for key negotiating issues	4 days	File record
Devise process for procurement issues (ITT)	20 days	File record
Finalize process for procurement issues (ITT)	3 days	File record
Identify required external expertise	44 days	No formal deliverable required
Confirm availability of technology for evaluation	28 days	File record

Task	Elapsed time	Deliverables
Devise documentation of decisions mechanism	11 days	No formal deliverable required
Finalize documentation of decisions mechanism	6 days	File record
Devise and finalize requirements and means for audit verification	20 days	File record
Devise format for final audit trail document	12 days	File record
Finalize format for final audit trail document	46 days	File record
Prepare final version of yellow book	12 days	File record
Finalize yellow book	6 days	Report – circulate to management
Agree yellow book	milestone	No formal deliverable required
Prepare outline for final evaluation report	13 days	File record
Finalize outline for final evaluation report	milestone	No formal deliverable required
Agree outline for final evaluation report	milestone	File record
Prepare mechanism for ex client references	11 days	No formal deliverable required
Finalize mechanism for ex client references	milestone	No formal deliverable required
Agree mechanism for ex client references	milestone	File record
Evaluation and report		
Develop assessment approach and mechanism	37 days	No formal deliverable required
Review of costs and allied statements	87 days	Report: file in project library
Valuation of assets	44 days	Report: file in project library
Prepare for selection panel meeting	21 days	No formal deliverable required
Establish embargo(s) on tender distribution	7 days	No formal deliverable required
Distribute ITT responses to evaluation team	milestone	No formal deliverable required
Prepare detailed index of the tenders (not required)	5 days	Report: file in project library
Prepare precis of standard/non-standard bids (not required)	5 days	Report: file in project library
Identify issues for clarification/investigation	19 days	No formal deliverable required
Identify reference team issues for clarification/investigation	8 days	No formal deliverable required
Identify financial issues for clarification/ investigation	8 days	No formal deliverable required
Identify security/confidentiality issues for clarification/investigation	8 days	No formal deliverable required
Collect issues for clarification/investigation from others	19 days	Report: file in project library
Examine non-standard bids – impact assessment on policies	2.5 days	Report: file in project library
Prepare for visits to referees/supplier sites/ guarantors	38 days	No formal deliverable required
Prepare new staff transfer paper – update policies	13 days	Report: file in project library
Selection panel meeting – issues arising/ education workshop	milestone	Minutes of meeting/file in project library
Conduct commercial stability assessments	38 days	Report: file in project library
Select references (by reference selection team)	11 days	No formal deliverable required
Take up references	19 days	No formal deliverable required
Meet suppliers for clarifications/ investigations	7 days	No formal deliverable required

Task	Elapsed time	Deliverables
Suppliers provide written clarifications [8 days]	milestone	No formal deliverable required
Visits to referees/supplier sites	5 days	No formal deliverable required
Visit guarantors	5 days	No formal deliverable required
Process completed questionnaires	32 days	Completed questionnaires – file in project library
Finalize reference spreadsheets	8 days	File record
Check/report documentation of references process	1 day	No formal deliverable required
Pass final reference evaluation results to core evaluation team	1 day	No formal deliverable required
Make arrangements – tenderers onto list 'X'	31 days	No formal deliverable required
Check/report documentation of security assessment process	1 day	File record
Pass final security evaluation results to core evaluation team	1 day	File record
Evaluate bids against adverse market conditions – risk assessment	30 days	File record
Prepare briefing and questions for suppliers (bid optimization)	17 days	No formal deliverable required
Check/report documentation of process re. commercial stability	1 day	No formal deliverable required
Conduct financial evaluation	46 days	No formal deliverable required
Test financial evaluation results	46 days	File record
Check documentation of final evaluation process/decisions	4 days	No formal deliverable required
Pass final financial evaluation results to core evaluation team	1 day	No formal deliverable required
Complete primary evaluation matrix	6 days	File record
Brief suppliers (bid optimization)	25 days	No formal deliverable required
Receive supplier written responses to briefing (bid optimization)	25 days	File record
Evaluate supplier written responses (bid optimization)	25 days	File record
Prepare preliminary evaluation report	6 days	No formal deliverable required
Publish commercial stability review	milestone	Report: file in project library
Core evaluation team presentation to full evaluation team	milestone	No formal deliverable required
Audit verification of overall results	55 days	File record
Publish commercial stability report	51 days	Report: file in project library
Refine evaluation report for selection panel	30 days	File record
Selection panel meeting – preliminary evaluation report	milestone	Minutes of meeting/file in project library
Selection panel meeting – briefing/ recommendation from evaluation team	milestone	Minutes of meeting/file in project library
Selection panel meeting – supplier presentations	milestone	Minutes of meeting/file in project library
Selection panel meeting – meeting 1	milestone	Minutes of meeting/file in project library
Clarify all outstanding issues [with 'supplier designate']	8 days	No formal deliverable required
Selection panel meeting – meeting 2	milestone	Minutes of meeting/file in project library
Ratification with board	20 days	File record
Selection panel meeting – meeting 3	milestone	Minutes of meeting/file in project library

Task	Elapsed time	Deliverables
Advise suppliers	1 day	No formal deliverable required
Debrief unsuccessful supplier	5 days	Minutes of meeting/file in project library
Audit review of evaluation of tenders	120 days	No formal deliverable required
Audit report: (a) Cross reference document (not required)	1 day	Report: circulate to management/file in project library
Audit report: (b) Collection and cross referencing	44 days	Report: circulate to management/file in project library
Audit report: (c) Identification of subject headings	44 days	Report: circulate to management/file in project library
Audit report: (d) Compilation of comprehensive index	44 days	Report: circulate to management/file in project library
Audit report: (e) Review of project papers	44 days	Report: circulate to management/file in project library
Audit report: (f) Placement of project documents	44 days	Report: circulate to management/file in project library
Audit report: (g) Record of subsumed documents	46 days	Report: circulate to management/file in project library
Audit report: (h) Timetable/prioritize library tasks	44 days	Report: circulate to management/file in project library
Audit report: (i) Agreed and allocate library responsibilities	44 days	Report: circulate to management/file in project library
Audit report: (j) Review project library resources	44 days	Report: circulate to management/file in project library
Audit report: (k) Advise new heading date procedures	44 days	Report: circulate to management/file in project library
Audit report: (l) Circulate author responsibilities	44 days	Report: circulate to management/file in project library
Audit report: (n) Implement security procedures for library	44 days	Report: circulate to management/file in project library
Audit report: (o) Review access and housing procedures	44 days	Report: circulate to management/file in project library
Audit review of project library/post evaluation	8 days	Report: circulate to management/file in project library

The tender process – security and confidentiality issues

Task	Elapsed time	Deliverables
Meet tenderers re. security and confidentiality issues	1 day	Minutes of meeting/file in project library
Prepare assurance certificates for selection panel	41 days	Assurance certificates/file copy to library

The tender process – commercial stability

Task	Elapsed time	Deliverables
Release draft template for evaluation of commercial stability	32 days	No formal deliverable required
Agree responsibility for completion of commercial stability work	1 day	No formal deliverable required
Agree draft template for evaluation of commercial stability	6 days	File record

Negotiation

Task	Elapsed time	Deliverables
Prepare paper – Negotiating team strategy	21 days	Policy paper – file in project library
Agree negotiating team strategy	1 day	No formal deliverable required
Establish negotiating team	18 days	No formal deliverable required
Establish back up team	18 days	No formal deliverable required
Produce draft terms and conditions	23 days	Negotiating document/file

245

APPENDIX A

Task	Elapsed time	Deliverables
Produce draft schedules	23 days	Negotiating document/file
Review financial remedies	23 days	No formal deliverable required
Review and confirm tranches profile	23 days	No formal deliverable required
Review and agree draft T&Cs and schedules	9 days	No formal deliverable required
Present Draft T&Cs and schedules to supplier	1 day	No formal deliverable required
Commence negotiations of T&Cs/schedules with preferred supplier	0.13 days	No formal deliverable required
Audit re-verification of costs/VFM	35 days	Report: file in project library
Audit review of contract negotiation	35 days	Report: file in project library
Agreement launch event		
Review launch process with prospective supplier	1 day	File record
Agree press release (internally)	1 day	File record
Agree press release with supplier	1 day	File record
Arrange signing ceremony	1 day	No formal deliverable required
Organize contract Day 1 event	8 days	No formal deliverable required

Appendix B: Sample reference questionnaire

Customer Company Ltd
[Department]

Assessing Proposals From

[ ]

Strategic Partnership Procurement

Reference Questionnaire
[ ]

[April 1996]

Customer Company Ltd Contact:
[   ]

0171 (Onshore)
+44 171 (Offshore)

Thank you for agreeing to help us with our procurement exercise and for giving time to the completion of our Questionnaire.

The department of [ ] at Customer Company Ltd employs over [ ] staff and supports [   ].

We are in the process of testing the market to see whether it is possible for us to engage, for a period of at least [ ] years, the services of a world class [ ] services company to help us achieve the following objectives:

- [A step improvement in value for money.
- Access to leading edge skills and tools.
- Optimize long-term opportunities for our staff.]

Customer Company Ltd seeks a relationship with its chosen supplier that has the characteristics of a 'partnership' and has the potential to endure for more than [ ] years.

Given this requirement and the need to meet some very demanding objectives, we would like to gain, in some detail, your perceptions of [bidding supplier] as a company and as a potential 'partner'.

Please be assured that the information you provide will be held by us in the strictest confidence and will not be shared with [bidding supplier]. We would be grateful if you would treat the information in a similar manner.

We have six primary areas of interest and they each form a section of the Questionnaire:

1. Relationship with customer.
2. Re-engineering capability.
3. Integration capability.
4. Ability to manage large-scale change programmes.
5. Ability to support multi-vendor environments.
6. Management of large-scale operational environments.

[ ] has nominated you specifically to provide information regarding section(s) [ ]. We would be grateful therefore if your primary focus could be directed to this section but would also be interested in your thoughts regarding any of the other sections if you feel able to give them.

We recognize that your response to many of the issues must necessarily be subjective and that, at best, you may be able to give only a broad indication of capability. Our evaluation process will take account of this and will ensure that the information you give will be interpreted with care.

In an attempt to save you time, simply ring the number which gives the best indication of performance as you judge it. In most cases 0 equals a poor perception of performance and 10 equals good.

Should you need to discuss any of the issues raised by this Questionnaire, please contact [   ] who will co-ordinate a response. The number is [   ].

Thank you again for your help.

Reference Questionnaire

Company Providing Reference

[ ]

_____

Name of Referee(s)   *Position*

--------------------   ----------
--------------------   ----------
--------------------   ----------

_____

Name of Customer Company Ltd
Evaluation Team Member(s)

--------------------   ----------
--------------------   ----------
--------------------   ----------

_____

Date of Interview

_____

SECTION 1: RELATIONSHIP WITH CUSTOMER

'Customer Relationship' will be examined under the following general headings:

Values

Those attributes of supplier organizations that guide the manner in which business is conducted and services are provided and that set the boundaries for professional and principled behaviour.

Corporate emphasis

An indication of the focus of supplier priorities as they relate to the deployment of resources and management attention.

Responsiveness

The manner in which suppliers respond to the varying needs of customers.

Reliability

The extent to which supplier performance, in all its aspects, is assured without undue customer intervention.

Consistency

The extent to which all aspects of supplier behaviour and performance can be predicted with certainty.

VALUES

(i) Trust/openness

0 1 2 3 4 5 6 7 8 9 10
Poor   Good

The extent to which the supplier has been shown to be open in its commercial dealings and dependable in conforming to its obligations and commitments.

(ii) Accommodating/flexible

0 1 2 3 4 5 6 7 8 9 10
Poor   Good

The extent to which the supplier has demonstrated a willingness to accommodate, without fuss, variations to plans, requirements or agreements of a non-commercial nature (i.e. variations do not affect the agreed price).

(iii) Commitment

0 1 2 3 4 5 6 7 8 9 10
Poor   Good

The extent to which the supplier has demonstrated an unequivocal commitment to, and focus upon, the business and service objectives of its client.

(iv) High standards of quality and service

0 1 2 3 4 5 6 7 8 9 10
Poor   Good

The extent to which the supplier sets for itself, and delivers, standards of service and quality above those likely to be required by its clients.

(v) Ethical

0 1 2 3 4 5 6 7 8 9 10
Poor   Good

The extent to which the supplier has set, and maintains, standards of behaviour and codes of practice that regulate and police the ethical behaviour of the corporation and its staff.

(vi) Maintenance of reputation/pride in organization

0 1 2 3 4 5 6 7 8 9 10
Poor   Good

The extent to which the supplier exhibits an awareness of its commercial reputation and a willingness to devote considerable effort to protect it.

(vii) Cultural maintenance

0 1 2 3 4 5 6 7 8 9 10
Poor   Good

The extent to which the supplier has a strong cultural identity and robust business processes for its maintenance and development.

CORPORATE EMPHASIS

(i) Customers

0 1 2 3 4 5 6 7 8 9 10
Poor   Good

The extent to which the supplier has focused its business processes and management thinking upon customer needs to the point where customers are conscious of the focus and feel its effects.

(ii) Staff

0 1 2 3 4 5 6 7 8 9 10
Poor   Good

The extent to which the supplier has established policies that assure effective staff development in a way that supports both its business and customer needs.

(iii) Delivery

0 1 2 3 4 5 6 7 8 9 10
Poor   Good

The extent to which the supplier has established a clear management focus upon delivery of services or projects to the point where customers understand the delivery mechanisms and have confidence in the delivery assurance monitoring and escalation arrangements.

(iv) Innovation

0 1 2 3 4 5 6 7 8 9 10
Poor   Good

The extent to which the supplier has demonstrated its ability and willingness to search for and provide innovative solutions even to the point where the solution proposed may fall outside the range of services offered by the supplier.

Negative

(v) Profit/shareholders

10 9 8 7 6 5 4 3 2 1 0
Poor   Good

The extent to which the supplier has demonstrated a tendency to put its requirements for profit ahead of customer needs rather than derive profit by meeting customer needs.

(vi) Quality (supported by robust audit arrangements)

0 1 2 3 4 5 6 7 8 9 10
Poor   Good

The extent to which the supplier has, or has not, committed itself to demonstrable quality standards and overt audit arrangements for their maintenance.

RESPONSIVENESS

(i) Speed of response

0 1 2 3 4 5 6 7 8 9 10
Poor   Good

The extent to which the supplier responds to issues and requirements within agreed parameters and without fuss.

(ii) Willingness to adapt

0 1 2 3 4 5 6 7 8 9 10
Poor   Good

The extent to which the supplier is able to react favourably to changes in circumstance or requirement.

(iii) Willingness to be inconvenienced

0 1 2 3 4 5 6 7 8 9 10
Poor   Good

The extent to which the supplier has demonstrated an ability to absorb, with good grace, a reasonable amount of unplanned work or compensate for customer deficiencies.

RELIABILITY

(i) Need for supervision/management

0 1 2 3 4 5 6 7 8 9 10
Poor   Good

The extent to which the supplier requires customer supervision or undue customer management input.

(ii) Delivery against agreed timescales

0 1 2 3 4 5 6 7 8 9 10
Poor   Good

The extent to which the supplier meets agreed service or project delivery timescales.

(iii) Delivery to agreed costs

0 1 2 3 4 5 6 7 8 9 10
Poor   Good

The extent to which the supplier meets agreed cost parameters.

(iv) Delivery to quality standards

0 1 2 3 4 5 6 7 8 9 10
Poor   Good

The extent to which the supplier meets agreed quality standards.

CONSISTENCY

(i) Stable values/emphasis/responsiveness/reliability

0 1 2 3 4 5 6 7 8 9 10
Poor   Good

The extent to which the supplier maintains a consistent performance in all attributes of values, corporate emphasis, responsiveness and reliability.

(ii) Low cycle time for key staff

0 1 2 3 4 5 6 7 8 9 10
Poor   Good

The extent to which the supplier changes senior customer facing managers within an eighteen-month cycle.

(iii) Consistent service performance

0 1 2 3 4 5 6 7 8 9 10
Poor   Good

The extent to which the supplier consistently maintains service performance within the agreed levels.

SECTION 2: RE-ENGINEERING CAPABILITY

'Re-engineering capability' refers to the ability of suppliers to bring about organizational and technical changes within the client's environment that result in significant performance improvements. It will be examined under the following general headings:

Evidence of performance improvements achieved

An indication of the performance improvements achieved under the following headings:

- Reduction in major development cycle time.
- Reduction in errors.
- Reduced unit cost of production.
- Improved user satisfaction with development process.

Extent to which supplier is dependent on one approach/tools

Extent to which supplier offers opportunities to exploit new technologies

EVIDENCE OF PERFORMANCE IMPROVEMENTS ACHIEVED

(i) Reduction in major development cycle time

0 1 2 3 4 5 6 7 8 9 10
Poor   Good

The extent to which the targets or expectations set for reducing major development cycle times were achieved.

(ii) Reduction in errors

0 1 2 3 4 5 6 7 8 9 10
Poor   Good

The extent to which targets or expectations set for reducing post-implementation errors were achieved.

(iii) Reduced unit of cost of production

0 1 2 3 4 5 6 7 8 9 10
Poor   Good

The extent to which targets or expectations set for reducing the unit cost of production were met.

(iv) Improved user satisfaction with the delivered product

0 1 2 3 4 5 6 7 8 9 10
Poor   Good

The extent to which user requirements have been met.

EXTENT TO WHICH SUPPLIER IS DEPENDENT ON ONE APPROACH/TOOLS

The extent to which the supplier is dependent upon, and promotes, one set of productivity and methodology tools.

0 1 2 3 4 5 6 7 8 9 10
Poor   Good

Score higher if the supplier is able to support a range of tools and methodologies.
Score low if large and small projects are forced to adopt the same tools and techniques.
Score low if there is no consistent methodology applied.
Score neutral (5) if you conducted a procurement and selected your supplier on the basis of the tools and methodologies offered.
Do not score if no experience (say, only one project completed).

EXTENT TO WHICH SUPPLIER OFFERS OPPORTUNITIES TO EXPLOIT NEW TECHNOLOGIES

[Develop against specific requirements.]

SECTION 3: INTEGRATION CAPABILITY

'Integration capability' refers to the ability of suppliers successfully to manage systems integration projects in the order of £[50] million to £[100] million lifetime contract cost. It will be examined under the following general headings:

Extent to which projects have been achieved

- Within timescale.
- Within budget.
- To user satisfaction.

Extent to which delivered projects

- Are easy to maintain.
- Have been integrated with other systems.
- Incorporate commodity off-the-shelf products.
- Achieve inter-operability and inter-working.
- Demonstrate conformance to standards.
- Are scaleable.

(i) Extent to which projects were achieved within timescale.

0 1 2 3 4 5 6 7 8 9 10
Poor   Good

(ii) Extent to which projects were achieved within budget.

0 1 2 3 4 5 6 7 8 9 10
Poor   Good

(iii) Extent to which projects were achieved to user satisfaction.

0 1 2 3 4 5 6 7 8 9 10
Poor   Good

(iv) Extent to which projects have been easy to maintain and amend.

0 1 2 3 4 5 6 7 8 9 10
Poor   Good

Do not score the following if there was no opportunity for the supplier to demonstrate a capability.

(v) Extent to which projects have been integrated with other systems already existing in your organization.

0 1 2 3 4 5 6 7 8 9 10
Poor   Good

(vi) Extent to which supplier is able to recommend commodity off-the-shelf products and has been willing to engage in discussion with users regarding the benefits of 80:20 solutions.

0 1 2 3 4 5 6 7 8 9 10
Poor   Good

(vii) Extent to which supplier promotes relevant standards and uses conformance to facilitate inter-working.

0 1 2 3 4 5 6 7 8 9 10
Poor   Good

(viii) Extent to which suppliers conform to agreed standards.

0 1 2 3 4 5 6 7 8 9 10
Poor   Good

(ix) Extent to which technical solutions have been capable of being scaled to provide for larger requirements without major redesign.

0 1 2 3 4 5 6 7 8 9 10
Poor   Good

SECTION 4: ABILITY TO MANAGE LARGE-SCALE CHANGE PROGRAMMES

'Ability to manage large-scale change programmes' refers to the ability of the supplier to manage large-scale programmes of organizational and cultural change within organizations acquired through an outsourcing agreement.

Please list your 'change' objectives and indicate the extent to which they have been achieved

Objective 1 _____ 0 1 2 3 4 5 6 7 8 9 10
_____ Poor   Good

Objective 2 _____ 0 1 2 3 4 5 6 7 8 9 10
_____ Poor   Good

Objective 3 _____ 0 1 2 3 4 5 6 7 8 9 10
_____ Poor   Good

Objective 4 _____ 0 1 2 3 4 5 6 7 8 9 10
_____ Poor   Good

Objective 5 _____ 0 1 2 3 4 5 6 7 8 9 10
_____ Poor   Good

Objective 6 _____ 0 1 2 3 4 5 6 7 8 9 10
_____ Poor   Good

Please indicate, to some extent, the complexity of the changes required by indicating approximately:

– the number of staff affected by the change   _____

SECTION 5: ABILITY TO SUPPORT MULTI-VENDOR ENVIRONMENTS

'Ability to support multi-vendor environments' refers to the ability of the supplier to manage and support environments that contain a wide range of equipment and systems from different manufacturers.

(i) Please indicate the total number of vendors supported on your behalf by your supplier.   Total vendors

(ii) Please indicate the *maximum* number of vendors supported on your behalf by your supplier in the delivery of any single operational service.   Maximum vendors

(iii) Please indicate the maximum number of vendors working to a common standard.   Maximum vendors

(iv) Please indicate whether your supplier supports products to different standards.

(v) General performance against service level agreements

The extent to which the supplier delivers operational services within agreed service levels.   0 1 2 3 4 5 6 7 8 9 10
Poor   Good

255

The extent to which the supplier delivers development services within agreed service levels.	0 1 2 3 4 5 6 7 8 9 10 Poor Good
The extent to which the supplier provides you with facilities to monitor the performance of routine service delivery.	0 1 2 3 4 5 6 7 8 9 10 Poor Good
The extent to which the supplier provides you with facilities to monitor the performance of projects.	0 1 2 3 4 5 6 7 8 9 10 Poor Good

SECTION 6: MANAGEMENT OF LARGE-SCALE OPERATIONAL ENVIRONMENTS

'Ability To Manage Large Scale and Multi-Site Operational Environments.'

(i) Extent to which operational services are provided within agreed service levels	0 1 2 3 4 5 6 7 8 9 10 Poor Good
(ii) Extent to which operational services are provided within agreed budgets	0 1 2 3 4 5 6 7 8 9 10 Poor Good

---

Questionnaire ends
Thank you again for your help

Signed:

Position:

Date:

Appendix C: Contract management process overview

The purpose of this appendix is to provide a high-level overview that describes the operational characteristics of contract management and may be used to guide and inform the development of its processes and mechanisms. In this context, contract management is intended to be a collective term for both the contract management team and the processes it runs.

Note that every effort should be made to keep contract management processes as simple as possible; their purpose is to monitor and report upon performance rather than attempt to micro-manage the supplier. It may be, therefore, that not all of the mechanisms that follow will be needed.

APPROACH TO DEVELOPMENT

Each macro- and sub-process should carry a unique identifier. One document per sub-process should be generated and referenced back to the parent macro-process. The collection of related sub-process documents should then be collated into a composite document that describes each macro-process.

A control sheet should then be prepared, listing all documents to be generated, their reference number, author and delivery date. The control sheet should be the primary means of control for progress review.

The overview described here can be developed in greater detail to reflect the constituent parts of each of the sub-processes and then further refined to take account of operational practicality and operational timescales.

SAMPLE CONTRACT MANAGEMENT MISSION STATEMENT

Contract management will fulfil a neutral but precise monitoring role to broker and initiate action within the relationship, driving processes that are geared to the elimination of inadequate planning and the stimulation of an unambiguous and mutually beneficial operation of the contract.

MACRO-PROCESSES

There are fifteen interrelated macro-processes, all of which will subdivide into sub-processes, tasks and activities. The macro-processes, with their reference numbers, are as follows (see also Figure C.1):

- Managing resource requirement (MP/01)
- Performance monitoring (MP/02)
- Cost monitoring (MP/03)
- Change control (MP/04)
- Monitoring unit costs (MP/05)
- Performance improvement (MP/06)
- Administration (MP/07)
- Tracking development of transferred personnel (MP/08)
- (MP/09) [Not used for the purposes of this appendix]
- Response to performance reporting and escalation (MP/10)
- Enable audit access (MP/11)
- Track and control third party use of assets (MP/12)
- (MP/13) [Not used for the purposes of this appendix]
- Strategic planning (MP/14)
- Accommodation (MP/15)

MANAGING RESOURCE REQUIREMENTS

Reference: MP01/Figure C.2 (pp. 261–3)

Sub-processes:

- SP01.1   Record allocated budgets
- SP01.2   Confirm committed plans
- SP01.3   Review resource requirement for period within committed SC (standard charge)
- SP01.4   Assess future SC/ASC (standard charge/additional service charge) requirement
- SP01.5   Confirm and commit SC with supplier
- SP01.6   Process request to consume resource
- SP01.7   Sanction work with supplier
- SP01.8   Monitor consumed SC
- SP01.9   Resolve supplier resourcing shortfalls
- SP01.10 Calculate expected invoice
- SP01.11 Pre-payment of invoices
- SP01.12 Sanction new service agreement
- SP01.13 Calculate SC cap

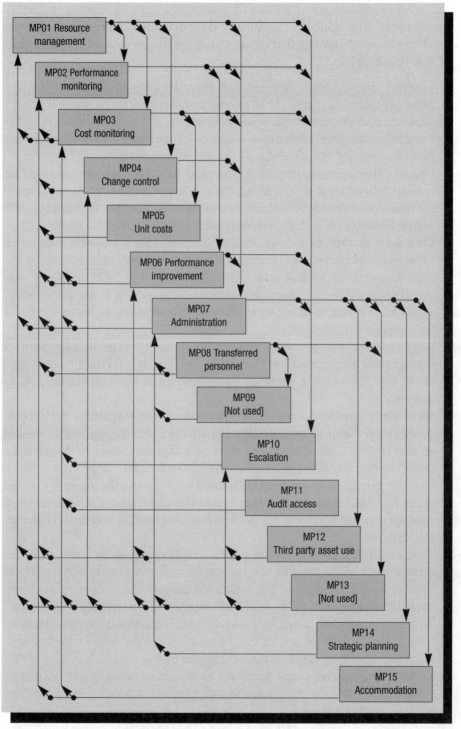

Figure C.1 Macro-process operational relationships

This process initiates and maintains the budgetary planning aspects of contract management. The allocated funds are recorded and contract management requests resource forecasts that establish both existing commitments and plans for new requirements.

1. Contract management receives and records budget allocations for the following planning cycle. This allows comparisons to be made between allocated budgets and intended commitments.
2. Contract management confirms resource commitments already made and requests new and amended plans from within customer.
3. Changes to existing (committed) plans and forward plans are recorded for each project or service, identifying the resources needed. The total demand for resource is established. If any anomalies arise, contract management will review the situation with the relevant users in order to resolve matters.
4. Contract management reviews plans for the period for which a commitment is to be made to the supplier. Contract management evaluates requests to use resources and checks that sufficient budget is available. The requester may be asked to delay its requirement in order to achieve a more cost-effective solution. Contract management also decides whether to 'broker' SC for unforeseen circumstances.
5. Once total resource requirements have been determined, contract management will express the demand in the form of a forward commitment of SC with the supplier. Contract management will also commit for ASC as appropriate.
6. Some plans submitted a year in advance will contain speculative work, yet to be approved. Contract management must ensure that the supplier is allowed to invoice only against approved work and that any resource destined for projects subsequently abandoned is sensibly redirected.
7. Contract management will have committed to utilize specific resources as part of the SC/ASC commitment. Near to the time the resource will be supplied, contract management must tell the supplier what work is to be undertaken by the resource
8. The supplier must report what SC has been used to date. Contract management will determine the reason for any under-consumption. Where the supplier is unable, for any reason, to provide the necessary resource, contract management will consult both supplier and user to seek resolution.
9. Where the supplier could not supply the requested resource, contract management will either ask for it to be supplied at some future date, agree an adjustment to SC or agree an acceptable alternative.
10. Contract management will calculate an expected invoice for committed resource and pass the details to the cost monitoring process for reconciling with the partner's invoice.
11. In certain circumstances additional funds may become available which were

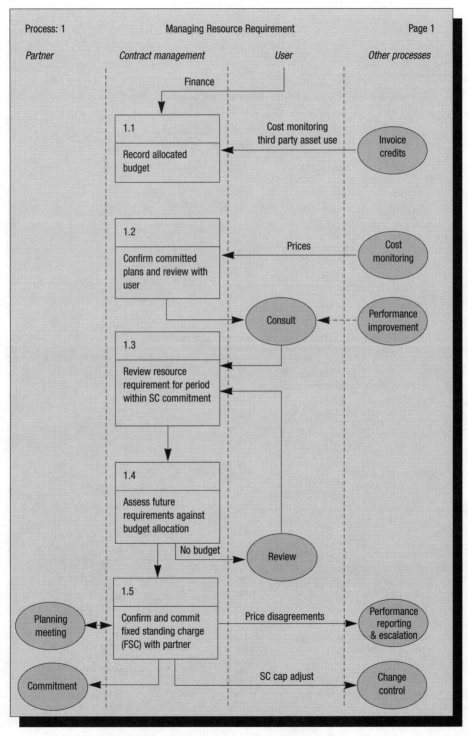

Figure C.2 Managing resource requirements

APPENDIX C

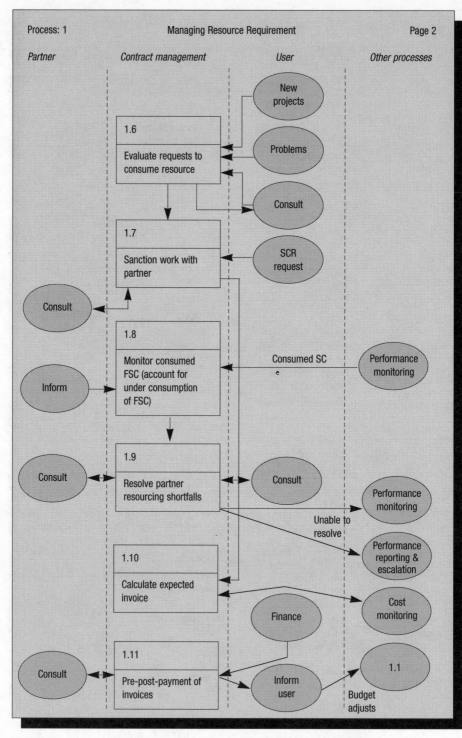

Figure C.2 Managing resource requirements (continued)

262

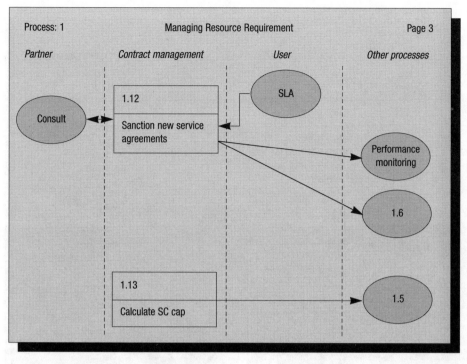

Figure C.2 Managing resource requirements264   264

not anticipated in the original budgetary planning. Contract management may negotiate special terms with the supplier in exchange for prepayment of resource already committed.

12. It is anticipated that, through mutual agreement, there may be changes to service level agreements and the managing resource requirement process will be used to sanction new SLAs, and ensure that they are measurable and capable of being monitored.

13. The charge capping arrangements of the contract, if relevant, may require contract management to pay attention to movements in volume and efficiency and the resultant effect on the base workload. Contract management should also ensure that adjustments to charges as a result of capping are set at the correct levels.

PERFORMANCE MONITORING

Reference: MP02/Figure C.3

Sub-processes:

● SP02.1   Receive and log performance issues

263

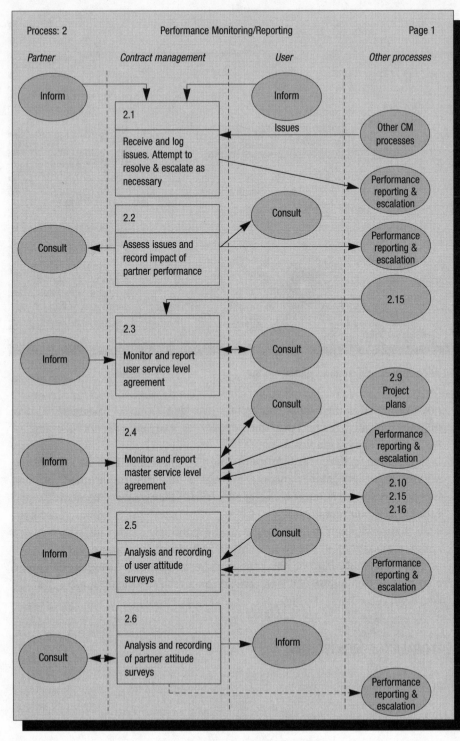

Figure C.3 Performance monitoring

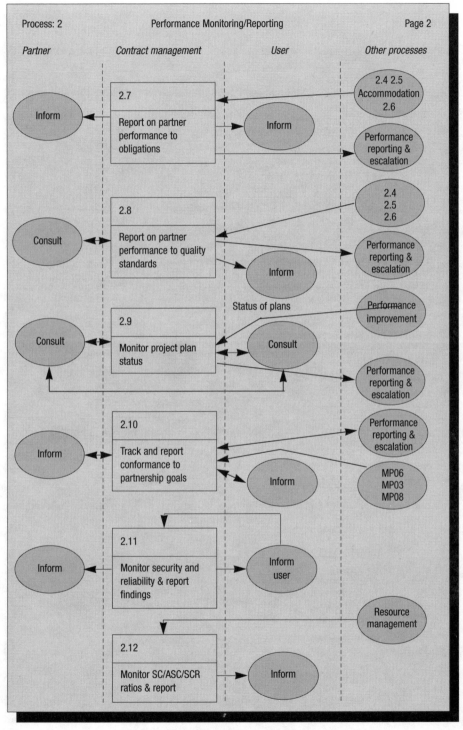

Figure C.3 Performance monitoring (continued)

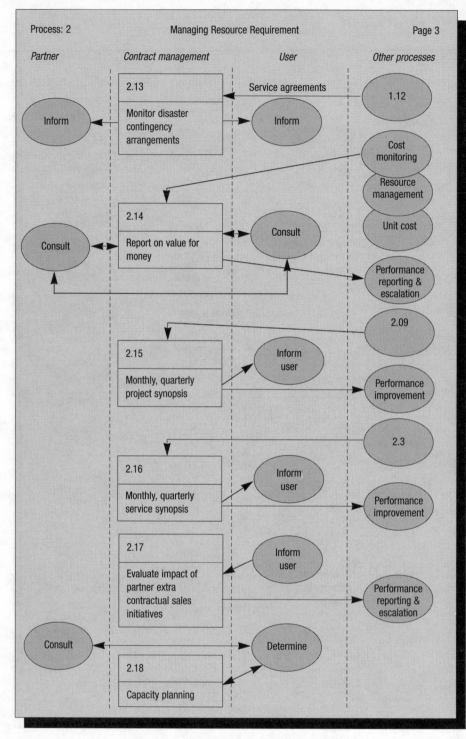

Figure C.3 Performance monitoring (concluded)

- SP02.2   Assess issues and initiate appropriate action
- SP02.3   Monitor and report user service level agreement statistics
- SP02.4   Monitor and report master service level agreement statistics
- SP02.5   Analysis and recording of user attitude surveys
- SP02.6   Analysis and recording of supplier attitude surveys
- SP02.7   Report on supplier performance to obligations
- SP02.8   Report on performance to quality standards
- SP02.9   Monitor project plan status
- SP02.10   Report conformance on achievement of partnership goals
- SP02.11   Report on performance to security and reliability requirements
- SP02.12   Record and report on cost of imperfect planning
- SP02.13   Monitor and report on performance to disaster contingency requirements
- SP02.14   Report on 'value for money'
- SP02.15   Report project synopsis monthly, quarterly, annually
- SP02.16   Report service synopsis monthly, quarterly, annually
- SP02.17   Monitor supplier extra sales initiatives

This macro-process gathers and collates information about the partner's performance.

1/2. Any performance issues of concern to either party will be reported to this process and an attempt will be made by contract management to resolve the problem. Where appropriate, the matter may be passed to the performance reporting and escalation processes.

3/4. Adherence to both master and user service level agreements (SLA) are monitored here and any breaches to either may be passed for escalation where the severity of the problem will dictate the required action.

5/6. Surveys will be conducted to determine whether there are perceived problems regarding the operation of the partnership. An evolutionary approach to the relationship will be adopted to prevent irritations becoming significant problems.

7/8. The supplier's performance in meeting contractual obligations and in adhering to quality standards will be ascertained. Any shortcomings will be reported to both the supplier and customer.

9. Ongoing projects will be monitored and project plans will be passed to contract management for evaluation. Any concerns may be conveyed to the supplier for early resolution and serious problems will be passed to the performance reporting and escalation processes.

10. Progress towards the principal objectives of the partnership will be assessed and reported upon.

11. The supplier's performance in meeting reliability targets and security arrangements will be reported upon.

12. The consumption of SC, ASC and SCR resource will be closely monitored

together with the effect of the planning arrangements under resource management to determine the precise purchasing ratio. Reports will be produced that both inform the planning processes prior to a purchasing commitment and identify the extent of any imperfect planning.

13. The supplier's performance in meeting disaster contingency requirements will be monitored and reported upon.

14. Measurements from other processes will be received and assessed to determine whether the customer is receiving 'value for money' from the relationship.

15/16. Monthly/quarterly reports will be produced to reflect project and service status.

17. Any supplier direct selling initiatives will be closely monitored to establish their effect on the relationship. Issues arising from such initiatives will be reported upon and details may be passed to the performance reporting and escalation processes for action to be taken.

18. Contract management will ensure it retains a complete view of the amount and disposition of processing capacity to aid decision making for management and other contract management processes.

COST MONITORING

Reference: MP03/Figure C.4

Sub-processes:

- SP03.1   Calculate gross margins and determine performance gains
- SP03.2   Agree performance gains
- SP03.3   Rebate performance gains to user (for hard charging)
- SP03.4   Calculate target margins
- SP03.5   Receive invoice and reconcile to expected invoice value
- SP03.6   From passed invoices determine trends and report on variable costs, handling charges and education costs
- SP03.7   Establish 'notional' charging
- SP03.8   Direct investigation under 'open book'
- SP03.9   Evaluate changes to metrics
- SP03.10   Implement agreed changes to metrics
- SP03.11   Evaluate potential for price change
- SP03.12   Maintain 'menu' of prices
- SP03.13   Monitor industry price movements
- SP03.14   Track and report purchases
- SP03.15   Invoice dispute procedure
- SP03.16   Financial remedies

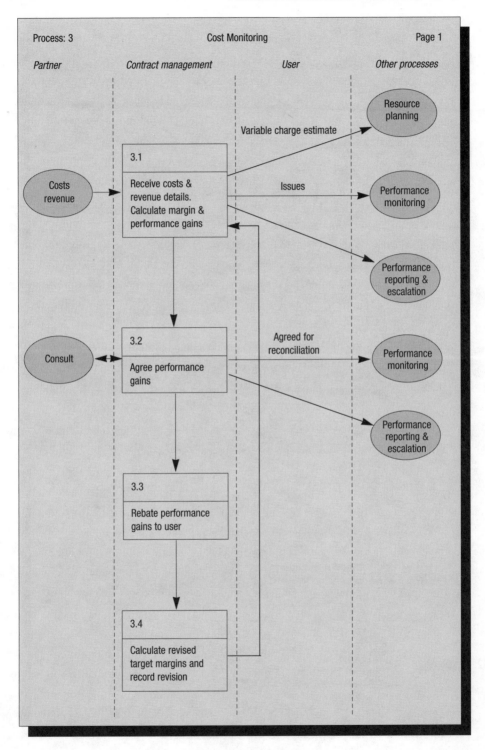

Figure C.4 Cost monitoring

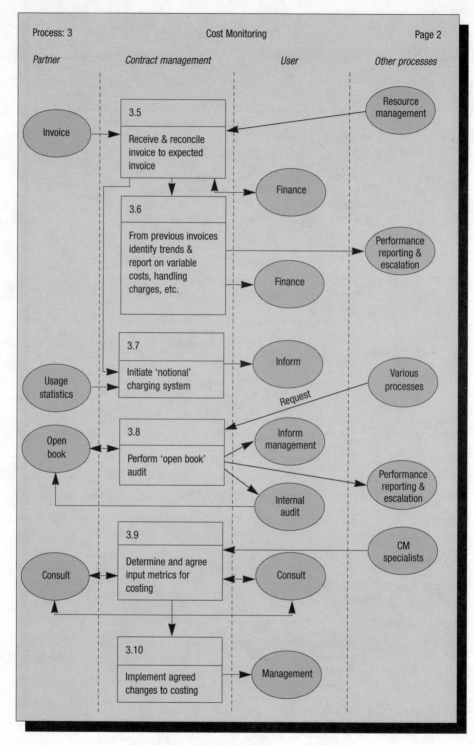

Figure C.4 Cost monitoring (continued)

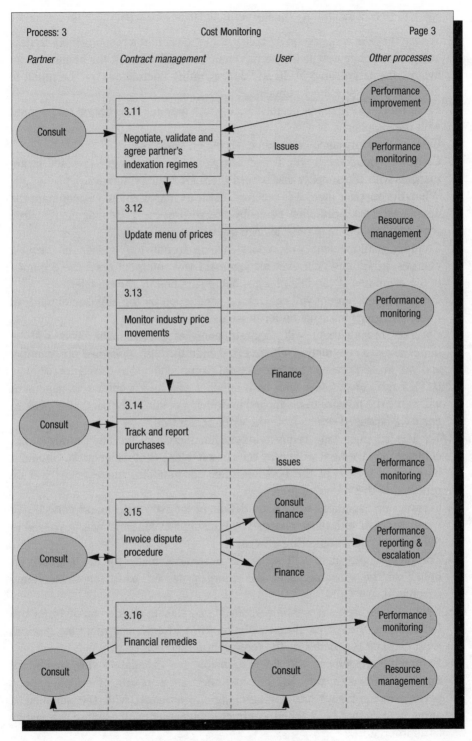

Figure C.4 Cost monitoring (concluded)

271

This macro-process monitors the cost-effectiveness of the partnership.

1. Where there is an 'open book' policy, it is the partner's responsibility to pass cost and revenue details to contract management to check the actual margin against the target margin. In addition, monthly fluctuations will be noted to determine any possible anomalies.
2. From these calculations performance gains may be determined and agreed with the supplier.
3. Calculate performance gains to be passed on to users.
4. Contract management will, if necessary, calculate and agree revised target margins with the supplier and record them for future reference.
5. When the supplier invoice is received, contract management will compare the details with the prediction made by macro process 1 (Managing resource requirement) and may raise invoice queries as necessary.
6. Contract management will report invoice trends and trends in variable charges. In addition, contract management will comment upon the accuracy of the estimates of variable charges being supplied by the supplier.
7. Contract management will control the production by the supplier of notional (hard charging) information for those users affected.
8. Contract management will facilitate audit of the supplier. This will be undertaken in conjunction with internal audit through a planned programme, and will make provision for 'exceptional circumstances' as they arise.
9/10. Through consultation with both supplier and user, contract management will agree the metrics to be applied in deriving costings for particular work to ensure a balanced return from the work performed.
11/12. The supplier may request indexation increases for any resource and contract management will verify the reasonableness of the request. Should it be decided to accept the revision, after consultation, the changes will be reflected in the 'menu' of prices.
13. Contract management will obtain details of industry prices and periodically compare them with those charged by the supplier. Findings will be passed to the performance monitoring process.
14. Contract management will reconcile purchases made by the supplier on behalf of the customer and the charges passed back for those items purchased.
15. Contract management will be responsible for raising queries on invoices and for resolving the issues. If no resolution can be found, contract management must escalate the matter by the most appropriate route.
16. Contract management will be responsible for calculating the amount of financial remedies due to the customer as a result of supplier poor performance (if any) and for agreeing the amounts with the supplier. If agreement cannot be reached, contract management will escalate the matter as appropriate.

CHANGE CONTROL

Reference: MP04/Figure C.5

Sub-processes:

- SP04.1   Receive and record change requests
- SP04.2   Evaluate the impact of requested change
- SP04.3   Obtain decision on requested change
- SP04.4   Implement rejection
- SP04.5   Implement acceptance and update contract
- SP04.6   Maintain change request logs and update files

This process supports changes to the contract, receiving requests either directly from the supplier or user, or indirectly via other processes.

1. Contract management receives change requests and verifies their source. Valid requests are recorded, invalid requests are rejected.
2. Requests are discussed and evaluated with recommendations being passed to the relevant sanctioning authority. Whatever the outcome, acceptance or rejection, both supplier and user are informed of the decision.
3. Contract management ensures that each request receives attention and that a decision is reached.
4/5. Acceptance of the request initiates an update to the contract with copies of all amendments being circulated to the supplier and customer. Similarly all interested parties are informed of a rejected request.
6. Contract management maintains records of all changes to the contract and the reasons for them.

MONITORING UNIT COST

Reference: MP05/Figure C.6

Sub-processes:

- SP05.1   Calculate supplier unit costs
- SP05.2   Report unit cost by resource type and produce trend analyses
- SP05.3   Calculate user unit costs
- SP05.4   Report calculated unit cost by resource type and trend

This process monitors progress towards the customer's target of achieving a [x per cent] reduction in unit costs over the first [y] years of the relationship. In addition, it will support the productivity debates and the comparisons of value compared with external organizations.

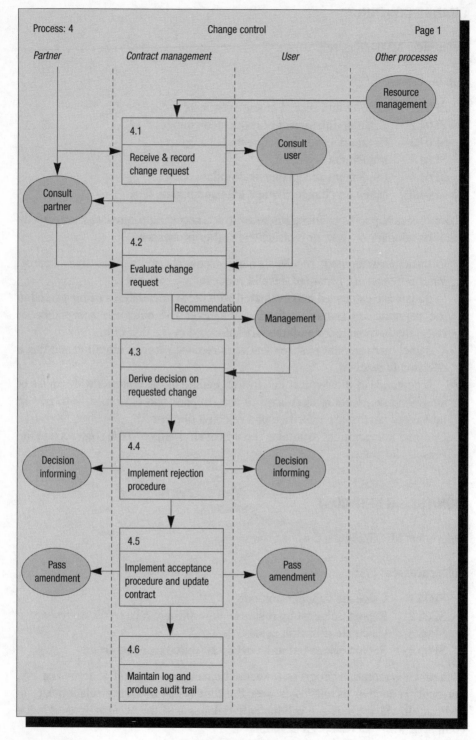

Figure C.5 Change control

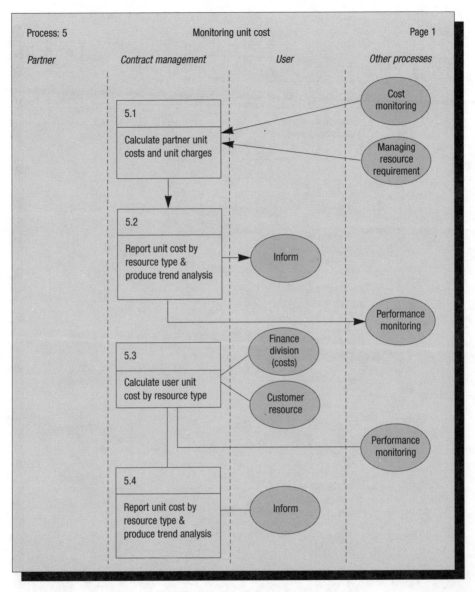

Figure C.6 Monitoring unit cost

PERFORMANCE IMPROVEMENT

Reference: MP06/Figure C.7

Sub-processes:

- SP06.1   Request and receive plans for improved performance
- SP06.2   Analyse performance improvement plans

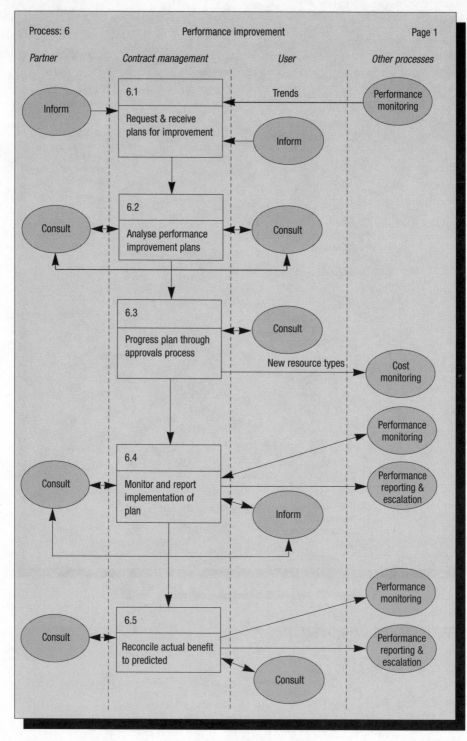

Process: 6   Performance improvement   Page 1

Figure C.7 Performance improvement

- SP06.3   Progress plans through the approvals process
- SP06.4   Monitor implementation of improvement plan
- SP06.5   Reconcile actual benefit to predicted benefit

This process receives statistics from other processes as well as suggestions from the supplier and user community regarding possible approaches for improving the performance of the partnership. Suggestions for improvements are evaluated in consultation with both parties to determine the potential of a given approach.

1. Contract management stimulates ideas for improved performance and receives and records their existence.
2. Contract management analyses plans and determines whether benefits are likely to be delivered and whether the approach seems workable.
3. If the approach is deemed to be beneficial and workable, contract management guides the plan through the departmental approvals process.
4. Progress and implementation is monitored by reference to the performance monitoring process.
5. Contract management continues to monitor the outcome of the plan once implementation is complete. Contract management verifies that the expected benefits have been, and continue to be, delivered.

ADMINISTRATION

Reference: MP07/Figure C.8

Sub-processes:

- SP07.1   Maintain contract management procedures
- SP07.2   Report any changes to contract management procedures
- SP07.3   Maintain contact log and registers
- SP07.4   Create, maintain and distribute contract management educational material
- SP07.5   Maintain documentation libraries and indexes
- SP07.6   Create, maintain and distribute summaries of contract terms and obligations
- SP07.7   [Not used]
- SP07.8   Administration of all contractually organized meetings
- SP07.9   Contract management sub-process integrity monitoring

This process provides a co-ordination point for the distribution of outputs from other processes controlled by contract management and for the administration of change within contract management processes. All distribution details together with documentation libraries and index systems should be centrally maintained by this process to eliminate possible duplication and ensure the integrity of the material.

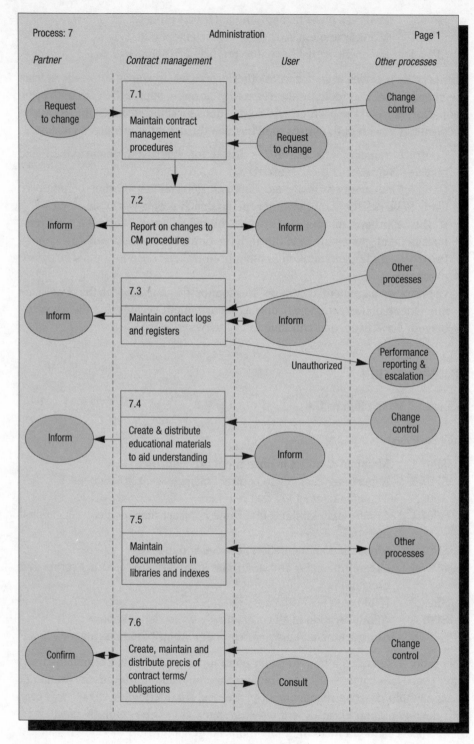

Figure C.8 Administration

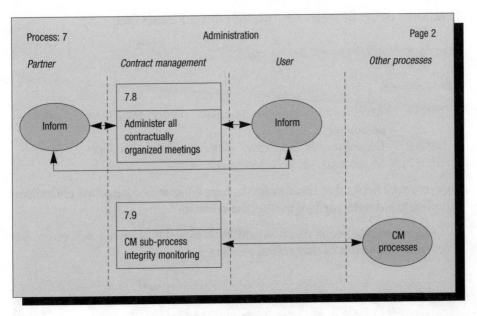

Figure C.8 Administration (concluded)

1/2. Contract management must ensure that changes in its procedures are subject to proper 'change control' practices. Educational material pertinent to the changed operation of contract management must be created and distributed to the partnership.

3. Contract management must maintain various contact points and registers for its processes. This provides for the filing and updating of information.

4. Educational material pertinent to the operation of contract management and the contract must be created and distributed. This includes both general educational material and specific information for those dealing with contract management.

5. Contract management must maintain various libraries relating to its processes. These need to be indexed and cross-referenced.

6. Contract management should produce 'Plain English' summaries of the contract and the obligations of both parties within it. Strictly, this could be part of education (4 above) but will be closely tied to contract change procedure (MP04).

7. (MP07.7) [Not Used]

8. Secretarial services will be provided to support all contractually organized meetings. Minutes must be circulated to all recipients on the circulation list.

9. Contract management must periodically review its processes to ensure they are still pertinent. In addition, the contact logs and distribution logs must be reviewed to ensure that they are up to date.

TRACKING DEVELOPMENT OF TRANSFERRED PERSONNEL

Reference: MP08/Figure C.9

Sub-processes:

- SP08.1   Receive and evaluate supplier report regarding transferred personnel
- SP08.2   Record trends and extract data for evaluation report
- SP08.3   Monitor staff interchange mechanism

This process checks that the supplier is complying with contractual obligations regarding the development of transferred personnel.

1. Contract management receives and evaluates the partner's report on the current disposition of transferred personnel.

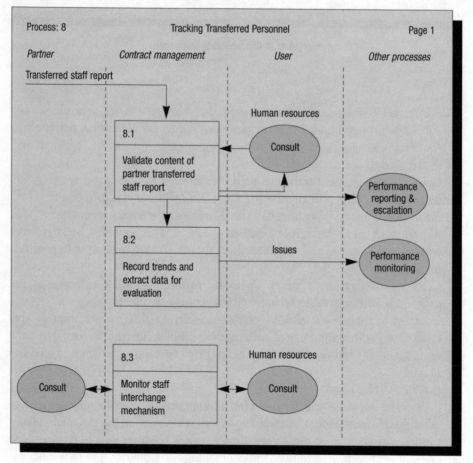

Figure C.9 Tracking transferred personnel

2. Contract management produces trend analysis and extracts data in preparation for the evaluation report.
3. Contract management monitors the value of interchanging staff between the two organizations.

RESPONSE TO PERFORMANCE REPORTING AND ESCALATION

Reference: MP10/Figure C.10

Sub-processes:

- SP10.1   Receive and log issues for escalation
- SP10.2   Evaluate the issues, establish the severity and determine course of action
- SP10.3   Initiate remedial action and progress to resolution

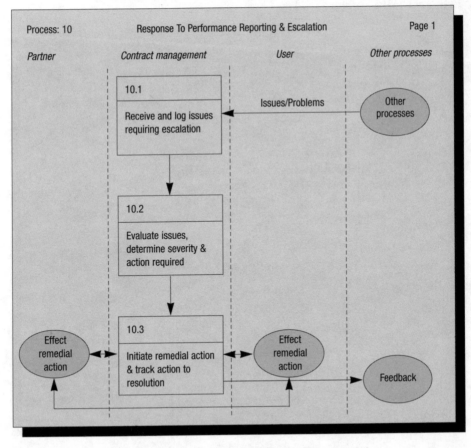

Figure C.10 Response to performance reporting and escalation

This process reacts to problems detected by other processes which require action and resolution.

1. Issues are received from other contract management processes, which have failed to be resolved elsewhere. They are logged and the primary escalation process engaged.
2. The issues are examined, their importance evaluated and contract management ensures all relevant information is available. The most appropriate escalation route is then chosen.
3. An escalation route will be initiated where appropriate. The escalation route will be monitored to determine whether a resolution has been found in a suitable time frame and if not further escalation will be initiated. Following resolution of the problem the results will be recorded and the process closed.

ENABLE AUDIT ACCESS

Reference: MP11/Figure C.11

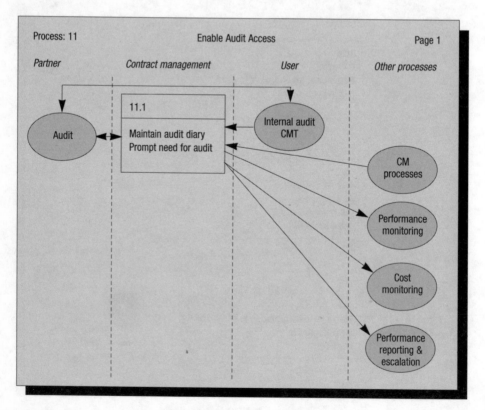

Figure C.11 Enable audit access

Sub-processes:

● SP11.1   Maintain audit diary and determine need for audit

This process provides the control point for audit activity. Audit requests will be logged and a history of findings maintained in an 'audit diary'. Details will be received from the appropriate auditing authorities, contract management and the performance monitoring activity, and passed to the performance monitoring process for analysis and reporting. Except in the most extreme cases, initial contact with the supplier to carry out an audit will be via contract management. Contract management and the appropriate auditing authority will agree the annual audit programme. Any additional audits required by contract management will be undertaken by an appropriate auditing authority.

TRACK AND CONTROL THIRD PARTY USE OF ASSETS

Reference: MP12/Figure C.12

Sub-processes:

● SP12.1   Maintain asset register
● SP12.2   Monitor third party usage of assets
● SP12.3   Monitor disposal of assets
● SP12.4   Check and agree rebates

This process establishes and maintains the asset register, identifying any third party use of equipment/resource. In addition, it controls the partner's disposal of assets.

1. The supplier must maintain a register of assets which it must copy to contract management on a regular basis. Contract management will check that changes to the register are in line with its expectations.
2. The supplier must notify contract management of any third party use of assets. Once notified contract management will ensure any rebates are obtained.
3. Contract management agrees whether assets may be disposed of and also the most convenient timing for disposal.
4. Contract management calculates any rebates or, more usually, confirms with the internal finance department whether the amortization period should continue and agrees this with the supplier. All actions taken will be recorded and reports will be passed to the performance monitoring and administration processes.

APPENDIX C

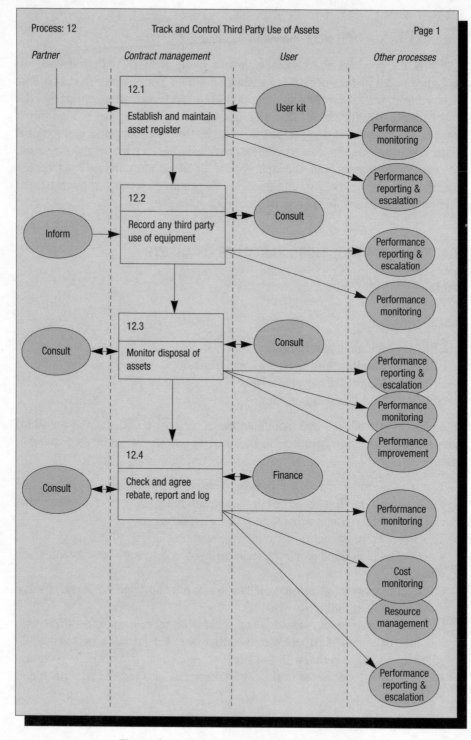

Figure C.12 Track and control third party use of assets

284

STRATEGIC PLANNING

Reference: MP14/Figure C.13

Sub-processes:

- SP14.1   Receive strategic plan and determine contractual implications
- SP14.2   Report on costs and impact of plans

This process considers the implications, on the partnership, of customer strategic planning activities.

1. Contract management receives long-term strategic plans or short-term highly confidential plans and makes a preliminary assessment regarding any necessary contract changes in order to accommodate the plan.
2. Following receipt of strategic plans, their impact is evaluated in terms of costs, resourcing and architectural issues and the findings are conveyed to the partnership for consideration.

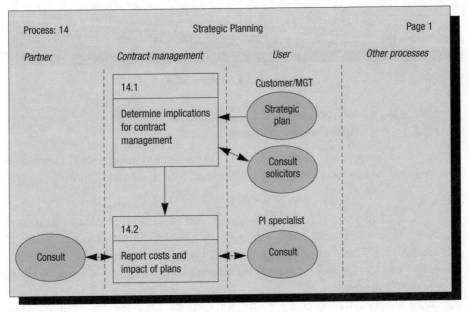

Figure C.13 Strategic planning

ACCOMMODATION

Reference: MP15/Figure C.14

Sub-processes:

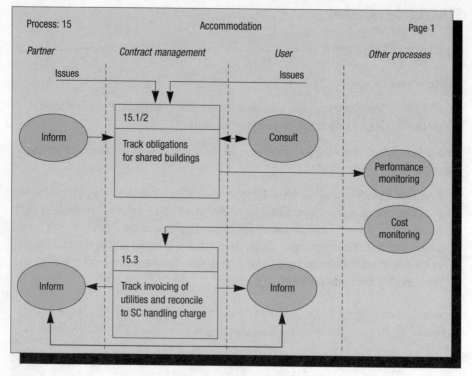

Figure C.14 Accommodation

- SP15.1 & 2   Monitor partnership obligations for buildings
- SP15.3   Monitor accommodation invoices

This process keeps track of shared and wholly occupied buildings. This process ensures that contractual obligations, enshrined in site service agreements, are met.

1/2. Contract management receives issues that local representatives have not been able to resolve, and attempts to resolve them. Where contract management fails to obtain a satisfactory solution, the matter may be escalated via the performance monitoring process and onwards to the escalation process.

3. Where the customer charges the supplier for services and utilities, this process reconciles this charge to the subsequent SC charge plus handling fee.

Appendix D: Illustrative implementation plan

Note that:

- The first column indicates the activity, event or milestone.
- The second column indicates likely elapsed time. The example comes from a very large procurement and the elapsed times shown here indicate a great deal of work that may not be necessary for less complex or valuable procurements. Note that 'elapsed time' is a function of inputs and delivery dates and does not reflect the effort needed to do the task.
- The last column indicates the identified deliverables.
- Explanatory comments or observations are shown in square brackets.

Task	Elapsed time	Deliverables
Implementation		
Review supplier draft implementation plan	10 days	File record
Implement open book accounting	15 days	No formal deliverable required
Plan board level meetings	14 days	No formal deliverable required
Agree joint management structure	16 days	File record
Agree (both parties) formal objectives for partnership	16 days	File record
Arrange ongoing quality review	1 day	No formal deliverable required
Arrange ongoing support	1 day	No formal deliverable required
Request changes to supplier's implementation plan	1 day	File record
Identify role and responsibilities	11 days	File record
Agree implementation plan	11 days	File record
Establish funding implications of contract/ negotiate with funding authority	10 days	File record
Identify key (implementation) milestones	11 days	File record
Establish monitoring process	8 days	File record
Develop performance reporting mechanisms	24 days	File record
Confirm content of each tranche	10 days	No formal deliverable required
Devise attitude surveys for transferred staff	2 days	No formal deliverable required
Monitor implementation (ongoing)	50 days	No formal deliverable required
Communications plan		
Agree agenda for senior managers forum	5 days	File record
Publish December magazine	milestone	Published document
Determine questions for telephone survey	10 days	No formal deliverable required
Conduct telephone survey	9 days	Record of survey/file in project library
Agree content for January magazine	5 days	File record
Publish January magazine	milestone	Published document
Senior managers forum	1 day	No formal deliverable required
Publish survey results	1 day	Record of survey/file in project library
Briefing for briefers: staff transfer	1 day	No formal deliverable required
Briefing for staff: staff transfer	6 days	No formal deliverable required
Agree content for February magazine	5 days	No formal deliverable required
Conduct telephone survey	2 days	Record of survey/file in project library
Publish February magazine	milestone	File record
Publish survey results to ER group	1 day	File record
Agree content for March magazine	5 days	No formal deliverable required
Agree agenda for senior managers forum	10 days	File record
Publish March magazine	milestone	Published document
Agree content for April magazine	5 days	No formal deliverable required
Conduct telephone survey	3 days	Record of survey/file in project library
Publish April magazine	milestone	Published document
Publish survey results to ER group	milestone	File record
Senior managers forum	milestone	No formal deliverable required
Conduct telephone survey	9 days	Record of survey/file in project library
Agree content for May magazine	2 days	File record
Publish survey results to ER group	1 day	File record
Publish May magazine	milestone	Published document
Agree content for June magazine	6 days	No formal deliverable required
Conduct telephone survey	9 days	Record of survey/file in project library
Publish June magazine	milestone	Published document
Publish survey results to ER group	3 days	File record

Task	Elapsed time	Deliverables
Senior managers forum	2 days	No formal deliverable required
Agree content for July magazine	21 days	No formal deliverable required
Conduct telephone survey	9 days	Record of survey/file in project library
Publish July magazine	milestone	Published document
Publish survey results to ER group	1 day	File record
Agree content for August magazine	5 days	No formal deliverable required
Conduct telephone survey	9 days	Record of survey/file in project library
Publish August magazine	milestone	Published document
Publish survey results to ER group	1 day	File record
Senior managers forum	2 days	No formal deliverable required
Agree content for September magazine	5 days	No formal deliverable required
Conduct telephone survey	9 days	Record of survey/file in project library
Determine and agree staff/supplier program	48 days	File record
Publish September magazine	milestone	Published document
Publish survey results to ER group	milestone	File record
Agree content for October magazine	5 days	No formal deliverable required
Conduct telephone survey	9 days	Record of survey/file in project library
Publish October magazine	milestone	Published document
Publish survey results to ER group	1 day	File record
Agree content for November magazine	5 days	No formal deliverable required
Conduct telephone survey	9 days	Record of survey/file in project library
Publish November magazine	milestone	Published document
Publish survey results to ER group	1 day	File record
Agree content for December magazine	5 days	File record
Publish December magazine	milestone	Published document
Agree content for January magazine	5 days	No formal deliverable required
Publish January magazine	milestone	Published document
Publish survey results to ER group	1 day	File record

Contract management – Phase 1 – Setting the parameters

Task	Elapsed time	Deliverables
Paper – Customer/supplier relationship	9 days	Policy paper as per title
Confirm and agree customer/supplier relationship	1 day	No formal deliverable required
Paper – Define CM responsibilities	3 days	Policy paper as per title
Confirm and agree CM responsibilities	1 day	Addendum to Project Handbook
Paper – Establish shape of CM team	9 days	Policy paper as per title
Confirm and agree shape of CM team	5 days	Updated policy paper – file in project library
Review CM team resource needs	14 days	No formal deliverable required
Identify CM team members	5 days	No formal deliverable required
Appoint contracts manager	5 days	No formal deliverable required
Appoint project team members	5 days	No formal deliverable required
Specify team budget requirements – 93/94	5 days	Report – Review with management.
Specify team accommodation	2 days	Report – Review with facilities management
Paper – Develop high level process design	6 days	Policy paper as per title

CM Phase 2 – Developing policy statements/process design

Task	Elapsed time	Deliverables
Paper – Define customer base	10 days	Policy paper as per title
Paper – Define mechanism for approving funding	15 days	Policy paper as per title
Paper – Define mechanism for prioritizing projects and services	15 days	Policy paper as per title
Paper – Define service requirements	25 days	Policy paper as per title
Paper – Define project management interfaces	25 days	Policy paper as per title

Task	Elapsed time	Deliverables
Paper – Define open book requirements	25 days	Policy paper as per title
Paper – Define audit requirements	45 days	Policy paper as per title
Paper – Specify requirements for estimating and metrics	15 days	Policy paper as per title
Paper – Specify requirements for technical architecture	15 days	Policy paper as per title
Paper – Specify requirements for post-implementation reviews	45 days	Policy paper as per title
Paper – Specify standards for inclusion in contract	25 days	Policy paper as per title
Paper – Define ongoing risk management requirements	25 days	Policy paper as per title
Paper – Define criteria for non-supplier procurements	15 days	Policy paper as per title
Paper – Define resource planning policy for partnership	15 days	Policy paper as per title
Plan second level process definition	1 day	Project plan detail for circulation
Impact of partnership on new planned services	50 days	Report: to be filed in project library
Prepare customers for hard charging	20 days	Report: to be filed in project library
Confirm process review team	19 days	No formal deliverable required
CM Phase 3 – Implementing contract management		
Provide accommodation needs	1 day	No formal deliverable required
Develop CM tool requirements	1 day	Policy paper – file in project library
Review CM processes against requirements – risk	5 days	Report: circulate to management/file in project library
Review CM processes against requirements – security	5 days	Report: circulate to management/file in project library
Review CM processes against requirements – SoSR	5 days	Report: circulate to management/file in project library
Develop customer workshops	4 days	Customer workshop documentation
Develop internal customer workshop	15 days	Internal workshop documentation
Review processes against suppliers' bids	15 days	Report: circulate to management/file in project library
Specify need for reference site visits (review CM methods)	10 days	Specification for review by management.
Review CM processes against existing management information systems	15 days	Report: circulate to management/file in project library
Appoint CM team	35 days	No formal deliverable required
Identify team training needs	5 days	Specification – for review by management.
Confirmation of issues for negotiation	27 days	Issues list
Conduct CM team training	116 days	No formal deliverable required
Develop contract management process – establish resource requirements process		
Review policy	2 days	Policy paper – file in project library
Second level process definition	2 days	Process documentation
Review second level process	1 day	Process documentation
Document in conformance with Project Handbook	21 days	Process documentation for review by management.
Implement process	25 days	No formal deliverable required

Task	Elapsed time	Deliverables
Develop contract management process – sanction work with supplier process		
Review policy	1 day	Policy paper – file in project library
Second level process definition	1 day	Process documentation
Review second level process	1 day	Process documentation
Document in conformance with Project Handbook	12 days	Process documentation for review by management.
Implement process	29 days	No formal deliverable required
Develop contract management process – monitor supplier project service and performance process		
Review policy	6 days	Policy paper – file in project library
Second level process definition	6 days	Process documentation
Review second level process	5 days	Process documentation
Document in conformance with Project Handbook	22 days	Process documentation for review by management.
Implement process	36 days	No formal deliverable required
Develop contract management process – monitor supplier costs and margins process		
Review policy	1 day	Policy paper – file in project library
Second level process definition	16 days	Process documentation
Review second level process	18 days	Process documentation
Document in conformance with Project Handbook	23 days	Process documentation for review by management.
Implement process	22 days	No formal deliverable required
Develop contract management process – ensure conformance to contract terms process		
Review policy	6 days	Policy paper – file in project library
Second level process definition	6 days	Process documentation
Review second level process	6 days	Process documentation
Document in conformance with Project Handbook	46 days	Process documentation for review by management.
Implement process	52 days	No formal deliverable required
Develop contract management process – respond to problems and trends process		
Review policy	1 day	Policy paper – file in project library
Second level process definition	6 days	Process documentation
Review second level process	6 days	Process documentation
Document in conformance with Project Handbook	6 days	Process documentation for review by management.
Implement process	11 days	No formal deliverable required
Develop contract management process – conduct open book process		
Review policy	10 days	Policy paper – file in project library
Second level process definition	5 days	Process documentation
Review second level process	6 days	Process documentation
Document in conformance with Project Handbook	6 days	Process documentation for review by management
Implement process	56 days	No formal deliverable required

Index